S0-AJO-414

THE GESTALT THEORY

Regarded by psychologists as a classic statement of Gestaltism, this challenging book explains the basic concepts of a theory which has profoundly influenced the progress and direction of modern psychology.

"The general reader, if he looks to psychology for something more than mere entertainment or practical advice, will discover in this book a storehouse of searching criticisms and brilliant suggestions from the pen of a rare thinker. . . . Thoughtful examination of the ideas of the volume will put the reader in the way of understanding the developments along the frontiers of theoretical psychology."   —*Atlantic Monthly*

One of the great figures of twentieth-century psychology, WOLFGANG KÖHLER left Germany in 1935 when the Nazis began to interfere with his research. As a student he invented a procedure by which the vibrations of the living eardrum could be registered. A few years later, he began his investigations of anthropoid apes, the results of which he described in *The Mentality of Apes*. From 1935 to 1958 he was Professor Emeritus at Swarthmore College, from which he received an honorary doctorate; from 1959 until his death in 1967 he was Research Professor of Psychology at Dartmouth College. *Gestalt Psychology* was his best known work and is here presented in its completely revised edition. He was also the author of *The Place of Value in a World of Facts*.

GESTALT
PSYCHOLOGY
WOLFGANG KÖHLER

AN INTRODUCTION TO NEW CONCEPTS IN MODERN PSYCHOLOGY

A MERIDIAN BOOK

NEW AMERICAN LIBRARY

TIMES MIRROR

NEW YORK AND SCARBOROUGH, ONTARIO

NAL Books are available at quantity discounts
when used to promote products or services. For
information please write to Premium Marketing
Division, The New American Library, Inc.,
1633 Broadway, New York, New York 10019.

TO MAX WERTHEIMER

Copyright, 1947, by Liveright Publishing Corporation
Copyright renewed 1975 by Lili Köhler

All rights reserved—no part of this book may be reproduced in any form without
permission in writing from the publisher, except by a reviewer who wishes to
quote brief passages in connection with a review written for inclusion in a maga-
zine or newspaper. For information address Liveright Publishing Corporation,
500 Fifth Avenue, New York, New York 10036.

This is an authorized reprint of a hardcover edition published by
Liveright Publishing Corporation. Originally appeared
in paperback as a Mentor Book.

Library of Congress Catalog Card Number: 80-80242

MERIDIAN TRADEMARK REG. U.S. PAT. OFF. AND FOREIGN COUNTRIES
REGISTERED TRADEMARK—MARCA REGISTRADA
HECHO EN FORGE VILLAGE, MASS., U.S.A.

SIGNET, SIGNET CLASSICS, MENTOR, PLUME, MERIDIAN and NAL BOOKS
are published in the United States by The New American Library, Inc.,
1633 Broadway, New York, New York 10019, in Canada by The New American Library
of Canada Limited, 81 Mack Avenue, Scarborough, Ontario M1L 1M8.

First Meridian Printing, March, 1980

1 2 3 4 5 6 7 8 9

PRINTED IN THE UNITED STATES OF AMERICA

0.1982
818g

L.I.F.E. College Library
1100 Glendale Blvd.
Los Angeles, Calif. 90026

CONTENTS

029381

I

A DISCUSSION OF

BEHAVIORISM

THERE SEEMS TO BE a single starting point for psychology, exactly as for all the other sciences: the world as we find it, naïvely and uncritically. The naïveté may be lost as we proceed. Problems may be found which were at first completely hidden from our eyes. For their solution it may be necessary to devise concepts which seem to have little contact with direct primary experience. Nevertheless, the whole development must begin with a naïve picture of the world. This origin is necessary because there is no other basis from which a science can arise. In my case, which may be taken as representative of many others, that naïve picture consists, at this moment, of a blue lake with dark forests around it, a big, gray rock, hard and cool, which I have chosen as a seat, a paper on which I write, a faint noise of the wind which hardly moves the trees, and a strong odor characteristic of boats and fishing. But there is more in this world: somehow I now behold, though it does not become fused with the blue lake of the present, another lake of a milder blue, at which I found myself, some years ago, looking from its shore in Illinois. I am perfectly accustomed to beholding thousands of views of this kind which arise when I am alone. And there is still more in this world: for instance, my hand and fingers as they lightly move across the paper. Now, when I stop writing and look around again, there also is a feeling of health and vigor. But in the next moment I feel something like a dark pressure somewhere in my interior which tends to develop into a feeling of being hunted—I have promised to have this manuscript ready within a few months.

Most people live permanently in a world such as this, which is for them *the* world, and hardly ever find serious problems in its fundamental properties. Crowded streets may take the place of the lake, a cushion in a sedan that of my rock, some serious words of a business transaction may be remembered instead of Lake Michigan, and the dark pressure may have to do with tax-paying instead of book-writing. All these are minor differences so long as one takes the world at its face-value, as we all do except in hours in which science disturbs our natural attitude. There are problems, of course, even for the most uncritical citizens of this first-hand world. But, for the most part, they do not refer to its nature as such; rather, they are of a practical or an emotional sort, and merely mean that, this world being taken for granted, we do not know how to behave in the part of it which we face as our present situation.

Centuries ago, various sciences, most of all physics and biology, began to destroy the simple confidence with which human beings tend to take this world as *the reality*. Though hundreds of millions still remain undisturbed, the scientist now finds it full of almost contradictory properties. Fortunately, he has been able to discover behind it another world, the properties of which, quite different from those of the world of naïve people, do not seem to be contradictory at all. No wonder therefore that now, as psychology begins to be a science, some of its most energetic students should wish to make it go at once the way of *natural* science. Indeed, if the scientists have found the naïve world impervious to their method, what hope of better success can we as psychologists have? And since the enormous feat of jumping from the world of direct, but confused, experience into a world of clear and hard reality already has been achieved by the physicist, it would seem wise for the psychologist to take advantage of this great event in the history of science, and to begin the study of psychology on the same solid basis.

A few words about the history of scientific criticism will help us better to define the material which psychology is to give up, and to indicate what it is to choose as a more adequate subject matter. Our naïve experience consists first of all of objects, their properties and changes, which appear to exist and to happen quite independently of us. So far as they are concerned, it does not seem to matter whether or not we see and feel and hear them. When we are not present or are occupied with other matters, they apparently remain just as they were when we gave them our full attention. Under these circumstances, it was a great step when man began to ask questions about the nature of seeing, feeling and hearing. And it was a revolution when he found that colors, noises and smells, etc., were merely products of influences exerted on him by his surroundings. Still, these surroundings seemed to subsist in their *primary* characteristics and to remain "the real world." When those *secondary* qualities were subtracted as purely subjective ingredients, the *primary* qualities seemed to remain directly given as characteristics of reality. But eventually the *primary* qualities of naïve realism turned out to be just as subjective as their *secondary* companions: the form, the weight, and the movement of things had to be given the same interpretation as colors and sounds; they, too, depended upon the experiencing organism and were merely end results of complicated processes in its interior.

What was left? The answer was that, henceforth, *no* phase of immediate experience could be regarded as part of the real world. Therefore, if both the *primary* and the *secondary* characteristics of the experienced world derived from influences which the environment exerts upon the organism, this environment could no longer be identified with man's experienced surroundings. His experienced surroundings were effects of such influences. Hence they could not at the same time be regarded as the causes from which the influences issue. As a result, science had to construct an objective and independent world of physical things, physical space, physical time and physical movement, and had to maintain that this world appears at no point in direct experience.

At this point we must remark that the same reasoning applies to the organism. On the one hand, our body is given to us as a particular thing in sensory experience. On the other hand, this particular sensory experience is caused by physical events in the physical object which we call our organism. Only the body as a part of sensory experience is directly accessible to us. About the organism, just as about other physical things, we know merely by a process of inference or construction. To the influence of other physical objects my organism responds with processes which establish the sensory world around me. Further processes in the organism give rise to the sensory thing which I call my body. Again others are responsible for the inner side of my experience, for feelings such as hunger and fatigue, for emotions such as fear and hope, and so forth.

We need not consider how the world of science, which does not appear in immediate experience, can nevertheless be investigated by the physicist. There can be no doubt as to the remarkable success of the procedure. Whereas the world of naïve man is somewhat confused, and reveals its subjective character in any critical discussion of its properties, in the world of the physicist no confusion and no contradiction are tolerated. Although the rapid changes which physical theory undergoes in our times may surprise us, we still have the feeling that most of these changes are improvements. Eventually, it appears, all important facts of the physical world will be included in a clear and unitary system of knowledge.

Let us now turn to psychology. For a while this discipline was supposed to be the science of direct experience, of its external and internal aspects, as contrasted with physical objects and occurrences. By description of direct experience the psychologist hoped to get not only an orderly survey of all its varieties, but also a great deal of information about the functional relations among these facts. He even aimed at formulating laws which govern the flow of experience.

This conception of psychology has been severely criticized by the psychological school of Behaviorism, which condemns both the subject matter and the purpose of psychology in the older sense. According to the Behaviorist, it has not been possible to give a convincing survey of direct experience; nor has anything come of the attempt to describe the relations among its varieties, or to formulate the laws of so-called "mental life." Obviously, the Behaviorist holds, a science of direct experience which has clear methods and reliable results does not exist. Endless discussions of minor and, less frequently, major items cannot be accepted as a substitute, particularly since facts of experience which are supposed to be the same for all are given utterly different descriptions by different authors. Take the example of images. One psychologist claims to have them in numbers, many of them almost as lively and concrete as percepts. Others tell us that in their direct experience there are no such things, and that the first man is probably deceived by words or other motor phenomena which are related to objects not actually present in experience. If in a simple case like this introspection can give no better result, what shall we expect from it when questions of greater importance but also greater intrinsic difficulty arise? As a matter of fact, the adherents of introspection themselves do not seem to trust their procedure. Apparently they have agreed upon facing important problems as seldom as possible, and to occupy themselves mainly with nuances in the field of sensation which can interest nobody but an Introspectionist. If mere description is to give us a science of direct experience, one naturally expects those who hold this view to attack at once the central facts of their subject matter. And yet they timidly keep to its periphery. In European countries, too, people have long since begun to joke about psychology's ponderous discussion of trifles. It *is* funny to see how, say in the case of simple comparison as a psychological event, hundreds of pages have been filled with descriptions of minute experiences, while the occurrence and the accuracy of the comparison itself have never been given an explanation. Even in a state of perplexity a science can be highly interesting. But this version of psychology has not only been a complete failure; it also has become a bore to all who do not make it their profession.

The Behaviorist likes to add that the insistence on introspection is closely connected with a philosophical bias. Whether or not we are aware of the fact, in its distinction from the world of physics the concept of direct experience is clearly related to such notions as mind and soul. Surreptitiously the term refers to the activities of a mental substance to which the laws of physics and biology do not apply. As a consequence, a great many superstitions of religious or metaphysical extraction have found it easy to hide within the meaning of the concept. As a child the psychologist has heard a great deal about the soul and its miraculous powers. All this still survives in his statements about direct experience, and makes his introspection a mere defense of medieval darkness.

If this were the only argument against introspection, the Introspectionist might answer that the criticism does not apply to the description of direct experience as such, but merely to a certain danger of which not all Introspectionists may be sufficiently aware. Increased self-criticism and a careful elimination of religious or philosophical interests in students of psychology would have to be recommended as remedies. At the same time such measures would serve as pacifying gestures toward stern Behaviorism.

But the Behaviorist has other reasons for not accepting direct experience as a field of scientific research. First of all, as a procedure, introspection lacks the chief methodological virtue of work in physics: a position of the observer outside the system which he observes. Introspecting and its objects are facts within the same system, and the chances that the former leave the latter undisturbed are exceedingly small. Any effort to study sorrow or joy by introspection may serve as an example. If the proper effort is made, such experiences do not remain the same; rather, they tend to disappear, as the selfsame person who has the sorrow or the joy tries to assume the attitude of introspection.

But even if this difficulty could be overcome, according to the Behaviorist we should still find the method useless, because it is so miserably and inevitably subjective. What is the principal characteristic of an objective statement which formulates the result of observations in science? That whoever happens to be interested in the statement can be forced to take it as having a precise meaning. For this purpose we merely have to give the exact definitions of the terms which we are using. Thus the atomic weight and the atomic number

of an element have clear definitions; thus again the analogy
and the homology of morphological structures. There is no
physicist or biologist who does not know the exact denotation
of these words. But now listen to psychologists who talk, let
us say, about the fuzziness which is characteristic of peripheral vision. What exact meaning can be conveyed by this
word so long as it has no accurate definition? Such a definition, however, seems to be impossible wherever one has to do
with the ultimate data of direct experience. If the psychologist
is asked for the definition of fuzziness he may attempt to define it negatively, for instance, as lack of clearness. But this
does not help us very much because we must now ask him
what he means by clearness. He may now tell us that a high
degree of clearness is a normal property of the central part
of an orderly visual field. Unfortunately, such a field may
have more than one normal property, and in the psychologist's pseudo-definition no *differentia specifica* is given—in
addition to which the word "orderly" needs definition just as
badly as do fuzziness and clearness. In any case, the psychologist has now resorted to the only thing which seems
feasible where, as in the field of direct experience, a true definition cannot be achieved: he has merely pointed in a certain
direction. If one cannot define a term, he may give a hint
about the conditions under which the thing in question can be
experienced. In case others understand the words by which
those conditions are described, they may now attach the un-
defined term to that phase of their experience to which the
term is actually meant to refer. But what a crude and vague
procedure this is, if we compare it with the elegant definitions
of exact science!

And still we have assumed that, given the same conditions,
a person who cannot know more than his own experience
will always find in it the same characteristics, objects and occurrences as another person finds in his. Two individual physicists seem to be able to make statements about one and the
same event. They seem, for instance, to make readings from
one and the same apparatus or scale. But in the case of direct
experience two people always have two facts in two separate
experiences. What is our evidence for assuming that under
given conditions the ultimate data of experience are the same
for several persons? Unfortunately, we shall never know
whether or not this is the case. On the one hand, color
blindness and similar phenomena show conclusively that such
an agreement does not generally exist. On the other hand, we
have no proof of agreement even in cases in which all imaginable tests give identical results such as precisely the same
verbal reports. One person may always report "red" where

another person also says "red." Still we know only that the first person has throughout a constant quality wherever and whenever the second person talks about red. We do not know that the first person has the same quality as is called red by the second person. Nor does it help us that what one person calls red seems to have the same exciting character as another person finds in what he calls red. For they may not use the term "exciting" with the same meaning, and actually have different experiences while their expressions are the same.

This is subjectivity in an extreme form. If everyone has his own direct experience, and if he is forever excluded from that of all other persons, direct experience is the private affair of each of us, and with respect to it a common science cannot possibly be achieved. Indeed, since about similar experiences in others so little can be derived from the direct experience of one man, we may go further and ask whether even our best friends have any direct experiences at all. Whatever we see or hear when we talk with them is a part of our experience. What in our experience appears as, say, their voice is first of all the result of physical events in the muscles of their mouths and throats. Such physical events must be understood from the point of view of pure physics and physiology. If so, how do we know that in our friends such processes are accompanied by direct experience?

The Behaviorist might add that he does not deny certain contributions which, before his time, the older forms of psychology have made to the advancement of this science. But he will also say that, when looking upon such achievements from the present point of view, one can easily discover a simple fact: nearly all of them are to the credit not of introspection and description but of objective experimentation. The meaning of this word is just as obvious in psychology as it is in natural science. Instead of inviting a subject to observe and describe his direct experience, we place him in a well-defined situation to which he will react in one way or another. We can observe and measure these responses without his giving us any description of his experiences. In this fashion Weber's law was discovered; this was the kind of experiment by which Fechner made psychology an experimental science; by research of this type, in the almost complete absence of introspection, memory and the formation of habits were investigated; and in the same manner Binet and Simon first measured individual intelligences. At present, even the Introspectionist himself gives us descriptions of colors and tones, pleasures and volitions, only so long as he has not found a method in which description is replaced by objective measurement.

Again, an individual Introspectionist seems to accept the descriptions of a fellow Introspectionist precisely to the extent to which the other has been able to verify his descriptions by more objective data. What, then, is the use of direct experience and description in any case?

From this criticism the Behaviorists do not all draw quite the same conclusions concerning direct experience as such. Virtually none, it is true, finds direct experience a matter of interest for science, since as the private affair of individuals it is not accessible to objective and therefore scientific observation by others. Only a few members of the school seem to go so far as to deny the existence of direct experience altogether. These particular people obviously hate the very concept. But such minor differences of opinion are of no particular importance. For, as to the question of method, all Behaviorists hold the same negative and positive opinions. In this respect their program is a simple consequence of the foregoing argument. With his objective experimentation the psychologist has tacitly placed himself on strictly scientific ground. His only weakness is that he has not yet become fully aware of the difference in principle between exact techniques and merely subjective groping. Physicists and chemists are interested in knowing how a system which they are investigating will react when exposed to certain conditions; they also ask how the reaction changes when these conditions are varied. Both questions are answered by objective observation and measurement. Now, precisely this is also the adequate form of research in psychology: a subject of a certain type (child, adult, man, woman, or animal) is chosen as the system to be investigated. Certain conditions, among which the most important are those of outside stimulation, are given and objectively controlled. And the resulting reaction of the subject is registered or measured just as are the reactions of systems in physics and chemistry.

Thus the only thing which psychologists must now recognize is the fact that this procedure alone can serve any serious purpose in their field. Behavior, i.e., the reaction of living systems to environmental factors, is the only subject matter which can be investigated in scientific psychology; and behavior in no way involves direct experience. The experimental work of the future will study even the highest forms of behavior in purely objective terms. This must be so since direct experience does not occur at a single point of an actual experiment. For some, this truth is somewhat obscured by the fact that in many experiments language reactions seem to be of some importance. If the experimenter himself enjoys what he calls direct experience, and if this experience includes a great many things which are associated with words, he will be inclined to take the words of his subject as signs of similar experiences on the part of this person. Nevertheless, such words must be regarded as responses of the subject; and as such they are purely objective physical facts, produced by certain processes in the larynx and the mouth of the subject. Though the experimenter knows that other objective processes such as those of innervation occur before certain muscles produce words as trains of sound waves, he will be wise if he does not go any further. According to our analysis, he will never know whether any direct experience accompanies those processes. Perhaps we should discipline ourselves to a less frequent use of language reactions in psychological experimentation, until eventually the danger of associating language with direct experience is overcome, and introspection has disappeared from psychology as a science.

Of course, not all reactions of a subject can be objectively observed with the same facility. Sometimes even strong stimulation will not produce overt behavior which we can register with present methods on the outside. In the majority of these cases, however, highly valuable information may be obtained from physiologists, who have studied the functions of the autonomic part of the nervous system and subsequent reactions in the most important visceral organs, including the endocrine glands. One of the main tasks of psychology will be to develop and to adopt available techniques until such visceral reactions can be registered with perfect ease. We also have evidence for assuming that what the Introspectionist calls "thinking" actually consists in slight innervations which the muscles concerned with verbal reactions undergo at the time.

So far, I hope, I have given a fair statement of the opinions which prevail among Behaviorists. It ought to be the more correct since at several points I sympathize with these opinions and am not very fond of introspection as here criticized. Much of current introspection seems to be rather sterile. In an odd contrast to its ambitions, it deflects research from more urgent problems. We will discuss later whether this is an intrinsic property of introspection or merely a consequence of errors which are particularly frequent among Introspectionists.

At present, we have a simpler problem before us. In the natural sciences, the Behaviorist tells us, methods deal with objective reality, whereas the introspection of direct experience—if there is such a thing—deals with something entirely subjective. Is this true? Is this the real reason why natural science has won the admiration of the world while psychology is still in an embryonic state? I cannot admit it. It seems to me that, starting with an admirable enthusiasm for exactness, Behaviorism has been completely misled at this point, and that, as a consequence, the energy spent in objecting to any use of direct experience has been spent in the wrong direction. For, whatever may have happened during the individual development of our keen Behaviorists, about myself I must give the following report, which brings us back to our starting point.

As a child, I had direct experience before I even dreamed of a world entirely beyond it, such as that of physics. At the time I did not, of course, know the term "direct experience." Nor could it have any meaning until I learned about the world of physics with which it then became contrasted. In my original world, innumerable varieties of experience appeared as altogether *objective*, i.e., as existing or occurring independently and externally. Other experiences belonged to me personally and privately, and were in so far *subjective*, such as dreadful fear upon certain occasions, and a warm, overwhelming happiness at Christmas.

In the next chapters we shall be occupied mainly with *objective* experience. This term, however, may easily be misunderstood. I shall therefore try to specify its meaning more precisely. In doing so, I shall even run the risk of repeating certain arguments, because this is the point where most of our difficulties arise.

The name "experience" seems to indicate that, though appearing as objective, the things around me were actually felt to be given "in my perception." In this sense they would still have remained subjective. But this was not at all the case. They simply were there outside. I had no suspicion whatever of their being merely the effects of something else upon me. I must go further. There was not even a question of their depending upon my presence, upon my keeping my eyes open, and so forth. So absolutely objective were those things that for a more objective world no place was left. Even now, their objectivity is so strong and natural that I find myself constantly tempted to attribute to their interior certain characteristics which, according to the physicists, are facts of the physical world. When, in these pages, I use the term "objective experience" it will always have this meaning. For instance, a chair as an objective experience will be something there outside, hard, stable, and heavy. Under no circumstances will it be something merely perceived, or in any sense a subjective phenomenon.

In some cases, it is true, the discrimination between the objective and subjective sides of direct experience may become dubious, as with after-images or with the prick of a needle in my finger. This does not make the discrimination less important. To compare with an example from natural science: in physics the discrimination between conducting substances and insulators remains of high value even though between the extremes we find a great many intermediate cases. In our present connection, the main point is the fact that in things, their movements, and so forth, the very highest objectivity is reached.

To repeat, when I first began to study physics I did not learn only about the physical world. Another lesson was necessarily connected with that study: I was introduced to a manner of thinking in which the term direct experience acquired its meaning. The physical world could not be identical with the objective world which I had had around me the whole time. Rather, I learned that physical objects influence a particularly interesting physical system, my organism, and that my objective experience results when, as a consequence, certain complicated processes have happened in this system. Obviously, I realized, I cannot identify the final products, the things and events of my experience, with the physical objects from which the influences come. If a wound is not the gun which emitted the projectile, then the things which I have before me, which I see and feel, cannot be identical with the corresponding physical objects. These objects merely establish certain alterations within my physical organism, and the final products of these alterations are the things which I behold in my visual field, or which I feel with my fingers.[1]

It remains nevertheless true that things in the latter sense were the first objects of which I knew. Moreover, I now understood that any other objects such as those of physics I could never know directly. Plainly, the characteristics of the physical world could be investigated only in a process of inference

[1] We have seen that the same warning applies to the relation between my organism as a physical system and my body as a perceptual fact. My body is the outcome of certain processes in my physical organism, processes which start in the eyes, muscles, skin and so forth, exactly as the chair before me is the final product of other processes in the same physical organism. If the chair is seen "before me," the "me" of this phrase means my body as an experience, of course, not my organism as an object of the physical world. Even psychologists do not always seem to be entirely clear about this point.

or construction, however necessary the construction might be. It was in contrast to this, the constructed, world that the world before me could now be called the world of direct experience.

But how can I say that a chair, for example, is an objective experience, if I must admit that it depends upon certain processes in my organism? Does not the chair become subjective on this ground? It does and it does not. At this very moment we have changed the meaning of the terms "subjective" and "objective." In a preceding paragraph "objective" denoted a characteristic which some parts of my experience, in contrast to others, possess as such (exactly as they have size, color, hardness, and so forth). But as the term "subjective" has been used just now it refers to the genetic dependence of all experience upon my physical organism. In this latter meaning, subjectivity is not itself an experienced attribute; rather, it is a relationship which we ascribe to *all,* and therefore also to objective, experiences once we have learned to regard them as results of organic processes. Quite often the two denotations of the term are confused in the most deplorable manner, as though what is genetically subjective ought also to appear as subjective in experience. Some Introspectionists, for instance, seem to think that, properly speaking, the chair before me must be a subjective phenomenon, which appears before me only as a consequence of learning or interpretation. On the other hand, since no such subjective chair can be discovered, the Behaviorist derides the Introspectionist for dwelling in a world of imaginary ghosts. The simple truth is that some of the experiences which depend upon processes in my organism have the character of objectivity, whereas others which depend upon different processes in the same organism have the character of being subjective. This contrast has nothing to do with the genetic subjectivity of both types of experience, i.e., with the fact that both depend upon events within the organism. After this, I hope, misunderstandings of the term "objective experience" will no longer be possible. When I talk about a chair, I mean the chair of my everyday life and not some subjective phenomenon.

On the other hand, we have seen, the chair of objective experience cannot be identified with the chair as part of the physicist's world. Now, since the world of direct experience is the first I knew, and since all I now know about the physical world was later inferred from certain events in the experienced world, how can I be expected to ignore the experienced world? After all, it still remains my only basis for any guesses about physical facts. If I choose, I can, of course, raise the question whether, in a certain sense, the physical world is perhaps the more important one. But even then I must admit that, from the point of view of acquaintance or access, the experienced world is prior to that of physics; also, that my only way of investigating physical realities is that of observing objective experiences and drawing from them the proper conclusions. To be sure, as physiology advances, I may become able to discover the nervous processes which underlie my observing and concluding, and thus to give a physical theory of these events. But again, since the world of physiology is part of the physical world, it can never become directly accessible to me. Any progress which I can make in physiology depends upon my observations of what I call a body in direct perceptual experience. If we listen to Behaviorists we may have the impression that to them the physical and physiological worlds as such are directly known, and that in their, the Behaviorists', case knowing has nothing to do with direct experience. None the less, I cannot change this report about my own case in which there is no direct access to physical and physiological facts. Naturally, with this defect I find it frightfully difficult to become a Behaviorist.

What, then, about the Behaviorist's statement that, in physics, observation deals with objective reality, whereas, in the case of direct experience, it deals with something that has no scientific value?

Let me describe my own procedure when I investigate the properties of a physical or chemical object. In this mixture of chemical substances, is there any considerable amount of $H_4C_2O_2$? I know about the presence of the mixture by way of certain objective experiences before me, and I find the positive answer to the question by smelling, i.e., in a further direct experience. Since this is a rather crude procedure, let us consider a case of accurate measurement. What is the intensity of the electric current which, under the given conditions, must flow in that wire? The position of a pointer on the scale of a certain apparatus gives me the answer in visual terms, the apparatus being part of my visual field, exactly as the wire and the given conditions manifest themselves as parts of objective experience. The same holds for all possible statements and measurements which I shall ever be able to make in physics. My observations of physical facts always remain in the same general class as those which refer to after-images, to the fuzziness which I find in peripheral vision, or to my feeling healthy. Hence, the exactness of my observations in physics cannot be related to an alleged avoidance of direct experience in physical research. I do not avoid direct experience when I am working in physics; for I cannot avoid it. Yet the procedure works. Thus at least some observations which refer to direct experience must constitute an entirely adequate basis for science.

If all concrete statements which I can make in physical research are primarily based on observations within the field of experience, some consequences are plainly inevitable. How do I define my terms when I work as a physicist? Since my knowledge of physics consists entirely of concepts and observations contained in or derived from direct experience, all the terms which I use in this science must ultimately refer to the same source. If I try to define such terms, my definitions may, of course, refer to further concepts and terms. But the final steps in the process will always be: pointing toward the locus of certain experiences about which I am talking, and hints where to make certain observations. Even the most abstract concepts of physics, such as that of entropy, can have no meaning without a reference, indirect though it may be, to certain direct experiences. I shall never be able to give a definition of terms in physics, or to understand such a definition when given by others, which differs in this respect from what I may use as definitions in psychology. Nevertheless, at this point also the method of physics is successful. I never have difficulty with definitions when physicists talk with me about their science. Hence, some definitions which ultimately refer to direct experience must be sufficiently safe for use in an exact discipline. The exactness of definitions in physics cannot result from the alleged fact that in this science definitions are independent of direct experience; for there is no such independence.

But the Behaviorist tells us that observation of direct experience is a private affair of individuals, whereas in physics two physicists can make the same observation, for instance, on a galvanometer. I deny the truth of the latter statement. Even from the point of view of Behaviorism the statement is incorrect. If somebody observes a galvanometer, he observes something different from the galvanometer as a physical object. For the object of his observation is the result of certain organic processes, only the beginning of which is determined by the physical galvanometer itself. In a second person, the observed galvanometer is again only the final result of such processes, which now occur in the organism of this second person. By no means do the two people observe the same instrument then, although physically the processes in one and the other are started by the same physical object. And yet, in most cases their statements about their observations agree so well that they never ask themselves whether a sufficient similarity of their two experienced galvanometers (and of both with the physical object) can be taken for granted. Again, the procedure works. The privacy of direct experience does not disturb anybody—in physics. When working in such a case with others, each individual physicist is naïvely convinced that his fellow-physicists "have that galvanometer before them." Thus he tacitly assumes that his fellow-workers have objective experiences highly similar to his own, and he does not hesitate to take the words of his colleagues as statements about these experiences. According to the Behaviorist this means, of course, that the physicist allows private affairs to play a part in exact science. Curiously enough, this does not seem to disturb the scientific procedure at all, just as it does not disturb the affairs of everyday life, where the same attitude occurs quite generally and naturally. In some cases, therefore, belief in specific experiences of others must be quite harmless, and cannot be regarded as an obstacle to scientific progress. Thus, if psychology does not advance more rapidly, the reason for it cannot be that belief as such.

There remains one consequence of the fact that observation in physics is observation within the field of direct experience. As a physicist who observes his apparatus, I do not fear that my activity as an observer has any serious influence upon the characteristics of what I observe—if only I keep myself as a physical system at a sufficient distance from the apparatus as another physical system. And yet, as direct experiences, both the apparatus to be observed and my activity of observing depend upon processes in the same system, namely, my organism. Again the Behaviorist must be wrong when he declares that, because of the inclusion of observer and observed facts in one system, the observation of direct experience has no scientific value. For in the case of physical observation the situation is similar: the material to be observed and the process of observing belong to the same system. Thus we see that the physicist and the psychologist are once more in exactly the same situation. It does not matter at all whether I call myself a physicist or a psychologist when I observe a galvanometer. In both cases my observation is directed toward the same objective experience. The procedure works in physics. Why should it not be used in psychology? There must be some instances in which the observation of facts within the field of direct experience does not seriously disturb these facts.

To be sure, this argument implies a remarkable limitation of the range of its own application. It does not mean that all forms of so-called introspection are justified; even less does it mean that the findings of introspection are quite generally independent of the activity of introspecting. Here the critical position of Behaviorism has only exaggerated the scope of a fair argument in unjustly applying it to all statements about direct experience. The critical point as such is well taken in many cases.

I have described how, even as a physicist, I must deal with direct experience. It is true, an extremist such as a Behaviorist could derive from this description some doubts as to the objectivity of methods in physics. But fortunately, such doubts had not yet arisen when in the time of Galileo, Newton and Huyghens the first really important steps were taken in physics. These great investigators just went about their business, pragmatically naïve and happily undisturbed by a Behaviorism in physics which would have blocked the whole development for the sake of epistemological purity. The procedure worked in spite of the fact that to justify its steps on logical grounds would sometimes have been a difficult task. Sciences which wish to carry on their research in a productive fashion generally show a healthy disdain for such scruples. It might be better for psychology, if after listening to a wholesome critical lesson from Behaviorism it would also return to its job with more naïveté, and use any techniques which yield results.

As a scientific attitude, the Homeric assault of Behaviorism against direct experience appears to me very strange. The Behaviorist does not generally show too great an interest in epistemological considerations. It is just one point which suddenly catches his attention: "How can I know about the direct experience of others? I shall never have a definite proof of the validity of such knowledge. But physics, that is another matter. There we are safe." The Behaviorist forgets that to prove the existence of an independent physical world is about as difficult as to make sure that other people have experiences. If I were an extreme purist, I might argue the former point precisely as the Behaviorist disputes the assumption of direct experience in others. For some reason it does not occur to him to apply his criticism to the assumption of the physical world. He does not say: "Thou shalt not work upon a physical world, the existence of which will always remain a mere assumption." On the contrary, he assumes the reality of this world with all the healthy naïveté which he lacks in psychology. The reason is, perhaps, that the achievements of physical science are imposing, and have become the ideal of Behaviorism. But, as a methodological purist, the Behaviorist ought not to regard mere achievements as satisfactory proof in such matters. Of course, personally I am in this respect as convinced as any Behaviorist has ever been. I am also fully aware of the fact that sciences often believe and postulate where epistemology may have its doubts. But from this point of view I can, of course, also believe that others have direct experiences. The decisive point is that this serves to make my work simpler and more productive. To repeat, I feel the more justified in this attitude since I find that my work in physics is also founded on direct experience; that in this science the assumption of direct experience in others is made as a matter of course; and that, therefore, the enormous superiority of physics over psychology cannot derive from any differences in this respect.

At this moment I see the Behaviorist smiling ironically. Probably he wants to say this: "With all his philosophy, Mr. Köhler will never make any headway against sound scientific Behaviorism." My answer is that the basis of Behaviorism is just as philosophical as my criticism: Behaviorism grows on epistemological ground. In this connection the only difference between the Behaviorist and me is one which concerns the width of our visual fields. The Behaviorist sees only a single theorem of epistemology—one person cannot observe another person's experience. As an extremist he dwells exclusively on this point and ignores the context from which it is taken. I am aware of this context; it is stated in the foregoing argument. And, obviously, I prefer to draw my conclusions from this wider view of the situation.

II

PSYCHOLOGY AS A
YOUNG SCIENCE

So FAR, direct experience has been shown to be the raw material of both physics and psychology. If in spite of this fact the physical sciences are so far ahead of psychology, what can we do in order to obtain similar achievements?

One advantage which contemporary physics has springs from a careful selection of the experiences which play a major part in the crucial moments of physical research. Naturally enough, the physicist ignores all subjective experience as defined in the first chapter, because feelings, emotions, and so forth, seem to have no analogues among the events of the physical world. All the difficulties of the psychologist who tries to observe and describe subjective phenomena are thus simply avoided by physical science.

But the selection and exclusion do not stop at this point. While during early developments most objective experience was taken as evidence of corresponding physical facts, a more critical view of the situation later tended to eliminate large parts of this material as well. At the present time, the process of selection has become extremely severe. For instance, the advancement of science has made it possible to transform qualitative observation into quantitative measurement almost everywhere. Virtually all physical measurements are now made in an extremely indirect fashion. Seldom does the physicist directly observe what must be regarded as the experienced counterpart of the physical variable in question; rather, his observation refers to a different experience which has the virtue of lending itself to more accurate determination. In this, knowledge of the relationship between the latter experience and the physical variable must, of course, be taken for granted. Of all objective experiences none seems better to fulfill the requirements of the physicist than the location of a visual line (a pointer) on a scale of other visual lines, especially if this location becomes a coincidence of the first line with one of the others. The range of experiences which are still being used in measurement has indeed been reduced to a minimum. It almost seems as if the same scale and the same pointer were used universally. This simple situation tells the physicist a hundred altogether different stories about the physical world. It may give evidence concerning "atmospheres" or "volts," "ampères" or "temperatures," and so forth, almost *ad infinitum*. Apart from observing coincidences, and checking the connection of his apparatus with the system under investigation, the physicist has only to read certain words and figures on the scale. No more direct experience than this enters into the procedure. Under such circumstances, there cannot be much opportunity for blundering. Because of this advantage, even so simple a fact as physical size is not measured directly. The physicist does not measure the length of an object by direct comparison with the length of a standard object. Such a comparison would not be accurate enough; moreover, it would be disturbed by optical illusions. He prefers the method of coinciding lines or points. Actually he defines physical length by this method, and then measures the length of an object by observing the coincidence of its boundaries with certain points on a scale.

If now we ask ourselves whether, in psychology, we are to imitate the procedure of the physical sciences, two answers must be given to this question, because the procedure has two aspects. In the *first* place, it involves making statements about physical systems on the basis of objective experience. Now, the behavior of men and animals can also be observed in objective experience—an observation in which the direct experience of the subjects plays no rôle. Plainly, such a study of behavior is perfectly legitimate and will therefore be further developed in the future. True, it existed before the days of Behaviorism; but this school is fundamentally right in praising the advantages of objective procedure as against introspection. Although Behaviorists have gone too far in failing to appreciate that, even in objective methods, direct experience of the observer remains the raw material, their error is of no particular importance so long as our question is given the proper *second* answer. Unfortunately, Behaviorism here tends to take the wrong position.

In present physics, we have seen, objective procedures are characterized by the use of a small group of selected objective experiences and, consequently, by the exclusion of all others because they do not satisfy the requirements of quantitative measurement. Ought we to do the same thing in psychology as the science of behavior? Evidently, the answer will depend upon the nature of the observed behavior. It is difficult to judge about a method as such. A method is good if it is adapted to the given subject matter; and it is bad if it lacks regard for this material, or if it misdirects research. Hence, what has been shown to be an excellent procedure in one science, or for some problems, may be altogether useless or even a hindrance in another science or for other problems. In this respect, behavior is easily seen to have distinctly different phases, and to give the psychologist correspondingly different tasks. Wherever indirect quantitative methods such as those of physics can be applied in conformity with our task, they must of course be applied. For instance, C. P. Richter and his collaborators have discovered a way in which the various drives of animals, and their variations in the course of time, can be investigated. The method consists in registering amounts of general or special activity.[1] Naturally, all students of behavior will be keenly interested in the future development of this technique. It is the correct procedure in cases in which total amounts of activity in relation to outer and inner conditions yield valuable information.

But what about other instances in which either our problems are not of the quantitative type, or where we have no way to replace direct observation by observation of other facts which are better adapted to accurate measurement? Obviously, the various qualitative types of behavior are no less important than are the quantitative differences within a given type. Once we know about such qualitative varieties, and also about the special type with which we are dealing in a given case, the question of quantitative measurement becomes extremely important. But in any case the discrimination of qualitative types must be accomplished in the first place. Thus during the observation of a puppy we may have to ask ourselves whether the behavior of the animal represents playful activity or a more serious reaction to existing conditions. Such a question does not necessarily imply "mental life" in the puppy; rather, it refers to a characteristic difference in what is actually being observed. The difference is one of quality of behavior. Again, while observing a man in a somewhat critical situation, it may be essential to observe whether he talks to us in a steady or in a shaky voice. At the present time this is essentially a qualitative discrimination. In the future a method may be discovered by which the steadiness of a voice can be measured. But, if such a method is to be properly used, we must still know from direct observation what we mean by steadiness or unsteadiness as temporary

[1] *Cf.* C. P. Richter, "Animal Behavior and Internal Drives," *Quarterly Review of Biology,* 2, 1927.

characteristics of voices. Otherwise, we should be in danger of measuring the wrong thing.

The application of indirect methods to many other forms of behavior is similarly restricted. Behaviorists, I take it, hold that we can investigate the emotional behavior of subjects without being concerned with their subjective experiences. At any rate, in this case psychologists have often tried to transfer observation to fields in which accurate registration and measurement are possible. Much work has been done to develop pneumographic, plethysmographic, galvanographic methods, and so forth. The result is not altogether encouraging, however; for again, our interpretation of the curves so registered depends entirely upon simultaneous direct observation either of the subject's experiences or of his behavior in a more general qualitative sense. By no means do we feel justified in drawing conclusions from the curves alone. At the present time such methods seem to be problems in themselves rather than aids for the solution of psychological problems. Generally speaking, it is still the easier and the more reliable procedure to observe anger in a subject's behavior as such than to measure, say, the adrenalin in his blood.

Why does this difficulty beset psychology while it does not seem to exist in physics? The answer is simple enough: physics is an old science, and psychology is in its infancy. It took the physicists centuries gradually to substitute for direct and more qualitative observations others which are indirect but very accurate. Their success was related to previously acquired knowledge about the physical world. Most indirect methods and measurements presuppose a vast background of information. Physics had to gather this information when its observations were still more qualitative and less accurate. Only in this way could it discover those important physical relations, on the basis of which qualitative direct observation is now so largely replaced by indirect and precise measurement. Oersted had to discover the deflection of a magnet in the neighborhood of an electric current before exact measurements of the intensities of currents became possible. His was a qualitative and direct observation; but an indirect quantitative procedure was its fruit. Even in our day, Röntgen did not at once make measurements when he discovered the X-rays. First of all he had to analyze their properties in qualitative experimentation. Later, of course, his rays could become a means of measuring the constants of crystals. Much too easily do we forget the fact that, at their start but also when more particular new fields come into sight, the natural sciences rely almost completely upon qualitative observation. To be sure, the quantitative indirect methods are now the most imposing features of the exact sciences, particularly to the layman who admires these disciplines from the outside. But we ought to realize that, in most cases, such methods represent mere later refinements of original methods, which were direct and qualitative. Only on this basis could the refined superstructure be erected. In the eighteenth century, Cavendish measured the resistances of different materials by comparing the shocks which geometrically equivalent pieces of these materials gave his arm, when he touched one pole of the battery with those pieces and the second pole with the other hand. Was this improper? On the contrary, in what was then a new field the procedure was perfectly sound. In this way he gained preliminary knowledge of facts which could then be used for the development of more precise methods.

It follows that, wherever we have a good quantitative problem in psychology and a correspondingly accurate method of measuring, we can immediately apply procedures which are comparable to those now used in physics. The problems which Galileo attacked in the seventeenth century could at once be solved quantitatively, because in this instance the qualitative experience of everyday life provided the necessary basis. But for the majority of psychological problems this is not the case. Where in psychology have we that knowledge of important functional relationships on which indirect and exact measurements could be based? It does not exist. Therefore, if the development of more exact methods presupposes the existence of such knowledge, the gathering of it must be our first task. For the most part, our preliminary advance in this direction will have to be crude. People who protest in the name of exactness do not understand our situation in psychology. They realize neither the nature nor the historical background of indirect quantitative methods. If we wish to imitate the physical sciences, we must not imitate them in their highly developed contemporary form. Rather, we must imitate them in their historical youth, when their state of development was comparable to our own at the present time. Otherwise we should behave like boys who try to copy the imposing manners of full-grown men without understanding their *raison d'être*, also without seeing that intermediate phases of development cannot be skipped. In this respect, a survey of the history of physics is most illuminating. If we are to emulate the natural sciences, let us do so intelligently.

Behavior is enormously rich in nuances. Only if we recognize this wealth and study it directly can quantitative procedures gradually be discovered which fit our subject matter. At present, and in this broader historical perspective, qualitative observation may often be more fruitful than premature measurements.

If organisms were more similar to the systems which physics investigates, a great many methods of the physicists could be introduced in our science without much change. But in actual fact the similarity is not very great. One of the advantages which make the physicist's work so much easier is the simplicity of his systems. His systems are simple because, to a degree, the experimenter himself determines their properties. I am far from believing that organic processes are of a supernatural kind. On the contrary, the most startling difference between the organism and a simple physical system is the enormous number of physical and chemical processes which, in complicated interrelations, occur at a given time in the organism. We are utterly unable to create simpler organic systems for elementary study. An amoeba is a more complicated system than all systems of the inanimate world. We also know that in studying, for instance, the properties of a nerve-muscle preparation, we are not investigating "a part" of natural behavior. The functional characteristics of such a preparation differ from the characteristics which the same nerve and muscle exhibit when functioning in normal behavior. Some Behaviorists have rightly said that it is the whole organism which we have to study. Unfortunately, in the whole organism one can seldom follow the change of one particular variable, as though it alone were affected by a certain change in outer conditions. The change of one factor usually involves concomitant changes in many others, and the latter changes again affect the former. Now, isolation of functional relationships and reduction of variables which take part in an event are the great artifices by which exact investigations are facilitated in physics. Since this technique is not applicable in psychology, since we have to take the organism more or less as it is, any kind of observation which refers to the behavior of our subjects as complex acting units will be right in our case.

Actually, however, young psychology could not resist the temptation which arose from the brilliant achievements of contemporary science. Every now and then a wave of short-sighted imitation swept it off its feet. Fechner himself was the first to copy adult physics when psychology was hardly born. Apparently he was convinced that measuring as such would make a science out of psychology. The result is well known. Measuring, which is tremendously fruitful as a refined continuation of previous qualitative observation, can easily become a dead routine without such a preparation. Today we can no longer doubt that thousands of quantitative psychophysical experiments were made almost in vain. No one knew precisely what he was measuring. Nobody had studied the mental processes upon which the whole procedure was built. It seems that in Fechner's day psychology became a science not as a result of his psychophysics, but merely on this occasion, and in spite of the premature quantitative program.

In the meantime, the lesson seems to have been forgotten. When observing the energy with which able psychologists measure individual intelligences, one is almost reminded of Fechner's time. From a practical point of view, it is true, their work is obviously not without merits. It seems that a crude total ability for certain performances is actually measured by such tests. For, on the whole, the test scores show a satisfactory correlation with achievements both in school and in subsequent life. This very success, however, contains a grave danger. The tests do not show what specific processes actually participate in the test achievements. The scores are mere numbers which allow of many different interpretations. Figuratively speaking, a given score may mean: degree 3 of "intelligence," together with degree 1 of "accuracy," with degree 4 of "ambition" and degree 3 of "quickness of fatigue." But it may also mean "intelligence" 6, "accuracy" 2, "ambition" 1 and "quickness of fatigue" 4—and so forth. Thus combinations of certain components in varying proportions may give precisely the same I.Q. Obviously, this matters, even for practical purposes. For instance, a child ought to be treated according to the nature and strength of the specific factors which co-operate in establishing his total I.Q. This is not a new criticism, of course, but in view of the influence which the tests have gained in our schools it must be repeated. We are still much too easily satisfied by our tests because, as quantitative procedures, they look so pleasantly scientific. Once more I must insist that this is a superficial view. If we compare the business of testing with the conduct of our ideal, the physicist, we find a striking difference. What questions does the physicist ask when he faces a new field of research? They are of this kind: Is light an oscillatory process? If it is, does it oscillate in the direction of propagation or at right angles to this direction? Is magnetism produced by the magnetic fields of elementary currents in molecular structures? Why does surface tension give liquids and liquid films regular forms? How can the spectrum of one element contain thousands of different lines? This is the type of question in which we find the physicist interested. In such questions he formulates his fundamental problems. It is true, when trying to find the answers, he uses at definite stages quantitative techniques which greatly help in the process. He also uses them in order to establish accurate laws. But all this is governed by his questions about the nature of events and things. Are given phenomena of one kind or another? Such are the main problems of experimental science, in the investigation of which measurement has become so important as a servant.

If we ask ourselves what problems concerning the processes involved in intelligent behavior we are solving by our tests, not very many of us will have an answer ready. Some psychologists have gone so far as to suggest that intelligence be defined as the X which is measured by the test, and that in science measuring is more important than all questions about the nature of events. This makes it quite clear that instead of imitating the essential pattern of research in physics we tend to copy merely its outer quantitative form. Suppose a physicist is interested in the various types of motors. We would not think too highly of the man if he were to restrict his investigation of motors to the following tests: measurement of their volume, of the temperature at their surface, of the ionization of the air in their neighborhood, of the maximum frequency with which they can rotate, and of their total weight. Probably no respect for him would be left if he were now to calculate from these data "power coefficients," to define "power" by his curious method, to ignore all questions about the processes which make the motors work, and to remain satisfied with this procedure for years. With this comparison I am, of course, exaggerating. I am doing so intentionally in order to call attention to the fact that quantitative methods *per se* are far from establishing the value of given activities. Unfortunately, human interests tend to be so narrow that preoccupation with only the quantitative phase of research immediately leads to further trouble. People who suffer from this ailment will soon fail to recognize problems which do not lend themselves at once to quantitative investigation. And yet, at the time such problems may be much more essential and, in a deeper meaning of the word, scientific than many purely quantitative questions. In the solution of those problems qualitative observation would constitute the first step; but since in contemporary physics qualitative methods seem to be despised, we lack the courage to undertake these tasks, however urgent they may actually be. Thus we are in danger of missing precisely those opportunities which, in our stage as an immature science, would be the greatest of all.

In animal psychology the situation has sometimes tended

to become somewhat similar to the one which we have just been discussing. In experimentation on animals virtually the only quantitative method is statistical. In other words, we do not measure in the strict meaning of the term; rather we count how many times an animal or a group of animals does this or that under given circumstances. Naturally, in order to have comparable cases to which the procedure can properly be applied, we put the animals in situations in which their behavior is restricted to a few possibilities. The actual performances we count, and the result of our experiments is given in frequencies for the various possibilities. The method as such is not open to criticism. But we ought to realize that, when used exclusively, it is likely to restrict our knowledge of behavior. With a given problem in mind, we necessarily choose experimental conditions in such a way as to exclude possibilities which are otherwise in the animal's repertoire. It is true, some psychologists do at least observe the remaining forms of behavior as such, and are thus aided in the interpretation of their quantitative results. But others refuse to do so, because in their opinion only quantitative observations are scientific. This leaves them with mere figures as their material. Even then the procedure may be valuable—provided they belong to those fortunate people who always hit upon interesting experimental problems. In others, however, the same attitude is likely to result in conservatism. Being in love with figures and curves, they will keep away from the true source of new ideas and new problems in a youthful science: a broad outlook upon its subject matter.

One can hardly exaggerate the value of qualitative information as a necessary supplement to quantitative work. In the absence of such information, behavior psychology will easily become as sterile as supposedly it is exact. Too great an interest in available quantitative methods is not a promising state of mind at a time when the development of psychology depends upon the discovery of new questions rather than upon the monotonous repetition of standardized methods. If it be said that behavior psychology does not need this advice, I reply that Watson has been criticized because his well-known observations on children were not made in the sanctified form of quantitatively controlled experiments. I do not think that these observations give an entirely adequate account of primary reactions and of early learning in children. But they do reveal interesting facts which we might never have learned from columns of abstract figures. Once an eminent psychologist was friendly enough to say a few approving words about my own work on intelligent behavior in apes. Still, he added, you have missed the main point by not applying the statistical method. To my mind this statement shows a certain inability to recognize the problems which I tried to treat in a preliminary way. These problems concern the characteristic forms of intelligent behavior in a particular species, as shown in various situations. Everything that is valuable in these observations would disappear if "results" were handled in an abstract statistical fashion. Under these circumstances, a warning against glorification of quantitative procedures alone still seems indicated. Quantitative research, I repeat, presupposes qualitative analysis in which fruitful problems are discovered.

In physics, measuring usually results from specific questions, questions which are in a way preliminary hypotheses concerning unknown phases of nature. Observed but enigmatic facts are, of course, over and over again explained in physics by assumptions about unknown parts of nature. But the physicist does not make such assumptions for their own sake. Any particular assumption which serves to explain certain observations has consequences quite apart from these facts. All interest is naturally concentrated on these consequences and on their examination. Take this example. What happens in electrolytical conduction? Arrhenius makes the bold hypothesis that in conducting solutions molecules are dissociated into independent ions. The charges of these particles explain the fact that the solution is a conductor. But if the ions are practically independent particles, their independence must have consequences as to the optic behavior of the electrolyte. These consequences are soon tested in new experiments. The example shows that a good hypothesis is just as essential to progress in science as observation and measurement are. In fact, the growth of physics can be described as a series of movements back and forth from the first to the second, and vice versa.

Organic systems offer countless puzzling facts to which the same procedure can be profitably applied. We know a few things about the effects of stimulation upon the sense organs of our subjects. We also observe their overt responses. But between these two terms there is more *terra incognita* than was on the map of Africa seventy years ago. Obviously, behavior depends upon the dynamics of the organism as well as upon outer conditions. To the degree to which the interior of the living system is not yet accessible to observation, it will be our task to invent hypotheses about the events which here take place. For much is bound to happen between stimulation and response. This response cannot possibly be understood in terms of peripheral stimulation alone. Those who know the history of physics will be inclined to believe that this task of finding fruitful assumptions about the hidden antecedents of behavior is about the most important of all. The whole future of psychology may depend on it. On this point all the creative force of Behaviorism ought to be concentrated in a fine emulation of physics. The critical attitude which Behaviorism shows toward introspection and direct experience is a merely negative feature of the school. Where are its specific positive ideas? If I feel a trifle disappointed by the work of Behaviorism, the reason is first of all a certain poverty in the functional concepts which the school applies to the explanation of behavior. It is scarcely a satisfactory achievement if the Behaviorist borrows from physiology the concept of reflex action (including the reflexes of inner secretion), and then adds conditioning as the function which is to explain the development of all new forms of conduct. Behaviorists, like many other people nowadays, seem to be convinced negativists. "Thou shalt not acknowledge direct experience in psychology" is their first commandment, and "Thou shalt not conceive of other functions but reflexes and conditioned reflexes" is the second. We need not return to the first thesis. The second commandment appears to me incompatible even with the modest knowledge of organic events which is now at our disposal. Nor do I understand for what reason the organism should be conceived of as such a poor affair. I cannot help feeling that, in excluding all but these two types of function, Behaviorism exhibits an unwholesome narrowness. While the school claims to be revolutionary, it actually is dogmatically conservative. Even now, as an adult science, physics permits itself at least one new idea about the nucleus of the atom per year. In spite of the youth of psychology, it seldom seems to occur to Behaviorists that new functional ideas could be needed in our science. Apparently, when Behaviorism was born, somebody put final truth about the functional possibilities of the organism into the cradle.

Why do I say that the functional concepts of Behaviorism are poor? My statement is caused by a comparison with the various processes which the physicist attributes to the inanimate world. And, I repeat, some simple physical systems are far richer in the variety of their functions than is the nervous system of man in the eyes of a Behaviorist. To be sure, no soap-bubble has so far ever been conditioned. Nevertheless, with the functional characteristics which the soap-bubble does exhibit it appears to me decidedly superior to the organism as seen by the Behaviorist. The same statement holds for innumerable other systems of the inanimate world. Even though they lack reflexes and conditioned reflexes, their conduct is often curiously reminiscent of animal behavior. But in Behaviorism it would be heresy to follow such a hint.

When beginning to imitate natural science, Behaviorism excluded not only direct experience from its program. Strangely enough, it also excluded the wealth of functional concepts which its ideal, physical science, offered for the taking. Even some members of the school are beginning to protest against this attitude.

An observer who looks without prejudice upon human and animal behavior will hardly find that reflexes and conditioned reflexes are the most natural concepts to be used in an explanation of the facts. But once a person is deeply convinced that the whole truth about the nervous system can be told in such terms, he has, of course, no real incentive for free observation of behavior. Since he feels no need of new functional concepts, why should he bother about a kind of information from which such concepts could arise. On the other hand, the restriction of observation to the counting of a few reactions, which alone are possible in customary experimental situations, will serve to protect the conservative scheme with which the Behaviorist works. Thus narrowness in observation protects narrowness in theory.

But even with a more impartial interest in the various forms of behavior, how are we to find new functional concepts? Is not the gap between observable conditions of stimulation and observable overt responses so large that hypotheses about connecting functions must be premature? It goes without saying that we will use all hints which are given by nerve physiology and endocrinology. But even the more recent discoveries in these fields do not tell us precisely what we need for our purposes. In such a situation virtually any assumption will be more useful than mere waiting. The hypotheses of empirical science are often based on somewhat meager evidence. Since such assumptions will be tested and continually corrected, they can surely do no harm. If they prove to be wholly or partly right, no one will have scruples about the legitimacy of their origin. If they are shown to be wrong or sterile, they can always be discarded and replaced by better ideas.

In actual fact, Gestalt Psychology has no particular difficulty in developing its principal hypotheses about the dynamics of the nervous system. In observations on the behavior of animals and man, direct experience of the subjects is not involved. At any rate, if such an experience exists, the experimenter does not assume that it exerts an influence upon the course of the physiological events which are interpolated between outside conditions and overt behavior. Assumptions about these events must be such as to explain the observed behavior without reference to non-physiological factors. Direct experience is not a force which could interfere with the chain of physiological causation. (Dualists make the opposite hypothesis. But I do not think that their way of thinking contributes much to the functional analysis of behavior.)

Although this is the way in which I have to think about my subjects, I cannot exclude my own direct experience when I observe their behavior. How could I exclude it, since even when employing the most indirect methods of physics, I have to rely on perceptual facts? Moreover, we have seen, in the study of behavior I have to use many forms of objective experience which are no longer used in the quantitative procedures of physics. But if my experience is acceptable as the basis of my statements about the behavior of others, why should I hesitate to utilize it when developing hypotheses about the functions of the nervous system?

Suppose I am being used as a subject. In this case, the experimenter will again wish to know what hidden processes in my nervous system mediate between observed stimulating conditions and observed behavior. But I can help him to build a bridge across the gap. Many phases of my overt behavior are accompanied by direct experience. Now we do not doubt that this experience is most closely related to some of the processes about which the experimenter wishes to have at least a working hypothesis. Under these circumstances, it seems natural to use my direct experience as a basis for theoretical operations. It is quite true, not all events in my nervous system which contribute to my behavior are accompanied by direct experience. To this extent any hypothesis to which we are led in this fashion will be of limited scope. It must be left to physiology to transcend these limitations in the future. Unfortunately, at the present time physiological views about the functions of the brain are about as speculative as our own guesses. Thus it will be advisable to make full use of the chance which inference from direct experience offers to the psychologist.

It is not proposed that for this purpose we introspect in the technical sense of the word. Only simple statements about experience, the kind of statements which all observers of people, of animals, of instruments, and so forth, are wont to make, will be used for our enterprise. Let us begin with objective experience. Under normal conditions, objective experience depends upon physical events which stimulate sense organs. But it also depends upon physiological events of the kind which we now wish to explore. The physicist is interested in the former fact: the dependence of objective experience upon physical events outside the organism enables him to infer from experience what those physical events are. We are interested in the latter fact: since experience depends upon physiological events in the brain, such experience ought to contain hints as to the nature of these processes. In other words, we argue that if objective experience allows us to draw a picture of the physical world, it must also allow us to draw a picture of the physiological world to which it is much more closely related.

Obviously, however, if the characteristics of concomitant physiological processes are to be inferred from given characteristics of experience, we need a leading principle which governs the transition. Many years ago, a certain principle of this kind was introduced by E. Hering. Its content is as follows. Experiences can be systematically ordered, if their various kinds and nuances are put together according to their similarities. The procedure is comparable to the one by which animals are ordered in zoology and plants in botany. The processes upon which experiences depend are not directly known. But if they were known, they could also be ordered according to their similarities. Between the two systematic orders, that of experiences and that of concomitant physiological processes, various relationships may be assumed to obtain. But the relation between the two orderly systems will be simple and clear only if we postulate that both have the same form or structure *qua* systems. Sometimes this principle is more explicitly formulated in a number of "psychophysical axioms."[2] In our connection, it will suffice if we give some examples of its application.

A sound of given pitch can be produced in many degrees of experienced loudness. In geometrical terms, the natural systematic order of all these loudnesses is a straight line, because in proceeding from the softest to the loudest sounds we have the impression of moving continuously in the same direction. Now, what characteristic of accompanying brain events corresponds to experienced loudness? The principle does not give a direct answer. Rather, it postulates that whatever the characteristic in question may be, its various nuances or degrees must show exactly the same order as the loudnesses do, i.e., that of a straight line. Also, if in the system of experiences a particular loudness is situated between two other loudnesses, then in the order of related brain events the physiological factor corresponding to the first loudness must also have its place between the processes corresponding to the two others. This gives the equality of structure of the two systems to which the principle refers.

[2] *Cf.* G. E. Müller, *Zeitschr. f. Psychol., 14,* p. 189.

It seems that the all-or-none law does not allow us to choose "intensity of nervous activity" as the physiological correlate of experienced degrees of loudness. But the principle can be equally well applied if the frequency or density of nerve impulses is taken as the correlate of loudness.

As another example, colors may be discussed in their relation to accompanying brain processes. This relation has been considered most thoroughly by G. E. Müller.[3] To be sure, his assumptions go beyond the principle now under discussion in that he makes hypotheses about *retinal* processes. The principle as such applies only to the brain processes which underlie visual experience directly. His theory is also more specific, since it includes a statement about the nature of the retinal processes as such. They are assumed to be chemical reactions. This transgression of the principle is perfectly sound for the following reason. If the system of color experiences and that of related physiological processes are to have the same structure, these physiological events must be variable in just as many directions or "dimensions" as the colors are. It is quite possible that chemical reactions constitute the only type of process which satisfies this condition. Thus the principle of identity of system structure serves to restrict the number of facts which may be considered when more specific hypotheses are desired.

Gestalt Psychology works with a principle which is both more general and more concretely applicable than that of Hering and Müller. These authors refer to the merely *logical* order of experiences which, for this purpose, are abstracted from their context and judged as to their similarities. The thesis is that when related physiological events are also taken from their context, and also compared as to their similarities, the resulting logical order must be the same as that of the experiences. In both cases, it will be seen, the order in question is the order of dead specimens as given the right places in a museum. But experience as such exhibits an order *which is itself experienced.* For instance, at this moment I have before me three white dots on a black surface, one in the middle of the field and the others in symmetrical positions on both sides of the former. This is also an order; but, instead of being of the merely logical kind, it is concrete and belongs to the very facts of experience. This order, too, we assume to depend upon physiological events in the brain. And our principle refers to the relation between concrete

[3] *Loc. cit.*

experienced order and the underlying physiological processes. When applied to the present example, the principle claims, first, that these processes are distributed in a certain order, and secondly, that this distribution is just as symmetrical in functional terms as the group of dots is in visual terms. In the same example, one dot is seen between the two others; and this relation is just as much a part of the experience as the white of the dots is. Our principle says that something in the underlying processes must correspond to what we call "between" in vision. More particularly, it is maintained that the experience "between" goes with a functional "between" in the dynamic interrelations of accompanying brain events. When applied to all cases of experienced spatial order, the principle may be formulated as follows: *Experienced order in space is always structurally identical with a functional order in the distribution of underlying brain processes.*

This is the principle of *psychophysical isomorphism* in the particular form which it assumes in the case of spatial order. Its full significance will become clearer in the following chapters. For the present I will mention another application of the same principle. It is a frequent experience that one event lies temporarily between two others. But experienced time must have a functional counterpart in brain events just as experienced space has. Our principle says that the temporal "between" in experience goes with a functional "between" in the sequence of underlying physiological events. If in this manner the principle is again generally applied we arrive at the proposition that *experienced order in time is always structurally identical with a functional order in the sequence of correlated brain processes.*

The field of application of the principle is not restricted to temporal and spatial orders. We experience more order than merely that of spatial and temporal relations. Certain experiences belong together in a specific fashion, whereas others do not, or belong together less intimately. Such facts are again matters of experience. The very moment I am writing this sentence, a disagreeable voice begins to sing in a neighbor's house. My sentence is something which, though extended in time, is experienced as a certain unit to which those sharp notes do not belong. This is true even though both are experienced at the same time. In this case our principle assumes this form: *units in experience go with functional units in the underlying physiological processes.* In this respect also, the experienced order is supposed to be a true representation of a corresponding order in the processes upon which experience depends. This last application of the principle has perhaps the greatest importance for Gestalt Psychology. As a physiological hypothesis about sensory experiences as well as about more subtle processes, it covers practically the whole field of psychology.

I have just taken an example from outside the realm of objective experience in the strict sense of this term. A sentence which I am formulating is not a part of objective experience in the way in which a chair before me is such an experience. And yet my statement about the sentence is no less simple and obvious than were the others, which referred to order in experienced space and time. This is not always so, however. The observation of subjective experiences cannot be recommended without limitation. In the present connection, only very simple statements in this field can be regarded as sufficiently reliable. Nor need we at present transcend the realm of objective experience. We have just seen that it provides an adequate basis of operations for our immediate purpose.

In the preceding paragraphs my own experience has served as a material which suggests assumptions about the nature of otherwise unobservable constituents of behavior. Now, the only way in which I can bring my observations in this field before the scientific public is through spoken or written language which, as I understand it, refers to this experience. But we have decided that language as a sequence of physiological facts is the peripheral outcome of antecedent physiological processes, among others of those upon which my experience depends. According to our general hypothesis, the concrete order of this experience pictures the dynamic order of such processes. Thus, if to me my words represent a description of my experiences, they are at the same time objective representations of the processes which underlie these experiences. Consequently, it does not matter very much whether my words are taken as messages about experience or about these physiological facts. For, so far as the order of events is concerned, the message is the same in both cases.

If we now go back to the observation of behavior, we have to deal with language as a particular form of behavior in human subjects. Here again we may safely regard language as a message which refers to facts outside the field of language. Only the most superficial view would treat words merely as phonetic events. When listening to a scientific argument, the Behaviorist himself will find that he reacts not to the phonetic characteristics of speech but to its symbolic meaning. For instance, he will regard as equivalent such nouns as "experiment" and *"Versuch,"* "animal" and *"Tier,"* although in both cases the first and second words are phonetically quite different. Why should this attitude be changed when the speaker happens to serve as a subject, and to give us a revealing report?

To repeat, the statements of a subject may be taken as indicative either of his experiences or of the processes which underlie these experiences. If the subject says, "This book is bigger than that other one," his words may be interpreted as referring to a "comparison-experience" of his, but also as representative of a corresponding functional relationship between two sensory processes. Since from our point of view the same order is meant in both cases, the alternative is of no particular importance. From the point of view of behavior psychology, the physiological interpretation must be given; but there is no reason why the other interpretation ought to be excluded. The behavior of a chick can tell me without words that he is able to react to one brightness in its relation to another. On the other hand, if in the course of an experiment a human subject tells me that one object appears to him brighter than another, the scientific import of this sentence is precisely the same as that of the chick's behavior. Why then should language, which is one of the most instructive forms of behavior, be ignored by the experimenter? Surely, by applying the same technique to man as we apply to the chick, we can avoid the use of language in human psychology. But why should we? The Behaviorist's dislike of language seems to have merely historical reasons. The Introspectionists have used "verbal reports" in their attempts to dissect experience. I am ready to admit that what they have called introspection has seemed to be of limited value. Unfortunately, as a result of such mistaken efforts, Behaviorists are now negatively conditioned not only to introspection as such, but also to other, entirely innocent, things which commonly accompany introspection. Hence their dislike of language.

III

A CRITICISM OF

INTROSPECTION

> Round about the accredited and orderly facts
> of every science there ever floats a sort of
> dust-cloud of exceptional observations.
>
> W. JAMES, *The Will to Believe.*

WILLIAM JAMES has well described how a sudden interest in certain "irregular" phenomena often marks the beginning of a new era in science. At such times, what has been exceptional often becomes the very center of scientific work. We shall now become acquainted with introspection as a procedure by which an artificial system of psychology is protected against a similar revolution. The protection is achieved by a technique which serves to discard particularly interesting observations. In discussing introspection, I do not intend to consider a particular school. What I have to say refers to all psychologists who treat experience in the manner which will be discussed in the following paragraphs.

For the most part, Introspectionists are likely to agree with my criticism of Behaviorism. In fact, some may have recognized their own arguments in the preceding chapters. What, then, is the difference between Introspectionism and the point of view of Gestalt Psychology? This difference will become obvious as soon as we consider how experience is to be observed. First of all, I propose to examine the way in which Introspectionists deal with objective experience, the field in which they have been particularly active. Surprisingly enough, the premises of their work will prove to be quite similar to those of Behaviorism.

The very moment we try to observe experience in an impartial fashion we are bound to hear objections from the Introspectionist. If I say that before me on my desk I see a book, the criticism will be raised that nobody can see a book. If I lift the book, I shall be inclined to say that I feel its weight as something external to my fingers and roughly in the place in which the book is also seen. These statements, my critic would remark, are typical of the language of untrained observers. He would add that for the practical purposes of common life such statements may be entirely satisfactory, but that none the less they differ widely from the descriptions which a trained psychologist would have to give. For instance, the statements imply that the terms "book" and "desk" refer to objects or things. In correct psychological discussion such terms are not admissible according to the Introspectionist. For if observation is to give us the simple and primary data of experience, we must learn to make the all-important distinction between *sensations* and *perceptions*, between the bare sensory material as such and the host of other ingredients with which this material has become imbued by processes of learning. One cannot see a book, the Introspectionist tells us, since this term involves knowledge about a certain class of objects to which the present specimen belongs, about the use of such objects, and so forth. Pure seeing has nothing to do with such knowledge. As psychologists, we have the task of separating all these acquired meanings from the seen material *per se*, which consists of simple sensations. It may be difficult actually to effect the separation, and to concentrate on the sensations with which alone we ought to be concerned; but the ability to do so is precisely what distinguishes the psychologist from the layman. Everybody must admit that originally the lifting of a book cannot have given the experience of a weight which is external to the lifting fingers. In the beginning there can have been only sensations of touch, and perhaps strain, within the fingers. It follows that the weight outside must be the product of a long development in which the pure sensations in our hand have gradually been connected with other factors. A similar consideration shows at once that among the genuine sensory data there can be nothing like objects. Objects exist for us only when sensory experience has become thoroughly imbued with meaning. Who can deny that in adult life meaning pervades all experience? Eventually it even leads to a kind of illusion. To Germans the German noun *"Igel"* sounds as though no animal but a hedgehog could have this name. The word "eagle," however, which in English has the same sound as *"Igel"* in German, sounds to an American or Englishman as though only an *"Adler"* could be called by this name.[1] In this instance it will be admitted that we must discriminate between the auditory experience as such, which is the same in both languages, and the attached meanings, which vary from one country to the other. Again, the sign + fairly looks its meaning of the operation of adding, especially if it is seen between numbers; and yet it might as well have been chosen as a symbol for the operation of dividing. If for a moment we hesitate to accept

---

[1] *"Adler"* is the German word for "eagle."

this last statement, we do so only because the connection of a particular meaning with this simple figure has been impressed upon us ever since we went to school. But once the enormous strength of the connection has been realized in the present situation, we shall be ready to admit that probably nothing in the naïve experience of an adult can be devoid of similar influences. Even the most imposing characteristics of given experiences may derive from this source.

Now, meaning in this sense depends upon personal biography. It represents a somewhat accidental trait of our experience. In psychology, we must therefore try to ignore it and to focus only on the actual sensations. The procedure by which this is achieved is called *introspection*.

When I was a student, all young psychologists learned this lesson most thoroughly, although in some cases the doctrine was transmitted implicitly rather than in a clear formulation. Unfortunately, if Introspectionism is right about this, direct experience as such has only limited value. Of all objective experience only selected parts are likely to survive when the great house-cleaning has been completed.

The main question is, of course, according to what criteria some experiences are to be selected as genuine sensory facts while all others are discarded as mere products of learning. Whatever the answer may be, we will now consider a few examples which in essential respects differ from those discussed in the preceding paragraphs.

Suppose, while standing at a street corner, we see a man approaching us. Now he is ten yards away, and presently five. What are we to say about his size at the two distances? We shall be inclined to say that at both distances his visual size was approximately the same. But such a statement, we are told, is utterly inacceptable. A simple consideration in geometrical optics shows that during the man's approach his visual height must have doubled, and that the same holds for his width. His total size must therefore have become four times the area which it was at ten yards. If this is to become entirely clear, we must repeat the observation in the laboratory. Here we replace the man by two cardboard rectangles. The sides of the first are two and three inches long; those of the second, six and nine. If now the first is held before our eyes at a distance of one yard and the second at three yards, they must have the same size from the point of view of optics; for their linear dimensions vary exactly as do their distances. It is quite true, the rectangle at the greater distance appears much larger than the nearer one. But this is precisely what the Introspectionist does not accept as a true statement about the sensory facts. Such a statement, he will say, cannot refer to actual sensory experience. He will also offer a proof that his opinion is right. He will invite us to look through a hole in a screen which he holds before our eyes. The two rectangles now appear on a homogeneous background, because the screen hides all other objects. Under these conditions the difference between the sizes of the rectangles will probably be somewhat reduced. If it does not entirely disappear, the experimenter may go further in helping us to see the sizes as they actually are according to his conviction. He may darken the room, and turn the light on only for a fraction of a second. This serves to exclude movements of the eyes and of the head. It is quite possible that now the rectangles have the same size. The Introspectionist may also invite us to practice in a certain fashion which I cannot here describe, and after some training the rectangles may indeed assume the same size, even if the screen with its hole and any other devices are omitted. Once this has been achieved, the Introspectionist will be satisfied. Now, he will say, you know what introspection means. After all, he will add, trained observers are bound to find the rectangles equal. Otherwise, people might go so far as to believe that the after-image of an object changes its size according to the distance from which they see it upon a screen, because in untrained observation the size of the after-image does seem to change when the distance of the fixation point from the eye is varied. Of course, according to the Introspectionist, it cannot actually change, since under these circumstances the area of the retinal after-effect remains strictly constant.

My next example may be regarded as a natural consequence of the first. When dining with friends, in what shapes do we see the plates on the table, to the left, to the right and opposite us? We shall be inclined to say that they are circular, just as our own plate. But this again is a statement which the Introspectionist will not accept. According to him, they must be elliptical; and he will add that once we have thought about their projection upon our retina we shall have to admit that this is true. In fact, some of the plates must be very flat ellipses, and even our own plate will become an ellipse as soon as our eyes do not look down upon it vertically. To this case a similar procedure may be applied as has been used in the preceding example. On a screen which is oblique to the direction of the eye is shown a circle; on another plane, at right angles to the direction of the eye, an ellipse is presented. The shape of the latter figure is chosen in such a manner that its projection upon the retina has the same shape as the projection of the circle from its oblique plane. An untrained observer will maintain that he sees the

circle as a circle and the ellipse as an ellipse. But the Introspectionist maintains that in actual sensory experience there
are two virtually identical ellipses. He will offer us a screen
with two holes in it, through which we can see both forms,
but which excludes the data by which the angles of the
planes could at first be recognized. Now both shapes do look
alike; both look like ellipses. Thus the Introspectionist seems
to have made his point. With some training, he will again
remark, anybody can see these real sensory facts, even without the screen, provided he assumes the right attitude,
the attitude of introspection. As a further elucidation, he will
remark that if an after-image is projected on planes of different angles in relation to the eye, the image will seem to
change its shape as we project it on one plane or another.
Since during these observations the retinal after-effect does
not change at all, only uninformed people will trust what
they seem to be seeing under these circumstances. Thus the
importance of observing given sensory experiences by way
of trained introspection appears to be convincingly demonstrated.

Another paradoxical experience has been widely discussed
ever since Helmholtz wrote his *Physiologische Optik*. An untrained observer sees not only sizes and shapes of objects
more constant than corresponds to the variations of retinal
sizes and retinal shapes; the same holds for the way in which
he seems to see brightnesses in their relation to the varying intensities of retinal projection. Suppose that a vertical screen is
placed on a table, near a window and parallel to it. On the
window side of the screen a black paper is laid on the table,
and symmetrically on the other side of the screen, a white
paper. The papers are selected in a special manner: the dark
one, which is exposed to the direct illumination from the window, reflects the same absolute amount of light as the white
paper, which receives so much less light. In spite of this fact,
the former paper appears black and the latter white. This
again is an observation which the Introspectionist refuses to
accept, because under the given circumstances the images projected upon the retina of the observer are both equally intense.
He assumes that the sensations, i.e. the brightnesses of the
papers, must therefore be the same. He also believes that this
equality can actually be demonstrated. Once more he will
take a piece of cardboard with two small holes in it, and will
hold it so that one of them is filled by a section of the black,
and the other by a section of the white paper. Now the surroundings of the papers, the vertical screen, and so forth, are
excluded from vision. And under these conditions the same
nuance of gray appears in both openings. Clearly, he tells us,

these are the true sensations. He is also likely to point out that after some practice most people can recognize the equality of the two brightnesses without the help of any special device. When this is the case, they have learned to observe in the attitude of introspection. At the time when painters were still interested in the representation of objects, they generally assumed this attitude in order to see the right brightnesses of things.

All these facts, the so-called constancies of size, shape and brightness, are from this point of view mere illusions, which must be destroyed if the true sensory phenomena are to appear. In this and in other respects they are comparable to a great many other "optical illusions," the diagrams of which fill pages in the textbooks of psychology. There is, for instance, the famous Müller-Lyer pattern, the figure with the arrow-heads, between which two equal lines seem to have strikingly different length. When this pattern is repeatedly inspected, and if the subject makes an effort to detach the objectively equal lines from their surroundings, he will soon find that the illusion becomes less striking, until eventually it may entirely disappear. It seems to follow that the inequality of the lines as first seen has not been a sensory fact. If we believe what the Introspectionists say, the same can also be demonstrated as follows: The two figures are drawn precisely one above the other. If now the observer focuses his attention upon the two left ends of the equal lines, he will find that an imaginary connection of these ends is vertical. If he makes the same test with the right ends, he will find the same result. If we have any knowledge of geometry, we seem thus forced to admit that both lines have the same length. Similarly, it can be shown that most other illusions disappear, if the observer is careful to assume the right analytical attitude. How, then, can these illusions be regarded as genuine sensory facts?

Here is a further example. During the past thirty years stroboscopic movement has been thoroughly investigated by German and American psychologists. Under appropriate conditions successive presentation of two lights at two points not too distant from each other results in an experience of movement from the first to the second. But if the observer adopts the attitude of introspection, he finds nothing but a "gray flash." Consequently, the Introspectionists say, any reports about actual movements in such a situation must be received with suspicion. Did not Benussi's subjects describe similar experiences when two points of their skin were touched in rapid succession? In their description the experienced movement did not for the most part occur along the surface of the skin; rather, it formed an arc through empty space and touched the skin only at the points of actual stimulation. As the Introspectionists see it, such an experience cannot possibly belong to the world of touch alone. All tactual experiences stay, of course, on the skin.

If all observations of this kind are illusions which deceive us not only as to the nature of given physical conditions but also about our own sensory data, then some powerful factor must be at work which obscures these data so long as they are not revealed by introspection. We already know what the nature of the distorting influence is. At least the Introspectionist is quite convinced that, just as in previous instances, it can only be *learning*. He argues as follows: The man who approaches us on the street does not seem to grow larger as for simple optical reasons he should. The circle which lies in an oblique plane does not appear as an ellipse; it seems to remain a circle even though its retinal image may be a very flat ellipse. The white object with the shadow across it remains white, the black paper in full light remains black, although the former may reflect much less light than the latter. Obviously, these three phenomena have something in common. The physical object as such always remains the same, while the stimulation of our eyes varies, as the distance, the orientation of the illumination of that constant object are changed. Now, what we seem to experience agrees with the actual invariance of the physical object much better than it does with the varying stimulations. Hence the terms constancy of size, constancy of shape and constancy of brightness. Clearly, this is just what we have to expect if such constancies spring from our knowledge of the physical situation, in other words, if they develop in some form of learning. Day after day, since early childhood, we have found that when we approach a distant object it proves to be much bigger than it seemed to be from a greater distance. In the same way we have learned that objects in oblique orientations do not exhibit those real shapes which they show when inspected from in front. Again in the same fashion we have become thoroughly acquainted with the fact that objects seen under abnormal conditions of illumination show wrong brightnesses or darknesses which are replaced by the right ones when conditions become normal. Such observations have been repeated so many times, and we have so fully learned what the real sizes, the real shapes and the real brightnesses are in each case, that gradually we have become unable to distinguish between our acquired knowledge and actual sensory facts. As a result, we now seem to *see* the constant real characteristics while the sensory facts as such which, of course, depend upon distance, orientation and illumination, are no longer recognizable. Thus meaning, knowledge or learning are just as effective in the present examples as they are when we seem to be aware of "things," of "weights" outside in space, and so forth.

We can accept the Introspectionist's claim that probably few experiences remain entirely uninfluenced by learning. After all, this is not a novel assumption. Moreover, he can point out that if untrained people seem to *see* what from this point of view is merely an effect of learning, this is merely an illusion which also occurs in other instances: we remember the symbol +, which *looks* like the sign for addition. But the Introspectionist has further arguments which seem to support his interpretation. All effects of past learning can be effective only to the degree to which they are recalled. Now, recall presupposes that some parts of the present situation can evoke what has been learned in the past. In the case of the constancies, such parts are, among others, the distances, the oblique orientations, and the various illuminations, as seen in each case. Obviously, then, if these distances, oblique orientations and varying illuminations are no longer visible, the normal sizes, shapes and brightnesses cannot be reactivated. But precisely this happens when the situations here under discussion are observed through holes in a screen. Under these conditions, the surroundings of the crucial surfaces and, with the surroundings, the distances, orientations and illuminations of the surfaces are excluded from vision. Consequently, there can be no recall of what we have learned about the situations; the constancies must disappear; and the surfaces must for once exhibit their true sensory characteristics. The same follows from the fact that the constancies can be destroyed by introspection. Obviously, in this procedure the sizes, shapes and brightnesses of surfaces are to a degree separated from their contexts. But, as we have just seen, this means separation from the factors which would otherwise cause recall of previously acquired knowledge. It is therefore only natural that under these conditions the pure sensory facts come to the fore.

If the size and the shape of after-images prove to be surprisingly variable when the distance and the orientation of the background are changed, this also appears as a direct consequence of the Introspectionist's explanation. After-images are localized upon the background. If the distance and the orientation of this background again operate as factors of recall, a given after-image must seem to assume different sizes and shapes when the distance or the orientation of the background is varied.

The same explanation helps us to understand why the

constancies do not survive under extreme conditions. Ten yards away a man appears to be scarcely smaller than at a distance of five yards; but fifty yards off he does look smaller, and a thousand yards away he is likely to become a tiny object indeed. Most of the time we are, of course, interested in objects in our neighborhood. Thus we learn little about things far off, and the result is that with increasing distance true sensory experience is less and less obscured by acquired knowledge.

It must be admitted that in all these arguments there is great persuasive force. Many psychologists do not for a moment doubt the truth of the explanation in terms of acquired knowledge. This explanation seems to satisfy a very natural tendency in human thinking. Physicists who have never studied psychology will give this explanation as soon as they become acquainted with the facts we are here considering. If you demonstrate the phenomena to a freshman, he will at once suggest similar interpretations.

The theory applies to countless facts. There is practically no visual situation which does not exhibit some of the experiences in question. When we open our eyes, we behold sizes, shapes and brightnesses all the time, and of these only a very few will escape the verdict which is imposed on them by the Introspectionist. It is not the facts themselves which are exceptional; only the demonstration of their surprising deviation from what one should expect them to be is something unusual. This demonstration is a matter of psychological sophistication; the facts themselves are affairs of every moment and of everybody.

Even so the extent of objective experience which is not to be trusted has not yet been exhausted in these paragraphs. The location of objects is open to similar criticism. When fixating a point before me, I see the objects around it in various places which correspond to the different positions of their images on my retina. If I now fixate another point, the same objects ought to appear in changed places since their images now occupy new positions on the retina. But actually the objects do not seem to have moved. When the eye moves, their location in space proves to be virtually independent of retinal position. Or take the speed of seen movement. The same physical movement may be seen from many different distances. When I am ten yards away from the moving object, retinal speed will be one half of what it is at a distance of five yards. And yet, in my experience the speed seems to be about the same in both cases. Clearly, the explanation which has been given to the constancies of size, shape and brightness also applies to this constancy of visual speed. Thus, of the objective experiences around us little is left that would be called a true sensory fact by the Introspectionist.

None the less, this is not yet the most serious consequence of the views held by Introspectionists. Apparently, the phases of experience which are interpreted as products of learning will not only be excluded from the sensory world; they will also be excluded from investigation in general. Most Introspectionists, it is true, would hesitate to acknowledge this as an explicit principle; but in their research they actually proceed as though they had adopted it. Once an experience has had the misfortune of being so interpreted, they seem to take no more interest in its existence than they would take in the subject matter of astronomy. This means that most objective experience plays virtually no part in the Introspectionist's psychology. In fact, wherever observation touches upon a somewhat unusual and therefore particularly interesting phenomenon, the Introspectionist is ready to offer his monotonous explanation, and henceforth he is extremely unlikely ever to give that phenomenon the slightest attention. Now, this is a serious situation. Whether the *empiristic explanation*, as the explanation by previous learning has been called, is right or wrong, in common life we are dealing almost exclusively with the first-hand objective experience which is discarded by the Introspectionist. Toward this common experience all our interests are directed. Millions of people will never transform the objects of their environments into true sensations, will always react to sizes, shapes, brightnesses and speeds as they find them, will like and dislike forms as they appear to them without recourse to introspection, and will therefore have no commerce with the particular sensory facts of which the Introspectionist is so fond. Thus, if his attitude were to prevail, such experiences as form the matrix of our whole life would never be seriously studied. Psychology would observe and discuss only such experiences as are, to most of us, forever hidden under the cover of merely acquired characteristics. Even the best Introspectionist is not aware of his true sensory facts unless he assumes his special attitude, which—fortunately for him—he drops when leaving the psychological laboratory. So far removed from common experience is his true sensory world that, if we should ever learn its laws, all of them together would not lead us back to the world we actually live in. This being the case, the Introspectionist cannot complain about his own fate. His psychology is quite unable to satisfy people for long. Since he ignores the experiences of daily life, and concentrates on rare facts which only an artificial procedure can reveal, both his professional and his lay audience will sooner or later lose patience. And something else will happen. There will be psychologists who will take him at his word when he says that this is the only right way of dealing with experience. If this is true, they will say, the study of experience can surely not interest us. We will do more lively things. We will study natural behavior. At the present time we know that what has just been described as a consequence of the Introspectionist's views is no longer a possibility but a fact. Behaviorism has come into existence very much in a reaction against Introspectionism.

Let us return to our discussion of Introspectionism as such. One would not be justified in calling its findings "unreal." When I apply the Introspectionist's methods I often find the same experiences as he does. But I am far from attributing to such facts a rare value as though they were more "true" than the facts of everyday experience. If common experience involves acquired knowledge, the experiences revealed by introspection depend upon the attitude of introspecting. One cannot show that they also exist in the absence of this attitude. Moreover, if for a moment we take it for granted that all the phenomena we have been discussing are actually products of previously acquired knowledge, does it follow that these phenomena are not actual facts, and therefore devoid of psychological significance? Is a certain amount of H_2O which I have before me no real chemical substance because I know that it has been formed by the oxidation of hydrogen? Would the hydrogen be a "true" chemical substance, but not the water? Is water not to be investigated by the chemist? I do not see why an experience which is imbued with acquired knowledge is to be regarded as less important than experiences which are not so influenced. Take the case of the symbol +, the appearance of which is surely affected by our knowledge of a mathematical operation. When seen between numbers it looks like "plus," i.e., its acquired meaning appears localized in the visual field. Clearly, this is a strange fact which immediately raises fascinating questions. Why are we not to investigate such problems? The situation is precisely the same with regard to all other experiences to which, correctly or incorrectly, the empiristic explanation is being applied. Why should we ignore the problems which they involve, when such labels as learning, meaning and previously acquired knowledge have been attached to them?

As a matter of fact, problems of this kind deserve special attention. Among the examples which have here been considered there are two kinds of phenomena. One, to which the symbol + belongs, is clearly defined by the fact that we actually know how during childhood a certain meaning creeps into a given experience. For the second type, which is represented by the majority of our examples, such an account has not been given. By no means has it been demonstrated that the objectivity of things, the localization of weights outside our hand, the constancies of size, shape, speed, location and brightness, and so forth, are really products of learning. To most of us it may seem extremely plausible that this is actually the case; but none of the observations and arguments which I have mentioned in this connection can be regarded as convincing proof of the empiristic thesis. Thus it is merely an hypothesis that facts of the second class are not essentially different from those of the first, and as an hypothesis it ought therefore to be clearly recognized.

The customary thing to do with an hypothesis is to subject it to tests. Does Introspectionism test its empiristic assumptions? We see no evidence that it does, or intends to do so, since once the assumption is made the Introspectionist is no longer interested in the facts. Consequently, if all psychologists were Introspectionists, such assumptions would never be examined. This is the more disturbing since many psychologists tend to lose their temper when their empiristic convictions are called hypotheses. If these convictions are no more than assumptions, what other explanations will the Gestalt Psychologist offer? Quite probably our criticism of the empiristic thesis is only the beginning, and more or less fantastic new notions about sensory function are to follow.

When a scientific discussion tends to assume this direction, it has always touched upon some particularly deep-rooted presupposition which one does not want to see regarded as an open issue. This makes it only the more obvious that the Introspectionist's attitude consitutes a danger to the advance of psychology. For a moment let us suppose that the constancies of size, shape, speed, localization, brightness and so on are actually *not* products of learning. The consequence would be that all these phenomena belong to sensory experience. But if so, sensory experience would be something fundamentally different from the aggregate of sensations which constitutes the Introspectionist's sensory world. It would follow that his conception of sensory function must be discarded. Of course, whether or not we have to draw this conclusion depends entirely upon the validity of the empiristic thesis. But precisely this thesis is apparently not to be freely discussed and tested. This is an extraordinary situation: as used by the Introspectionist, the empiristic explanation serves as a bulwark which protects his particular views about sensory function. It seems that Introspectionists adhere to the empiristic thesis not so much because it is as such attractive as because their firm belief about a certain nature of sensory facts does not permit them to acknowledge certain experiences. These "irregular" experiences are constantly being explained away by the empiristic assumption, and therefore this assumption must be right. That this is the correct interpretation of the Introspectionist's attitude will be seen as soon as his arguments in favor of the empiristic hypothesis are closely examined. These arguments have little to do with learning, but very much with convictions about the world of pure sensory experience.

Take the constancy of brightness as an example. A white paper on which a shadow lies appears as white, a black one in bright illumination remains black, even if under these conditions the white paper may reflect less light than the black one does. In this experience, do the white and the black *per se* tell the Introspectionist that they are products of previous learning? By no means. His argument is entirely indirect: since the observation is incompatible with his beliefs about the nature of true sensations, it cannot be accepted. What can he do with it? The Introspectionist is not at all embarrassed. Interpreted as a mere product of learning, the constancy of brightness becomes at once quite harmless.

Let us follow his argument in more detail. In the present observation one can change the brightness of the papers by looking at them in a special fashion. Therefore, the Introspectionist says, the brightnesses as first seen can not have been genuine sensory experiences. This statement obviously implies a presupposition about the nature of sensory facts. Such facts, the Introspectionist assumes, must be independent of changes in the attitude of the observer. But at this point his reasoning is not entirely consistent. If in the attitude of introspection an apparent white can be transformed into a dark nuance, and an apparent black into a relatively bright one, the opposite change occurs spontaneously as soon as that attitude is discontinued. Thus the true brightnesses which are said to be revealed during introspection are just as changeable as the brightnesses which were seen before, and are now seen again. From a purely logical point of view, the experiences found during introspection might therefore just as well be rejected, since they disappear when the observer returns to his everyday attitude. The Introspectionist, however, is far from treating both experiences with the same measure. He holds that what he experiences during introspection is true experience, and that it persists when he falls back into a more naïve attitude, although now it is again obscured by the effects of knowledge. Hence, there must be a further belief which makes him prefer his special sensory experiences.

This other belief is easy to find. Why is the Introspectionist surprised by the constancies of size, shape, localization, speed, and brightness? Why does he not take these facts at their face value? Obviously, because under the given conditions of stimulation he expects to have experiences quite different from those which he actually has. Visual size, he would say, should be proportional to retinal size; changes in retinal shape should be followed by changes in seen shape; localization in the visual field should vary with retinal position; visual speed with retinal speed; and visual brightness with retinal intensity. Now, while the everyday experience of the layman contradicts these expectations all the time, the special attitude cultivated by Introspectionism succeeds in obtaining those other experiences which we always ought to have. This is the fact which makes the Introspectionist prefer his particular findings, and which also makes him believe in a permanent, though hidden, existence of such "pure sensations." Thus it becomes apparent that the procedure and the results of introspection are sanctioned by their agreement with certain premises about the relation between stimulation and sensory experience. The same premises lead, of course, to the condemnation of many phenomena such as the constancies. Nobody can understand the ways of Introspectionism who is not aware of this decisive point. As a young student, how many times have I read that the Müller-Lyer illusion does not represent a true sensory fact because it can be destroyed by analytical observation and corresponding practice. If this be taken as a proof, one kind of experience is obviously given a higher value than another. Why should this be the case? The answer is that one experience agrees with what peripheral stimulation makes one expect, while the other does not. The one that does not agree is discarded with the aid of empiristic assumptions or other devices of a similar kind. A second fundamental conviction, then, which underlies the scientific decisions of Introspectionism is this: the characteristics of true sensory experiences depend only upon corresponding characteristics of peripheral stimuli.

The Introspectionist's belief takes a still more extreme form. How does he proceed in order to find the true sensory facts, say, in the case of brightness constancy? He tries to isolate parts of the white and of the black paper so that they are no longer related to their specific environments. Isolation, it seems, is also the procedure by which the Müller-Lyer illusion can be destroyed, and similarly in all the other cases. Such an analytical attitude will have effects similar to those of a screen with a hole, which conceals the specific surroundings of objects and gives them instead a new homogeneous environment. If now the disturbing facts disappear, this effect of isolation is explained by the exclusion of all factors which otherwise distort the true sensory situation. How do these factors operate? According to the Introspectionist, they act as cues for the processes of recall which import previously acquired knowledge. We have to realize that at this point the Introspectionist's interpretation is once more one-sided. Without any doubt, isolation of facts in the sensory field affects these facts. Under these circumstances they tend to be more strictly related to local stimulating conditions. But for this two entirely different explanations may be given: (1) Either true sensory experience always depends upon local stimulation alone, and it is only the recall of previously acquired knowledge which depends upon factors in the environment. This is the Introspectionist's view. (2) Or sensory experience in a given place depends not only on the stimuli corresponding to this place, but also on the stimulating conditions in the environment. I will at once remark that this is the view held by Gestalt Psychology. With the second interpretation as with the first, isolation and the introduction of a homogeneous environment will tend to make local experience correspond better to local stimulation. The Introspectionist, however, considers only one alternative. He prefers the thesis which allows him to believe that local sensory facts are strictly determined by local stimulation. His partiality in this respect is also obvious when it is not empiristic assumptions but other hypotheses by which he protects his picture of a simple sensory world. In a well-known example, when subjects make eye movements along the main lines of the Müller-Lyer pattern, which are objectively equal, these movements prove to have different amplitudes for the two parts of the pattern, and the difference corresponds to the difference of their appearance, i.e., to the illusion. From this it has been concluded that the illusion is not a visual fact; that, rather, it is caused by such asymmetrical eye movements, or at least by corresponding innervation tendencies. This statement is biased because, in case the two lines actually have different visual length in the first place, the eye movements or innervation tendencies will, of course, be similarly asymmetrical. Only a prejudiced person can draw the conclusion that such observations prove the indirect genesis of the Müller-Lyer effect. And what is the prejudice of such a person? He will under no circumstances admit that the length of a line depends upon more conditions than the length of its retinal image. The most fundamental assumption of Introspectionism is therefore this: true sensory facts are local phenomena which depend upon local stimulation, but not at all upon stimulating conditions in their environment.[2] Only if we know this rule can we understand on what occasions the Introspectionist begins to introspect. Very seldom do we find him introspecting when simple relations between local stimulation and sensory facts obtain without a special effort. But where *prima facie* such relations do not obtain he will always take recourse both to his introspective procedure and to the assumptions which serve to protect his main thesis.

Our inquiry has led to a remarkable result. At first the tenets of Introspectionism appear to be sharply contrasted with the views of Behaviorism. If the Introspectionist is not the advocate of direct experience, who else should be able to play this rôle? In actual fact, however, his enthusiasm for direct experience is obviously limited. Introspectionism follows the orders of an authority to whom the testimony of experience as such means little. This authority subjects direct experience to a screening process, finds most of it defective, and condemns it to corrective measures. The authority is commonly called physiology of the sense organs. This branch of physiology has very definite ideas about the sensory functions of the nervous system. When the Introspectionist mentions physiology, he seems to talk about a helpful servant. But when we look at the facts, the servant is the Introspectionist's master.

This being the case, does Introspectionism differ quite as much from Behaviorism as was our first impression? If we compare the physiological premises of Introspectionism with those of Behaviorism, we shall soon realize that, on the contrary, in this respect the two schools have much in common.

The main concepts of Behaviorism are those of the reflex and the conditioned reflex. The principal characteristic of reflex action consists in the fact that nerve impulses travel from a receptor along prescribed paths to prescribed centers, and from these along further prescribed paths toward an effector organ. This conception explains the order of organic reactions in their dependence upon given stimuli: the order is enforced by a particular arrangement of the conductors. It is true, Behaviorists do not suppose that such anatomical arrangements are entirely rigid and constant. But although a certain diffusion of excitation is admitted, the only biological value of this "tolerance" is seen in the fact that other conditions,

[2] This is the famous mosiac hypothesis. Some Introspectionists have said that Gestalt Psychology must also acknowledge certain relations between stimulating conditions and sensory facts. Quite! We do not argue against relations between such conditions and sensory facts in general, but only against a rigid relation between *local* stimulation and *local* experience.

which can make the connections quite rigid, have thus a certain range of possibilities to work upon. In this fashion, order of function is to a degree prescribed by the reflex arc; but, at a higher level of the nervous system, connections may be built (or blocked) by another factor. This other factor is conditioning.

With this picture we can now compare the ideas which underlie the Introspectionist's criteria for true sensory experience. First, local sensation depends upon local stimulation. It does not depend upon other processes in the nervous system, not even upon those which issue from adjacent parts of the same sense organ. The only assumption which can explain this independence of local sensation is conduction of processes along insulated pathways from one point of the sense organ to one point in the brain, where activity is accompanied by sensory experience. But this is only the first half of a reflex arc, so that in this respect Introspectionism entirely agrees with Behaviorism. Now, if often experience does not seem to obey this principle, the reason lies in a second principle. At a higher level of the nervous system, connections which did not exist originally may still be formed in individual development. As a consequence, certain experiences will regularly be followed and accompanied by others, particularly in the form of recall which adds its material to those experiences. Essentially, this principle is the same as that of conditioning, inasmuch as in both cases the formation of new connections is the main point. Hence, here again we find no real difference between Introspectionism and Behaviorism.

During their lively dispute as to whether introspection or the objective observation of behavior is the right procedure in psychology, it does not occur to either party that another question might be much more urgent, namely, whether their common assumption about the functions of the nervous system are adequate. Both seem to regard these assumptions as self-evident. And since their essential premises are taken for granted by both, we cannot be surprised to find the same conservatism in Introspectionism as disturbed us in Behaviorism.

Most Introspectionists do not seem to realize that psychology is a very young science, and that therefore its future must depend upon discoveries which are unsuspected at the present time. At least in sensory experience, the essentials of all possible observations are finally given to them before they begin to observe. Accordingly, they show a negativistic attitude whenever observations do not agree with the established truth; and their experimentation tends to become a merely defensive procedure. If others point to new facts which do not fit, they are eager to remove the disturbance by introspection and auxiliary assumptions. Criticism of new observations is a healthy procedure in science; but I have known Introspectionists who spent their scientific lives in bitter defense of their dogma.

Under these circumstances, I do not see why Introspectionism should be preferred to Behaviorism. In their fundamental concepts the two schools are so much alike that all their disputes remind me of unnecessary quarrels in a family. At any rate, the principal questions of Gestalt Psychology refer to an issue which is never mentioned in their discussions, because for these schools it does not yet exist: Is it true that the processes underlying experience and behavior depend upon the connections of nerve paths, and that changes in the conductivity of these connections constitute an individual's development?

IV

DYNAMICS AS OPPOSED TO
MACHINE THEORY

IT SOMETIMES HAPPENS that people are conservative and right at the same time. But it seems highly improbable that our young science is right in holding conservative views, when these views are constantly contradicted by actual experience, and must all the time be protected by such devices as the empiristic hypothesis.

Once the arguments of Introspectionism are submitted to thorough examination they prove to be hardly convincing. In one of our examples, an experience of movement resulted when two points on the subject's skin were touched in succession. This experience was not admitted as a true sensory fact because the movement had the form of a curve through empty space, only the ends of which were felt on the skin (*cf.* p. 77 f.). But why should the experiences which arise from stimulation of a sense organ invariably be localized in the place in which this sense organ is localized as an experienced object? In vision, this is not the case; forms or colors are not seen where we feel our eyes to be. Neither, for the most part, are sounds heard where we localize our ears. Behind the Introspectionist's argument there seems to be some confusion of the peripheral processes caused by stimulation with the sensory experiences which follow, and therefore also of the physiological locus of the former with the experienced location of the latter.

The example shows that the apparent self-evidence of such arguments prevents their critical consideration. In the present instance any such examination destroys that self-evidence at once. In this chapter I will try to show that the same holds for the main assumptions of Introspectionism and Behaviorism. These assumptions are by no means axiomatic, although they agree with a common prejudice which probably has an age of more than a thousand years.

We have seen that these convictions can be kept alive only

so long as they are defended by empiristic explanations of opposed facts. Now, much experimental work on the experiences discussed in the preceding chapter bears upon these explanations. For instance, in order to learn that sometimes white is black and vice versa, an individual would obviously need time and many lessons, particularly since he has to learn it so thoroughly that eventually the products of his learning will appear in his visual field as specific nuances of brightness which replace the true sensory facts. Thus we should expect that young or very primitive subjects do not, to any considerable degree, show brightness constancy. But when I tested chickens, they proved to possess approximately as good a brightness constancy as I do.[1] Similar experiments on size constancy with children (from two years up), and with young apes, also gave positive results.[2] Though it would be difficult to demonstrate that learning has no influence whatsoever upon the phenomena in question, it seems now extremely unlikely that such phenomena are altogether effects of previously acquired knowledge. To repeat, I do not deny that objective experience is imbued with other acquired characteristics. But where this influence is not actually proved to exist, no indirect arguments can be accepted in lieu of such a demonstration.

Since in these instances the empiristic explanation has lost so much of its plausibility, a radical change in fundamental principles appears to be unavoidable. In other words, the phenomena we have here discussed, such as the constancies of size, shape, location, speed and brightness, the stroboscopic movement, the well-known optical illusions, and so forth, must now be given the same weight in our understanding of sensory processes as the "normal" sensations of the Introspectionist. We readily grant that at a given distance and on a homogeneous background visual size depends principally upon retinal size, that (apart from contrast and other similar exceptions) in a given illumination brightness depends upon retinal intensity, and so on. In these cases, size, brightness, etc., are found to vary with the properties of local stimulation, because influences which are exerted by surrounding stimuli are not of a kind that would interfere with this simple relation. For the same reason, when the attitude of introspection is adopted, experiences may be found to correspond to local

[1] "Optische Untersuchungen am Schimpansen und am Haushuhn." *Abhandl. d. Preuss. Akad. d. Wiss.*, 1915.

[2] *Op. cit.* and Frank, *Psychol. Forsch., 7,* 1926; *10,* 1927. Beyrl, *Zeitschr. f. Psychol., 100,* 1926.

stimulation, because this analytical attitude can temporarily suppress the influence of surrounding stimuli.

By no means do we admit, however, that this isolation of local facts represents a more "normal" state of affairs. Rather, if in objective experience observations are taken at their face value, our fundamental assumptions about the processes underlying such experience must be sharply opposed to the premises of Introspectionism and Behaviorism. Our view will be that, instead of reacting to local stimuli by local and mutually independent events, the organism responds to the *pattern* of stimuli to which it is exposed; and that this answer is a unitary process, a functional whole, which gives, in experience, a sensory scene rather than a mosaic of local sensations. Only from this point of view can we explain the fact that, with a constant local stimulus, local experience is found to vary when the surrounding stimulation is changed.

"Unitary process" and "functional whole" are, however, terms which may sound a bit vague to most scientists. It therefore seems advisable to present our thesis in more detail. This discussion will be greatly facilitated if we first ask ourselves just why the now prevailing views have seemed so utterly convincing to one generation after another.

The chief reason seems to be that sensory experience tends to be an orderly affair, and that the same holds for the behavior to which it gives rise. Now, since the early days of European science man has been convinced that, when left to what is often called their own blind play, the processes of nature never produce orderly results. Does not the accidental intercourse of forces in the physical world produce chaos and destruction everywhere? Science has been able to formulate some laws which isolated processes always follow. But where many factors operate at the same time, there seems to be no reason why things should develop in the direction of order rather than chaos.

On the other hand, we know that chaos can be prevented, and order enforced, if proper controls are imposed upon acting factors from the outside. As soon as man begins to restrict the possibilities of function by rigid constraining conditions of his choice, he can compel the forces of nature to do orderly work. But it is generally taken for granted that this is also the only way in which order can be imposed upon physical events. This has been man's conception of nature for thousands of years; and in our day we still impose order on nature in the same fashion when we construct and operate the machines of our factories. In such machines, nature is allowed to cause movement, but the form and order of this movement are prescribed by the anatomy of the machines, which man, not nature, has provided.

From this point of view, a young science will tend to presuppose the existence of special constraining arrangements wherever the distribution of processes in nature is found to be orderly. Aristotelian astronomy is a good example. The movement of the stars exhibits a remarkable order, so different from what one expects to occur in free nature that the assumption of controlling arrangements seemed necessary to the Greek theorists. Obviously, they thought, the possibility of a star running wild or a planet going astray is excluded by something that constrains their course. In Aristotelian theory the stars are therefore fixed on rigid crystal spheres which turn and take the stars along. No wonder that the stars have regular orbits. Even engineers appear in the picture: Aristotle speaks of stellar deities who keep the machinery in working order. Three hundred years ago this conception still filled many with pious awe. And yet the functional significance of its crystal spheres was the same as that by which order is imposed on function in the machines of a mill. Man has a pathetic longing for rest and safety. For a long while this need was satisfied by the primitive hypotheses of Aristotelian astronomy, however crude and narrow they may now appear to us. What was so shocking in Galileo's astronomical discoveries? That he found so much going on in the sky, and that as a consequence the astronomical order was so much less rigid than people had been able happily to believe before. If the heavens began to show such a lack of rigid reliability, if they approximated the restlessness of terrestrial conditions, who could feel secure in his most important beliefs? Thus primitive fear inspired the furious attacks which the Aristotelians of his time directed against Galileo. It seems quite possible that the excitement produced by Harvey's discovery of the circulation of the blood contained a similar element of fear, because this discovery suddenly disturbed the conception of man as a rigid structure. With so much unrest in his interior, did not life as a whole become a most precarious affair?

The same motive expressed itself in the tendency of early biological thought to explain all remarkable characteristics of organic life, and most of all its striking order, by special arrangements which enforce this order. Descartes' "mechanical" interpretation of organic functions may have been bold enough in some respects; but he was only conservative in assuming that—apart from the influence of one engineer, the soul—the orderly play of processes in the organism is enforced by arrangements, connections, and channels. Figuratively, the organism was for him what the sky had been for Aristotle—full of crystal spheres. He did not know the laws of dynamics, it is true. But though we know much more about these laws, the main changes in biological theory since his time seem to have been refinements of his way of thinking rather than discoveries of essentially new concepts concerning the order of function in biology. What is our own situation in this field? To be sure, the machine conception of life now meets with some scepticism. On the other hand, biologists do not yet appear to have a much better explanation of organic order.

The possibilities of alternative explanation will be more readily recognized if we try to get a more precise picture of machine theory as developed in astronomy and biology. In a physical system events are determined by two sorts of factors. In the first class belong the forces and other factors inherent in the processes of the system. These we will call the *dynamic* determinants of its fate. In the second class we have characteristics of the system which subject its processes to restricting conditions. Such determinants we will call *topographical* factors. In a conducting network, for instance, the electrostatic forces of the current represent its dynamic phase. On the other hand, the geometrical pattern and the chemical constitution of the network are topographical conditions which restrict the play of those forces. It will at once be seen that, while in all systems of nature dynamic factors are at work, the influence of special topographical conditions may be at a minimum in one case and predominant in another. On an insulated conductor electric charges are free to distribute themselves in any way which respects the boundaries of the conductor. If actually the charges assume a particular distribution which represents an equilibrium, this happens for dynamic reasons. In a steam engine, on the other hand, the piston can move only in one fashion which is prescribed by the rigid walls of the cylinder.

We are thus led to a classification of physical systems which has the greatest relevance for our problem. We assume that, in all systems with which we are concerned, processes are strictly determined by factors of *some* kind. But we must always remember that systems vary tremendously as to the relative influence of limiting topographical conditions, on the one hand, and dynamic factors, on the other. To the degree to which topographical conditions are rigidly given, and not to be changed by dynamic factors, their existence means exclusion of certain forms of function, and the restriction of processes to the possibilities compatible with those conditions.

The most extreme case is that of a system in which pre-established topographical arrangements exclude all possibilities except one. As an example of this type I have just mentioned a piston, the motion of which is prescribed by the walls of a cylinder. In this case the steam in the cylinder tends to expand in all directions, but owing to the given topographical constraints it can do work only in one direction, the one in which the piston is free to move. In such a system nothing but motion as such is dynamically determined. The direction of the motion is prescribed by the cylinder.

This extreme relation between dynamic factors and imposed topographical conditions is almost or entirely realized in typical machines. The variety of different one-way functions which may be enforced in one such system or another is enormous. But the general principle is everywhere the same. Sometimes, it is true, dynamics is allowed a bit more freedom than the absolute minimum. Still we do not construct machines in which dynamic factors are the main determinants of the form of operation.

Clearly, it was a machine in this sense of which Aristotle first thought when he considered the order of celestial movements. His spheres were topographical conditions which he supposed to enforce that order. Since Descartes neurologists have worked with similar assumptions wherever neural function in animals and in man exhibited striking order. As they saw it, neural dynamics as such would never make for co-ordinated function. Thus the assumption of special anatomical conditions became a matter of course in any case in which the nervous system showed orderly behavior.

Under these circumstances, it is not particularly astonishing that both Introspectionists and Behaviorists work with premises in which the machine type of function is tacitly taken for granted. Consider vision, for example. So many stimuli impinge upon the retina at a given time. And yet, there is generally no confusion in the visual field. One object appears here, another there, apparently just as they are distributed in physical space. Points which are neighbors in physical space are neighbors also in the visual field. The center of a circle in physical space appears as the middle of a similarly symmetrical figure in vision, and so forth. All this order is as remarkable as it is necessary for our commerce with the world. Now, the order in which the images of objects are projected upon the retina is easily explained by the existence of the pupil, the lens, and so on. But what about the processes which are propagated from the retina to the brain, and here determine visual experience? Since this experience still seems to show the same order, there must be factors which everywhere prevent confusion. Only one kind of factors seems capable of achieving this: the visual nervous system must consist of topographical arrangements in enormous numbers, and these arrangements must keep nerve function everywhere on the right track. If from each point of the retina nerve impulses are conducted along prescribed pathways toward equally prescribed termini in the brain, and if in the totality of these termini the geometry of retinal points is repeated, then dynamic factors are completely prevented from influencing the distribution of the neural flow, and thus the result will be order. This order is a matter of anatomy rather than of factors inherent in the flow.

In the case of touch and hearing similar considerations would lead to similar results. We will now turn to the facts of learning and habit formation. In trying to explain these facts, psychologists have said that in some parts of the nervous system, for instance between its visual and auditory sectors, pathways are not fixed once for all in early youth. According to this view, either no paths are at first ready for conduction, or else from one point of the tissue several paths conduct processes equally well in several directions, so that no particular order is prescribed. In the adult, however, a great many associations are established between the two sectors, and the accuracy of recall shows that now events occur in a directed and orderly fashion. The thing we have before us on the table is called a book, and its parts, pages. It is a serious pathological symptom if someone cannot recall these names when the objects are before him as visual facts. The normal order in the play of the associations suggests this explanation: Where at first no conducting paths, or several paths of equal conductivity, were given, learning has singled out one path by making it better conducting than all the others. Consequently, processes will now follow this one path. If for the time being we disregard the question how learning actually does this kind of thing, the order of association and recall is explained by the assumption. Obviously, the explanation is given in terms of topographical conditions. It is true, in the present case these conditions are not supposed to exist in infancy; it is also true that the changes by which the conditions are established remain a bit obscure; but once we grant that they are established when associations are formed, the direction of events is now as rigidly enforced and as independent of dynamic factors as is conduction in the visual sector as such. Just as a railroad train remains on its tracks because these constitute a way of least resistance, and just as the enormous power of the engine has no influence upon the direction of the train, so order in association and recall is a matter of pathways, and the nature of the processes which travel along these pathways has no influence upon their course.

We will now discuss the consequences of this view. First of all, all order which is found in mental events is now explained in terms of either inherited machine arrangements or secondarily acquired constraints. Thus, if a given performance is not an instance of learning as such, its causes must lie either in original topographical conditions or in past learning, i.e., in acquired changes of such conditions.[3] It will be seen that this alternative coincides with that of nativistic and empiristic explanations.[4] The discussions between nativists and empirists leave no doubt that a nativistic explanation has always meant an explanation in terms of inherited anatomical facts. If in a given case such an explanation does not seem to be acceptable, then only one other possibility is left, namely, that of learning. It never occurs to the authors in question that function might be orderly when neither inherited nor acquired arrangements in the nervous system are responsible for the fact. Often, the consideration of such a further alternative is regarded with deep suspicion, as though the introduction of vitalistic notions were imminent.

What happens at the end of a one-way street depends upon the events which happened at its entrance at an earlier moment. According to the present picture of sensory function, objective experience must be composed of purely local sensory facts, the characteristics of which are strictly determined by corresponding peripheral stimuli. For the sake of the maintenance of order, processes in individual pathways and in corresponding cells of the brain have been separated from one another and from the surrounding tissue. It follows that no processes in other parts of the nervous system can alter sensory experience; more particularly, sensory experience cannot be influenced by any changes of the subject's attitude. If we enumerate the intensive and qualitative characteristics which the elements of the field exhibit at a given time, the result must be an exhaustive account of the field. Thus sensory experience is a mere mosaic, an entirely additive ag-

[3] In the first class we may include anatomical arrangements which are not ready at the time of birth, but gradually develop to their final form by maturation.

[4] The term "empirist" has not, of course, the same meaning as the term "empiricist." While the latter refers to a philosopher who claims that all knowledge grows from outside experience, the former refers to a psychologist who tends to explain a maximum of mental facts by previous learning.

gregation of facts; and this mosaic is just as rigid as is its
physiological basis. We have every reason to add that in
this picture sensory experience is also incredibly "poor." Any
function by which the various parts of the field could be
interrelated is made impossible. The only dynamic events
which can happen are located in elements; and their distribution as a whole is no more than a geometrical pattern.

In the machine theory of the nervous system, connections
between cells in the brain and effector organs (such as the
muscles) are of the same type as the connections between
points of sense organs and those cells. Under these circumstances, a thoroughly adequate formula for research in psychology will be as follows: we have to discover what reactions in the effector organs go with given stimuli. This is the
well-known *stimulus-response formula* which has for long
enjoyed considerable prestige in American psychology. It
agrees entirely with the view that the nervous system is devoid of any characteristic processes of its own.

The fact that in this theory the dynamic factor is reduced
to minimal importance has one more consequence. In physics,
dynamic interrelations depend upon the characteristics of
the interrelated processes and materials. For example, in a
solution which contains Na_2SO_4 and $BaCl_2$, $BaSO_4$ will be
precipitated because of certain characteristics of Ba, $SO_4^=$
and H_2O which, in their mutual relations, determine what
happens in the mixture. Two electric currents cause mutual attraction of their conductors, if both flow in the same direction; but repulsion occurs, if the currents have opposite directions. The rule is general that "characteristics in relation," as
exemplified in these cases, are decisive for interaction. It will
be obvious that since the machine theory excludes any dynamic interrelations among the parts of a field, such a field can be
put together in any arbitrarily chosen fashion. In a mere
mosaic each element is entirely indifferent to the nature of
its neighbors. No other consequence of the theory shows
quite so clearly what is involved in the exclusion of dynamic
interrelations. For we have just realized that if such interrelations exist, physical facts are surely not insensitive to the
characteristics of other facts in their neighborhood. This point
will again be mentioned when we discuss association and
recall in another chapter.

When confronted with this picture of their assumptions
about physiological functions, most psychologists will hesitate
to agree. They will declare that preliminary guesses about the
processes of the nervous system ought not to be taken too
literally. Who does not admit, they would say, that in some
parts of the tissue there are leaks in the conducting connec-

tions? My answer is that if the first tentative picturing of nervous function uses analogies only of one kind, the machine type, then other analogies have probably never occurred to the theorists. Preliminary or final, it is a machine picture with which we are here dealing, and no essentially different principle is ever mentioned. As to the question of leaks, this concept contributes no more than a certain lack of precise function in the machine. It still presupposes as the normal case that order is enforced by separation of local events; and it is far from pointing out positive consequences which lack of complete separation would have. In this fashion our ideas about nervous processes may become more nebulous than a consistent machine theory is; but I cannot see that this means a new way of explaining order of function. Just what is supposed to happen if all conductors leak a bit at certain points? Would not local processes simply mingle? If not, what else do the theorists expect to happen? I am afraid that they will have difficulties in answering this question.

Let us once more compare theory with observation. It was quite clear to us that constancy of brightness and constancy of size are, as facts, incompatible with the assumptions of the machine theory; for in both cases sensory experience is surely not determined by corresponding local stimuli alone. Precisely because of this predicament, we remember, recourse was taken to empiristic explanations. But since, in the meantime, animal psychology has offered strong evidence against these explanations, it must now be admitted that neither the empiristic nor the nativistic assumptions can be right. Thus we must try to find a kind of function which is orderly and yet not entirely constrained by either inherited or acquired arrangements. If such an alternative exists, we shall have to apply it also to other observations, such as the constancies of shape, speed, location, and so forth. They are, on the whole, so similar to the constancies of brightness and size that an explanation which fits the latter is extremely likely to throw light also on the former. This means, of course, that the alternative between nativistic and empiristic assumptions must be quite generally mistaken.

The Introspectionist's thesis that changes of attitude do not influence true sensory experience is also incompatible with actual facts. The thesis almost amounts to an arbitrary definition of true sensory experience. As a matter of sheer observation, I can "by introspection" transform the white in the shadow and the black in full light into two similar grays. There can hardly be a more radical influence of attitude upon sensory experience than this transformation. The same holds for all instances in which introspection destroys natural experience and thus finds its true sensations. That this is what happens in introspection is widely recognized at least with regard to one observation. When analyzing a musical sound, we may hear several notes in succession which emerge from the original unit. Many admit that in this case a special attitude transforms one sensory datum into another; and that the sound heard as one is just as good a sensory fact as the overtones which appear during analysis. But if this be granted, how can we object to similar evidence in other instances?

As to the statement that sensory experience is a mosaic of purely local facts in the sense that each point of a sensory field depends exclusively upon its local stimulus, I must repeat that no grounds have ever been given for this radical assumption. Rather it seems to be the expression of an *a priori* belief about what ought to be the nature of things, experience to the contrary notwithstanding. As far as observation goes, local retinal stimulation does not alone determine what the size, the shape, the location, and the brightness of local experience is to be; neither does retinal speed alone determine seen speed, as it ought to, if only the geometry of retinal facts determined spatial experiences. As a matter of observation, a great many so-called illusions may be cited as showing that local processes depend upon *sets* of stimuli. To a degree this controversy will eventually be settled by pragmatic principles: that side will win whose principles prove more fruitful in the further development of psychology.

In the case of one observation almost all psychologists agree that local sensory experience is determined by more than merely local stimulation. The case is that of color contrast, which at the present time most psychologists suppose to be an effect of interaction in the nervous system. Here the point-to-point correlation between retinal stimuli and sensory experience is no longer defended, because the determination of local experience by conditions in a larger area is too evident. But after this concession, how can we proceed as though nothing serious had happened? It took science some time to accept obvious evidence even in this case. Helmholtz refused to do so. In order to save his fundamental premise, i.e., the point-to-point determination of local sensory facts by local stimuli, he made, of course, use of empiristic hypotheses. But in our time, after the first step has been taken, we should realize not only that one theory of contrast has taken the place of another, but also that a fundamental principle in the whole field of sensory experience can no longer be held. When in the future an experience is found to be at variance with local stimulation, we shall have to consider the possibility that, just as contrast, such an experience depends upon a set of stimuli rather than upon local stimulation alone. In a similar way we may eventually understand why in some cases particular attitudes of the subject affect sensory experience. Once it has been shown that sensory experience in a given place is influenced by stimulation in a larger area, there is, of course, no reason why such an influence should not also be exerted by processes which go with a particular attitude.

In the following chapters we will discuss further facts which point in the same direction. There is, in the first place, what is now generally called the *organization* of sensory experience. The term refers to the fact that sensory fields have in a way their own social psychology. Such fields appear neither as uniformly coherent continua nor as patterns of mutually indifferent elements. What we actually perceive are, first of all, specific entities such as things, figures, etc., and also groups of which these entities are members. This demonstrates the operation of processes in which the content of certain areas is unified, and at the same time relatively segregated from its environment. The machine theory with its mosaic of separate elements is, of course, incapable of dealing with organization in this sense.

Furthermore, it has been shown that many sensory experiences cannot be related to purely local conditions of stimulation because such local conditions never give rise to anything like those experiences. The facts to which I am alluding are attributes only of certain areas in space and of stretches in the dimension of time. Now, extended physical processes, the parts of which are functionally interrelated, may also have characteristics of their own, characteristics which cannot be related to merely local conditions. But the machine theory of the nervous system excludes this possibility, because the assumption of extended processes with functionally interrelated parts is incompatible with the principal tenets of the theory.

In the machine theory, we have seen, any local sensory fact is strictly determined by its stimulus. Consequently, the characteristics of stimuli in their relations to one another can play no part in the determination of local sensory experience. They can do so only if processes in the brain are free to interact. Interaction in physics, we remember, depends throughout on the "characteristics in relation" of the interacting facts. Now, if we review available knowledge in the field of sensory experience, we find that in countless instances local sensory data depend upon the relation between local stimuli and stimuli in the neighborhood. This holds for the case of contrast and that of tonal fusion, also for the observations which have been discussed in the preceding chapter.

The constancy of brightness, for instance, depends upon the relation of the illumination and brightness of the surrounding field to the brightness of the object under observation. It will soon become apparent that organization as we defined it a moment ago also depends upon local characteristics in their relations to one another.

In view of these facts, we are surely not exaggerating if we say that the machine theory of the nervous system is quite unable to do justice to the nature of sensory experience. Everything in this field points toward a theory in which the main emphasis lies on dynamic factors rather than on anatomically prescribed conditions. Moreover, in many observations field dynamics is almost directly revealed to the subject. This is the case, for instance, when sudden stimulation, or a change of stimulation, is followed by sensory events rather than states. Suppose that a bright figure suddenly appears in the dark. Such a figure has neither its full size nor its right place at once. It appears with an energetic movement of extension as well as of approach. Again, when it suddenly disappears, it does so with a movement of contraction and recession. In terms of the machine theory such observations are entirely incomprehensible. Or take the fact that in touch, as well as in vision and hearing, objects and events change their places when other objects and events are added. The physiologist von Frey has shown that when two points of the arm are touched at the same time the distance between them is much shorter than corresponds to their locations when given alone. Scholz and Kester have both measured the mutual attraction which two lights or two sounds exhibit when presented under certain conditions. Without the great historical prestige which the machine theory still enjoys, nobody would hesitate to take these observations as evidence of dynamic interaction. The stroboscopic movement, which obviously belongs in the same class, is now generally known as the fact on which Max Wertheimer based his first protest against the mosaic theory of sensory experience.[5] If two stimuli are successively projected upon different places of the retina, the subject generally sees a movement which starts from the locus of the first and ends in the region of the second (*cf.* Ch. III). Under favorable conditions subjects will not report about two impressions. Rather, one thing will be seen moving from one place to the other. How can a theory which interprets sensory fields as mosaics of independent local facts deal with such observations? The stroboscopic movement has been widely discussed, and empiristic argu-

[5] *Zeitschr. f. Psychol., 61,* 1912.

ments have, naturally, played a great part in the debate. But there is no longer any question about the main point: if objective conditions and the attitude of the observer are not entirely inadequate, the stroboscopic movement is a striking phenomenon. After all, the art of motion pictures is based on the stroboscopic effect. There are, of course, people who do not trust observation when it contradicts the postulates of machine theory. Perhaps such opponents can be convinced by the fact that, when repeated in a given area, stroboscopic movements give negative after-images of their occurrence just as ordinary movements do. Historically, Wertheimer's investigation was the beginning of Gestalt Psychology. In the present discussion I am following another line merely because I doubt whether the stroboscopic movement represents the best material to be used in a first introduction.[6]

There are, of course, several arguments which have served to defend the machine theory. Sometimes it has been said that this theory gives us a particularly clear and simple picture of nervous function, a picture which everybody can understand, since in practical life order is everywhere enforced by arrangements *ad hoc*. I must confess that such a policy of the least scientific effort seems to me unacceptable. When our questions refer to the actual nature of a certain subject matter, the comfort and the habits of the scientist do not count at all. Furthermore, only the psychologists, neurologists and physiologists save time and effort by assumptions which explain order by constraining arrangements in the tissue. They simply hand their problems down to somebody else; for, whenever a problem of function is interpreted as one of constraining arrangements, the science of biological developments, of ontogeny and phylogeny, is implicitly asked to explain the origin of the histological arrangements. Thus the avoidance of difficulties in some sciences here means more difficulties in others. Also, sooner or later functional problems must be treated in functional terms. It may perhaps be possible to explain the ontogeny of anatomical structures by special arrangements which operate in the egg and germ; but nobody will attempt to explain phylogeny by arrangements which have forced it to take a certain course.

As a further argument it could be pointed out that, as a matter of obvious anatomy, the organism does contain

---

[6] Benussi has contributed greatly to the investigation of these problems. His work on similar facts in the field of touch has been mentioned above. Some extremely important characteristics of the stroboscopic movement have been discovered by Wertheimer and Ternus (*Psychol. Forsch., 7*, 1926).

special arrangements which guarantee adequate function. Surely, such facts cannot be denied. As an example, the mere existence of connecting fibers between the sense organs and related parts of the brain proves the fact. But let us not forget that there is another conducting system in the organism which clearly shows the limitations of machine theory. In the blood vessels a great many substances are continually being transported from certain places to others. To be sure, the blood vessels as such constitute an arrangement "for transportation"; but within this system there are no special arrangements for carrying each component of the fluid to its right place. In this case, selection and order depend solely upon the relation between the various chemical parts of the blood and the state of the various tissues at the time. Hence, the existence of large organs in the anatomical sense does not prove that all details of function are kept in order by machine arrangements.

Often we are told that the fibers of nerves actually are separate conductors in which essentially independent impulses travel. Now I wonder whether we can still maintain that impulses in the various fibers of a given nerve travel quite independently of one another. Quite apart from this, physiological investigations leave no longer any doubt that in ganglionic tissue the functions of individual nerve cells are dynamically interrelated.

If the facts of sensory experience can be explained neither by inherited nor by acquired arrangements, what is the decisive factor in sensory function? Let us return to our statement that in physical systems the relative influence of topographical conditions, on the one hand, and of purely dynamic factors, on the other, varies enormously. In typical machines the rôle of topographical conditions prevails to such an extent that dynamic factors serve only to cause displacements along a path laid down by those conditions. Such machines represent, however, an altogether special type of physical system. Outside the narrow world of man-made machines there are innumerable other physical systems in which the direction of processes is by no means completely determined by topographical arrangements.

Let us consider a drop in a current of water which moves along a narrow pipe. Why does the drop move? If we ignore inertia, it moves because pressure in the water is higher behind the drop than it is in front. So long as the walls of the pipe exclude all other possibilities, this difference of pressure can have effects only in one direction. Let us suppose, however, that there is no pipe, and that the drop now becomes part of a much larger volume of water. In its new environment the drop will probably also move. But in this situation it is exposed to many gradients of pressure, and its movement will be in the direction of the resultant gradient. This movement is, of course, just as strictly determined as was the movement in the pipe, but now there are no particular constraining arrangements at each point which prescribe its direction. In the new situation, any drop within the current takes its particular course for dynamic reasons; it follows the resultant force at each moment and in all places. But how are these forces themselves determined at each point? They are determined by all displacements and corresponding changes of pressure, which have occurred the moment before. In fact, to a degree they are also determined by the way in which our particular drop has just been moving. All this means, of course, that it is free interaction among the parts of the water on which its flow at each point depends. To be sure, somewhere in such a system displacements are usually constrained by rigid limiting conditions, for instance, by walls which force the surface of the liquid to move along *their* surface. If, however, no such constraining conditions are given in the interior of the volume, then it is left to interaction alone to determine what happens at each point. Naturally, nothing can happen at any point which is incompatible with the constraints given at the surface. But this is the only way in which these limiting conditions influence the flow. Their influence makes itself felt by the enforced behavior of the flow in their immediate neighborhood, and by the dynamic consequences of this behavior in all other parts of the volume. It is events of this type which are almost entirely prevented in machines; and the now prevailing neurological theories assume that they are also prevented in the nervous system. Gestalt Psychology sees no convincing grounds for this assumption. In actual fact, this school suggests that such processes are of paramount importance in physiology and psychology.

In a pipe, a drop of water moves in a way which tends toward equalization of the differential pressure. Such is the operation of forces at all points of all systems. When the drop is surrounded by a larger volume of water, not only its own movement but also that of the current as a whole illustrates the same rule. But now the *direction* of the flow at each point also depends upon the tendency of the dynamic factors to bring about equalization of pressure.

Pipes can be so constructed that virtually any particular order may be imposed on the flow in the whole system. In this case, the resulting order is enforced by *exclusion* of free, i.e., dynamically determined, behavior. Naturally, we must ask ourselves whether order ·can also result when the distribution of events depends upon the play of free inter- action. Have the Aristotelians and the theorists of neural function been right in assuming that free interaction invari- ably leads to disorder? At first, what happens around us in nature seems to corroborate their opinion: when forces and processes blindly meet, the result is for the most part chaos and destruction. But the situations of which this is true are commonly more or less of this type: In the beginning we see a thing at rest or a process which uniformly takes its course. Suddenly a new factor impinges from the outside upon the thing or the process; after a short while another such dis- turbance, independent of the first, makes. itself felt, and so forth. Under these circumstances, it is true, almost anything may happen, and the end result of such accumulated acci- dents is likely to be destruction. This, it seems to me, is the picture which most men have in mind when they refer to the free play of forces in nature—as though accidental impact were the only form of interaction.

For our present discussion, however, other situations are much more interesting. For instance, if in a large vessel water moves in one way or another, there is at a given moment a certain amount of pressure at each point, and everywhere the differences between local pressures tend to change the distribution of the water and its flow. Now suppose that the vessel itself does not change, and that no outside factors accidentally impinge upon the system, what will be the result of the continual interaction among the parts of the water? If we try to find the answer by imagining the water divided into small volumes, each of which moves with the resultant gradient of pressure at its place, and thereby changes this gradient; if we notice that in this way the pattern of the flow will generally not remain the same even for a smallest frac- tion of a second; then we shall soon be inclined to dismiss the task as being beyond our capacity, and to conclude that no more order can result in this situation than is the case where events depend upon accumulated accidents. How- ever, in this we are entirely wrong. We are merely projecting our own confusion into the course of objective events. Thus we become guilty of anthropomorphism. The physicist takes quite a different view of the situation. Both observation and theoretical calculation make him conclude that, in general, dynamic interaction within a system tends to establish order- ly distributions.

Let us return to an example which has been mentioned in the beginning of this chapter. To Aristotelian theorists the striking order of astronomical movements appeared inexplicable without the assumption of rigid constraints by which the stars are kept on the right tracks. Now, in modern times nobody believes in the crystal spheres which were once supposed to serve as such constraints. But the planets still move along their orderly orbits. Obviously, they have not learned to move in this orderly fashion. It follows that, quite apart from pre-established or acquired constraints, there must be other factors which tend to establish, and to maintain, this remarkable order of function. In the modern conception of the solar system, it is, of course, the free play of gravitational vectors which has caused, and still maintains, the order of planetary movements.

If a number of straight wires are suspended in an irregular distribution, in which they point in different directions, an electric current which enters the wires will immediately give them parallel directions. This is an orderly result of electrodynamic interaction.

Or assume that oil is poured into a liquid with which it does not mix. In spite of the violent interaction of molecules at the common surface of the fluids, the boundary remains sharply defined. Obviously, this orderly distribution is not enforced by any rigid constraints; rather, it results precisely from the dynamic factors which operate in the boundary region. If the specific density of both liquids is the same, the surface forces will change the shape of the oil until a perfect sphere is formed which swims in the other liquid. Any number of further examples could easily be added. There is no question that so long as dynamics remains undisturbed by accidental impacts from without it tends to establish orderly distributions.

What is the explanation of this tendency? I will try to indicate the answer in a few words. In such systems there is at a given time a certain resulting force at each point. All these resultant forces together constitute a continuous pattern of stress. For the system as a whole, the immediate effect can have only one direction: all local changes must be such that, when considered in their totality, they bring the system nearer the balance of forces. The factor of inertia, it is true, may cause temporary deviations from this simple rule. But, then, in many systems inert velocities are at once destroyed by friction, so that the actual development exhibits the rule in pure form, and an orderly balance is soon reached. (It is important to know that this applies to the nervous system. There are no processes in this system which are influenced by inert velocities.) The fact that the final result always constitutes an orderly distribution has been simply explained by Ernst Mach: In orderly distributions, the pattern of forces is just as regular as is the distribution of the material. But, clearly, in regular patterns forces are more thoroughly balanced than they are in irregular distributions. Hence, since undisturbed interaction operates in the direction of balance, it must operate toward orderly distribution both of forces and materials.

Dynamic self-distribution in this sense is the kind of function which Gestalt Psychology believes to be essential in neurological and psychological theory. More particularly, it is assumed that the order of facts in a visual field is to a high degree the outcome of such a self-distribution of processes. From this point of view, a stationary visual field corresponds to a balanced distribution of underlying processes. When conditions change, resulting developments will always be in the direction of balance.

How is this view related to the fact that visual processes depend upon retinal stimulation? Self-distributions of processes, it will be remembered, do not generally occur without *any* imposed constraints. In our particular case, the patterns of retinal stimuli establish similar patterns of photochemical reactions in the eye. Neurologists assert that between the retina and the visual sector of the brain conduction is approximately a matter of separate pathways, and that, as a consequence, the patterns of retinal processes are to a degree repeated in the visual brain. If this is true, dynamic self-distributions will begin here; and the conditions to which they are subjected will be the patterns which impulses from the retina impose upon the visual cortex.

We have no reason to deny that the task which this theory faces is enormously more difficult than anything with which the machine theory has to deal. When any question as to the distribution of processes is answered in terms of anatomical arrangements, not much knowledge about the nature of the processes involved will be needed. On the other hand, a theory in which dynamics plays an essential part cannot possibly be developed without knowledge of the principles of self-distribution in general, or without assumptions about the nature of the participating processes. In the absence of sufficient physiological evidence concerning these processes, hypotheses about their nature can be derived only from the facts of sensory experience. In the situation as now given, such hypotheses can also be tested only by further observations in this field. It will take us some time before we feel firm ground under our feet. It must be remembered, however, that any perplexities which we may find on our way need by no means be related to the fundamental concept of dynamic self-distribution. They may be caused by wrong assumptions about the particular processes to which this concept is to be applied in the case of the human brain.

Dynamics plays so slight a part in contemporary theory that the terms which have been used in the preceding paragraphs may sound a bit mysterious to many a psychologist. As a result, there will be suspicions as to the intentions of Gestalt Psychology. For this reason it seems advisable to make at this point the following statement: the concepts to which we have referred in this chapter are not in the least related to Vitalistic notions. On the contrary, in the future our dynamic concepts may serve to deal with objections which Vitalism has raised against the scientific interpretation of life. If this happens, the machine theories of life will lose ground—after all, Vitalistic arguments against these theories have sometimes been fairly convincing. But Vitalism will not profit—for from its objections against the machine theories it has wrongly concluded that the main problems of biology cannot be solved in terms of natural science. Our concepts suggest new ways of dealing with these problems precisely in such terms.

V

SENSORY ORGANIZATION

DYNAMIC DISTRIBUTIONS are functional wholes. Take, for example, a simple electric circuit. The differences of potential and the densities of the current distribute themselves along the conductors in such a way that a steady or stationary state is established and maintained. No part of this distribution is self-sufficient; the characteristics of local flow depend throughout upon the fact that the process as a whole has assumed the steady distribution.

If a similar conception is to be applied to the processes which underlie sensory experience, we must avoid a mistake. In his protest against psychological atomism William James once said that in the sensory field local experiences are interwoven with their neighbors in a manner which is beyond the grasp of purely intellectual theory. He also thought that original sensory experience is uniformly continuous, and that all cuts and boundaries are later introduced into the field for pragmatic reasons.

From the point of view of Gestalt Psychology, such a statement does not correspond to the facts. Notwithstanding the general dynamic interdependence throughout the field, there are boundaries in it at which dynamic factors operate toward a measure of segregation rather than uniform continuity. For this there are good examples in physics. Everything favors the assumption that the same happens in the nervous system.

The visual field exhibits two kinds of order. One is the order with which the machine theory is occupied when it tries to explain how a given process keeps its right place between its neighbors, and does not go astray. There is, however, another order in the field which tends to escape our attention, although it is no less important than the first. In most visual fields the contents of particular areas "belong together" as circumscribed units from which their surroundings are excluded. James did not admit that this *organization* of the field is a sensory fact, because he was under the influence of his empiristic prejudice. Nowhere is this prejudice more detrimental than it is at this point. Under its sway not a few readers will have difficulties in acknowledging the import of the following paragraphs.

On the desk before me I find quite a number of circumscribed units or things: a piece of paper, a pencil, an eraser, a cigarette, and so forth. The existence of these visual things involves two factors. What is included in a thing becomes a unit, and this unit is segregated from its surroundings. In order to satisfy myself that this is more than a verbal affair, I may try to form other units in which parts of a visual thing and parts of its environment are put together. In some cases such an attempt will end in complete failure. In others, in which I am more successful, the result is so strange that, as a result, the original organization appears only the more convincing as a visual fact.

The reader will say: "Of course, you are talking about psychological facts; but something may be a psychological fact without for this reason belonging to sensory experience. Surely, you will admit that a piece of paper, a pencil, a cigarette are objects which are known by use. For many years you have handled such objects. Thus you have had more opportunity than you needed for learning that they are units in a practical sense. This previously acquired knowledge you now project into your field of vision. Why, then, do you lay so much stress upon your observation? It is widely known and, as just shown, quite satisfactorily explained. Probably it was known, and so explained, when Aristotle wrote his textbook of psychology."

My answer will take more time than this argument does. So long as arguments of this kind are still accepted, even the most elementary theses of Gestalt Psychology will not be adequately understood. To be sure, the piece of paper, the pencil, and so forth, are well-known objects. I will also grant without hesitation that their uses and their names are known to me from numerous contacts in previous life. Much of the meaning which the objects now have unquestionably comes from this source. But from these facts there is a large step to the statement that papers, pencils, and so forth, would not be segregated units without that previously acquired knowledge. How is it proved that before I acquired this knowledge the visual field contained no such units? When I see a green object, I can immediately tell the name of the color. I also know that green is used as a signal on streets and as a symbol of hope. But from this I do not conclude that the color green as such can be derived from such knowledge. Rather, I know that, as an independently existent sensory fact, it has acquired secondary meanings, and I am quite willing to recognize the advantages which these acquired meanings have in practical life. In exactly the same fashion, Gestalt Psychology holds, sensory units have acquired names, have become richly symbolic, and are now known to have certain practical uses, while nevertheless they have existed as units before any of these further facts were added. Gestalt Psychology claims that it is precisely the original segregation of circumscribed wholes which makes it possible for the sensory world to appear so utterly imbued with meaning to the adult; for, in its gradual entrance into the sensory field, meaning follows the lines drawn by natural organization; it usually enters into segregated wholes.

If the empiristic explanation were correct, specific entities would be segregated in the field only to the extent to which they represent known objects. This is by no means the case. When I look into a dark corner, or when I walk through mist in the evening, I frequently find before me an unknown something which is detached from its environment as a particular object, while at the same time I am entirely unable to say what kind of thing it is. Only afterwards may I discover its nature in this sense. Actually, such visual things will sometimes remain unrecognized for minutes. It follows that my knowledge about the practical significance of things cannot be responsible for their existence as detached visual units. The same argument may be restated in a more general form. Whenever we say to ourselves or others: "What may that something be, at the foot of that hill, just to the right of that tree, between those two houses, and so on?" we ask about the empirical meaning or use of a seen object and demonstrate by our very question that as a matter of principle, segregation of visual things is independent of knowledge and meaning.

Yet many are so fond of their empiristic convictions that, in this predicament, their explanation will immediately assume another form. "The unknown entity which you see in the mist," they will say, "appears as something separate because it is darker than the gray mist around. In other words, no special knowledge about particular groups of sensations as meaning specific objects need be assumed in our explanation. You seem to underrate the extraordinary achievements of learning, if you restrict its effects to specific instances. Since early childhood we have often observed that sets of sensations which have approximately the same color, and differ in this respect from their environment, tend to behave as units, i.e., to move and to be moved, to appear and disappear, at the same time. Such is the case with stones, with papers, with plates, with shoes, with many animals, with the leaves of plants. Approximately homogeneous sets of sensations tend to correspond to physical objects which behave as units for physical reasons. It is only an example of the well-known generalizing power of memory if, as a result of such experiences, we treat all homogeneously colored areas as units until we actually seem to *see* them as such units. It is therefore not astonishing that, in the mist, for instance, an area of darker nuance is seen as an individual something, although we may not recognize it as a particular kind of thing."

I do not believe that this modification of the theory is satisfactory. In a great many cases units are formed and segregated under circumstances to which the explanation does not apply. Take all visual units which consist of separate parts. If on a clear night we look up at the sky, some stars are immediately seen as belonging together, and as detached from their environment. The constellation Cassiopeia is an example, the Dipper is another. For ages people have seen the same groups as units, and at the present time children need no instruction in order to perceive the same units. Similarly, in Fig. 1 the reader has before him two groups

Fig. 1

of patches. Why not merely six patches? Or two other groups? Or three groups of two members each? When looking casually at this pattern everyone beholds the two groups of three patches each. What about generalized effects of learning in these instances? No previous learning can have separated Cassiopeia from the other fixed stars around it. As far as everyday experience goes, all fixed stars move together. Quite generally, one cannot possibly assert that we have learned to regard a number of separate similar patches as one group because they regularly move together. They are very far from doing so. On a table I now see five flies which, from my distance, appear as black dots. Presently these dots begin to

move separately, and to move in different directions. So do
three yellow leaves which a breeze lifts from the ground; so
again three similar stones which my hand moves one after
the other. My general experience is that, as often as not,
similar members of a group are movable, and move, independently. If nevertheless in such cases groups are again
formed and segregated, this happens in spite of our previous
knowledge about the actual behavior of their members.

When discrete entities unite in a group, the part which
equality (or similarity) plays in the unification cannot be explained in terms of learning. But the same factor has a uni-
fying influence in the case of continuous areas, whether or
not they represent known objects. Consequently it is futile
to apply the empiristic explanation to this formation of continuous homogeneous things; for the formation of groups
proves that equality favors grouping quite irrespective of acquired knowledge.

The grouping of separate entities plays a decisive rôle in
a well-known test for color blindness. A rectangular field is
filled with dots which lie at approximately equal distances
from one another. For normal vision several of these dots
form a group, and are, as such a group, segregated from
the rest. Since the group has the shape of a written number,
it can be read without any difficulty. The dots in question
have approximately the same hue, and differ in this respect from the others. This is the reason why they unite
in a group, the characteristic shape of which is immediately
recognized. In the visual field of color-blind people, however,
who do not perceive those differences of hue, no such group
can be formed, so that they are unable to see and to read
the number. In this example the general acquaintance with
numbers is the same for both normal and color-blind subjects. The striking difference as to grouping must, therefore,
be caused directly by the given differences as to sensory
content.

Groups which consist of separate members have a special
interest for theory inasmuch as they prove that a given unit
may be segregated and yet at the same time belong to a
larger unit. In our last example one dot represents a continuous detached entity. None the less it is a member of a
larger whole, the number, which is detached from a wider
area. There is nothing peculiar about such a subordination
of units. In physics, a molecule constitutes a larger functional
whole which contains several atoms as subordinate wholes.
Functionally, the atoms belong to the molecule-unit; but in
this unit they do not altogether lose their individuality.

After casual observations of others, Wertheimer was the

first to recognize the fundamental importance of spontaneous grouping in sensory fields. He also showed by many examples what principles the grouping follows. Most of his illustrations refer to the grouping of separate dots and lines, because when such patterns rather than continuous objects are used demonstrations are less open to objections in terms of previous knowledge. But he also emphasized that the same principles hold for the formation of other sensory wholes. I know of no better introduction to this subject than was given in Wertheimer's paper.[1] Some of his principles are easy to understand. The one which claims that equal and similar items tend to form units, and to be separated from less similar items, has already been considered. Where this principle does not apply, relative proximity is often decisive. In one of our examples (p. 83) two groups of three members each were formed, because among the six patches some distances were small as compared with others. The patches which were separated by relatively small distances formed group-units. Sometimes it seems more natural to define a principle of grouping not so much in terms of given conditions as in terms of the direction which grouping tends to take. As the physicist is accustomed to say that surface tension tends to reduce the area of liquid surfaces, so we say that in the sensory field grouping tends to establish units of certain kinds rather than others. Simple and regular wholes, also closed areas, are formed more readily and more generally than irregular and open wholes. The order of sensory fields, in this sense, shows a strong predilection for particular kinds of organization, just as the formation of molecules and the pull of surface forces in physics operate in specific directions.[2]

The nature of grouping as an elementary sensory fact was most convincingly demonstrated in experiments which Hertz made with a certain species of birds (*Garrulus glandarius*).[3] A number of small flower pots were put on the ground upside down. The tame bird, perched on the branch of a tree, was allowed to see how food was placed under one of the pots by the experimenter. Soon he would come down, lift the

---

[1] *Psychol. Forsch., 4,* 1923.

[2] In one form of the empiristic explanation it is said that we have learned to regard as wholes whatever always moves together. Wertheimer has pointed out that, if some parts of the field begin to move at the same time and in a uniform way, they become at once a moving unit. In other words, if a "common fate" actually determines sensory grouping, it does so as a factor of primary sensory organization rather than *via* processes of learning.

[3] *Zeitschr. f. Vergl. Physiol., 7,* 1928.

pot, and take the food. This is, of course, a simple form of "delayed reaction" as investigated by Hunter years ago. In the present experiments, however, the main point was not so much the delay of the reaction as its dependence upon particular patterns in the field. The bird reacted without difficulty when there was one pot only. But when there were more than one, everything depended upon the question whether or not the right pot was an outstanding and specifically characterized member of the totality. If it was put in a straight line with the others so that, for human vision, it became absorbed as an indifferent member of the whole series, the bird lifted one pot after another in a haphazard fashion. This happened even when the distance between the pots was as large as 25 cm. As soon, however, as in human vision the right pot became something strikingly segregated from the rest, the bird selected the right object at once. So, for instance, in the case of Fig. 2, in which the right pot was 10 cm. removed from the straight line of the other pots. Apparently in his vision, too, this line was a compact whole

Fig. 2

from which the right pot could readily be distinguished as a thing by itself. Even in the situation of Fig. 3, where the

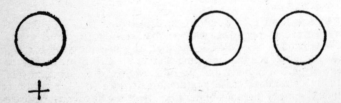

Fig. 3

right object stood 6 cm. from the next, and this 2 cm. from
the last, grouping was clear enough to permit correct reaction.
But in the case of Fig. 4 where the right object was only 3 cm.

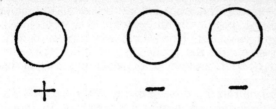

Fig. 4

distant from the next and this 2 cm. from the last, responses
became a matter of chance. Quite generally, the bird was
unable to single out the right pot unless quite specific grouping helped him to do so. On the other hand, so long as grouping was entirely clear in human vision, the bird reacted

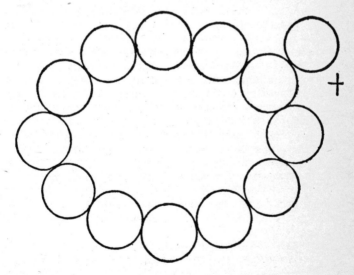

Fig. 5

promptly and correctly even when the right object was in immediate contact with its next neighbor. In the situation of

Fig. 5, for instance, 12 pots were arranged in the form of an ellipse, and the right pot was put close to one of the other twelve. In the visual field of the experimenter the situation appeared as one compact group to which a single object was added outside. In this situation the bird chose the right object at once. The example is particularly instructive in showing that individual distances as such are not the decisive factors. The grouping which results in the pattern as a whole determines the bird's responses. How Hertz was able to demonstrate similar effects by the application of other principles, such as differences in size or color, may be seen in her paper.

If I am not mistaken, these experiments open an altogether new field of research in animal psychology. In further experimentation it ought to be possible to decide to what degree birds and other animals see *continuous* entities when such specific things appear in the visual field of man. It would, of course, be difficult to understand the behavior of the bird in Hertz's experiments, if in his field of vision the pots as such were not detached units.

The elementary nature of continuous wholes is demonstrated by observations on the first reactions of congenitally blind adults who begin to see after an operation. The problems which in these cases interest the ophthalmologist most are those of visual depth, and of an original similarity between forms in vision and forms in touch. Results have been discussed in several ways, but one phase of the observed facts has hardly been given adequate attention. When during the first post-operational tests the patient is shown an object which he knows by touch from previous life, he can seldom give a satisfactory response. With very few exceptions he does not recognize such forms when now given only in vision. Still there is something very significant in his reactions: when asked about "that thing" which he has before him, he understands the question. Obviously, he has before him a specific entity to which he refers the question, and which he tries to name. Thus, if the object has a simple and compact form, he need not learn what "aggregate of sensations" he must regard as one thing. Elementary visual organization seems to be given to him at once.

In Wertheimer's paper on sensory grouping the problem of grouping is also discussed in the case of wholes of a different sort. Experienced *time* has certain characteristics in common with experienced space, particularly with the spatial dimension which is indicated by the words "in front" and "behind."

Words which refer to relations in this dimension are used as terms for temporal relations everywhere and in all languages. In English we may have something "before" or "behind" us both in the spatial and the temporal meanings; we look "forward" in space as in time; and death approaches in time just as somebody approaches us in space. From the point of view of isomorphism, one would expect that there is a corresponding kinship between the physiological correlate of the temporal and that of this particular spatial dimension. At any rate, temporal "dots" form temporal groups just as simultaneously given dots tend to form groups in space. This holds for hearing and touch no less than it does for vision.

One can easily show that the factors on which grouping depends in time are about the same as those on which it depends in space. Suppose that I knock three times at short intervals on my table, and that after waiting for a second I repeat the performance, and so forth. People who hear this sequence of sounds experience groups in time. Physically, all these sounds are, of course, independent events. They are about as unrelated as the stars of Cassiopeia. In other words, there is no grouping in the physical sequence. Also, from a purely logical point of view, other forms of grouping are quite as possible as the one which is actually heard. But these do not occur in the experience of an observer who listens in a passive attitude. The groups as actually heard are therefore instances of psychological and, according to the thesis of isomorphism, also of physiological organization. In the present example, the operating principle is that of proximity in time, which is, of course, strictly analogous to the principle of proximity in spatial grouping. If the intervals between sounds are made equal, groups will again be formed as soon as differences of intensity or quality are introduced in the series, especially if they occur in regular repetition. Thus, equality plays the same rôle in the organization of temporal sequences as it does in a stationary visual field.

In the most general case of sensory organization, both space and time are involved in a given experience of grouping. Here is a simple example: In a dark room we move a tiny lamp, which appears as a bright point in the surrounding black. Let us suppose that the point moves at a constant speed in the form of Fig. 6. Under these circumstances an unprejudiced observer will describe what he sees as three similar figures or three movements (I, II, III). Perhaps he will then correct himself and say that there were seven movements (1, I, 2, II, 3, III, 4). But he will not say that he saw 53, or 16, or 29 movements. Now, if we consider the number of stimuli which successively impinge upon his retinae as independent events, any of the larger numbers is at least as correct as three or seven. But in this visual experience there

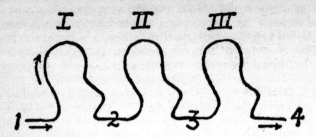

Fig. 6

is no series of mutually independent facts. What the observer actually sees is characterized by the small numbers three or seven; in other words, the movement appears organized in a specific fashion. The same holds for visual experiences such as these: "he nodded twice" or "he shook his head a few times." Quite apart from the fact that these movements convey certain particular meanings, as visual phenomena they involve an organization to which the words "twice" and "a few times" refer.

This seems to be the proper place for mentioning a further indirect explanation of organization which is suggested by some psychologists. They seem to believe that the overt movements which we make in responding to stimuli are responsible for the facts in question. Others would say that it is rather a particular kind of sensory experience, namely, the kinesthesis which occurs during such movements, that gives us the impression of a specific organization. In view of certain obvious objections it is sometimes added that mere tendencies to move may suffice; or, in the second explanation, that mere recall of past kinesthetic experiences can give a field its organized appearance.

In either case, whether movements as such or kinesthetic experiences are regarded as decisive, it is obviously important to consider how these factors are supposed to establish organization in a visual field. As far as I can see, it would have to be assumed, in the first case, that our movements are organized in the way in which the visual field seems to be organized; and, in the second case, that the same holds for our kinesthetic experiences. Whatever the process may be by which organization is believed to be introduced into the field of vision, it cannot be imported without existing beforehand in the region in which it is said to have its origin. So long as we consider movements of sequences of kinesthetic experiences as series of independent momentary events, which merely follow one another, their occurrence will never help to explain the segregation of visual units and groups. Take as an example the bright point which moves in dark space. If it be said that in this case the observer talks about three or seven movements because he makes or experiences three or seven eye-movements, it is tacitly taken for granted that eye-movements, or the experiences of such movements, are organized in the way in which the visual field appears organized. Otherwise, why should such movements impose upon the visual field three or seven rather than 53 or 29 units? Apart from organization, the latter numbers would not be more arbitrary than the former.

I have been told that the observations of Gestalt Psychology are not at all new, and that they have long been explained by the kinesthetic experiences which we have during eye-movements. This sounds as though a mere hint at the kinesthetic experiences which accompany vision could be accepted as an explanation of visual organization. Actually, instead of solving the problem, the reference to eye-movements merely shifts it from one place to another. For now the problem of unification and segregation must be solved in the field of kinesthetic experience.

I am far from denying that the problem of organization arises in the field of movements and kinesthetic experiences just as it does in vision. On the contrary, I feel convinced that the facts in these fields will remain quite incomprehensible unless the present point of view is applied. But why should movements and kinesthesis be the only materials which are capable of being organized, and which must therefore be treated in terms of Gestalt Psychology? If organization is possible in one field, why not in others? In the next chapter these questions will occupy us again.

After this discussion the reader will not be surprised to learn that serious lesions in the visual center of the brain produce a kind of "blindness" in persons who at the same time are by no means deprived of vision. Careful examination of such a case by Gelb and Goldstein showed that the patient's field of vision had undergone a radical change in that organization had disappeared almost completely.[4] Where he fixed his attention, the patient was able to grasp some small fraction of a line, for instance, but he could no longer see extended wholes with clear-cut shapes. It is a particularly interesting observation that he had spontaneously begun to rely more on motor experience than on vision. Following the fractions of contours which were clear to him with move-

[4] *Zeitschr. f. d. ges. Neurol. u. Psychiatrie, 41,* 1918.

ments of the head, he was able to build up motor wholes
and to recognize these. If his name was written on a black-
board, he would in this fashion follow the first letters and
soon guess the rest. But it was possible to exclude this procedure by a simple trick. A few lines of the same color as the
letters were drawn across the name. Since the patient never
saw the name as a simultaneously given object, he could also
not see it as one thing, and the crossing lines as a different
pattern. As a result he followed parts of a letter and then
parts of a crossing line indiscriminately. The effect was that
under these conditions he could not read the name. Incidentally, the example shows to what degree motor function
which accompanies vision depends upon visual organization.
Generally speaking, organization is a matter of extended
regions of the field. When only local fractions are to some
degree organized, the control which organization in a larger
area normally exerts upon eye-movements is made impossible.

But why do the entities which are formed in visual organization generally correspond to objects in the practical meaning of the word? Is there a mysterious harmony between the
laws of sensory dynamics and the way in which physical
things are formed in nature? No such assumption need be
made since there are so many exceptions to the correspond-
ence of sensory organization and physical facts. Take all the
groups of separate members such as the constellations in the
sky, or the dots and patches which form group-units (Fig. 1).
Or take grouping in ornaments, the parts of which are, of
course, for the most part physically independent of one another. In countless cases organization is a sensory fact when
there is no corresponding physical unit. Not only groups but
also continuous sensory wholes may occur in the absence of
corresponding physical units. To repeat, sometimes we see
from a distance a strange object which later, when we approach it, splits into a well-known thing and parts of other
objects. At first this thing and parts of its environment were
unified and segregated as an unknown entity. The example
also shows that occasionally an actually existing physical
object has no partner in the visual field, because parts of its
surface have combined with surrounding areas which happen
to have the right characteristics for the unification. The puz-
zle-pictures which years ago amused the readers of magazines
were examples of this kind of thing. In modern wars it has
become a real art to make objects such as guns, cars, boats,
etc., disappear by painting upon these things irregular de-
signs, the parts of which are likely to form units with parts
of their environment. In such cases the objects themselves
no longer exist as visual entities, and in their place appear

meaningless patches which do not arouse the enemy's suspicion; for similar patches are constantly produced by accidental combinations of parts which fuse, for instance, because of their similarity.

On the other hand, it is not difficult to explain why visual units at least *tend* to correspond to physical objects. The things around us are either made by man, or they are products of nature. Objects of the first class are fabricated for our practical purposes. Naturally, we give them forms and surfaces which make them likely to be seen and recognized as units. For this to happen, the principles of sensory organization need not be known explicitly by the manufacturers. Without such knowledge they will conform their work to these principles. As a consequence, the objects which they fabricate will generally appear as segregated visual units. Moreover, it is not at all easy to produce a somewhat compact object which, in a simple environment, does not fulfill the general conditions of segregation. Camouflage is a difficult art.

With objects which nature has produced the situation is not altogether different. A condition which is fulfilled by many natural things is this: within the area of such a thing surface properties tend to be more or less of one kind, while the surface properties of adjacent areas are for the most part of a different kind. The difference is due to the fact that the common origin of the parts of one object is likely to give them common surface characteristics. As a rule, these are not exactly repeated in adjacent surfaces, which have a different origin. In this fashion one condition of visual segregation is given in the case of most objects. Even if a stone lies half-embedded in sand, which consists of tiny fractions of the same kind of stone, the difference of coherence, and therefore of visual detail, between the surface elements of the stone and those of the sand will in most cases be sufficient to make the stone a segregated visual unit. Along the boundary between a natural object and its environment some discontinuity of properties will generally prevail. This discontinuity separates the environment from the interior of the object by a closed outline. Since such a discontinuity suffices to make any area appear as a segregated entity, it must also have this effect when the boundary is that of a physical object. Without such a discontinuity there is, of course, no reason why segregation should take place. But this is no objection to our reasoning. It is virtually impossible to find objects which fail to fulfill any of the conditions of sensory segregation, and are nevertheless seen as specific entities. Experience shows that whenever the conditions of organiza-

tion operate strictly against the formation of a certain visual
unit, this unit will not spontaneously be seen, even if it is
well-known as such, and camouflaged only by the special
circumstances of the moment. In a more detailed discussion
of this problem, visual depth and the segregation of things in
three dimensions would have to play an important part. For
the present, however, we can only mention this topic because in the field of depth perception both experimentation
and theory are still in a comparatively primitive state.

In the preceding paragraphs I have laid some stress upon
the fact that sensory organization constitutes a characteristic
achievement of the nervous system. This emphasis has become necessary because some authors seem to think that, according to Gestalt Psychology, "*Gestalten*," i.e., segregated
entities, exist outside the organism and simply extend or
project themselves into the nervous system. This view, it must
by now be realized, is entirely wrong.[5]

Once this has been made quite clear, however, we may, of
course, ask ourselves to what degree sensory organization has
an objective value even though it is an achievement of the
nervous system. Between the physical objects around us and
our eyes, light waves are the only means of communication. There is no organization among these stimuli; the formation of specific units occurs in neural function. None the
less, in some respects the results of organization may tell us
more about the world around us than the light waves are
able to do. We do not always learn more about an object
the nearer we approach it. For instance, when a lens is put
between a bright object and a screen, the image of the object on the screen does not become optimally clear when the
screen is placed as near as possible to the lens (and thereby
the object). At a certain distance the projection tells more
about the object than nearer by. Similarly, sensory organization may give us a more adequate picture of the world than
light waves do, although these waves are the only messages
which come to us from the objects, and although sensory organization occurs only after the arrival of the waves.

The waves of light, I repeat, do not as such contain the
slightest indication of the fact that some are reflected by

[5] One chapter of *Die physischen Gestalten in Ruhe und im
stationären Zustand* has the title: "Denn was innen, das ist
aussen." Perhaps these words of Goethe have produced the mis-
apprehension. The title refers to the thesis of psychophysical
isomorphism, i.e., to the similarity between sensory experience
and accompanying physiological processes. It cannot simply be
applied to the relationship between such processes and the physical environment.

parts of one physical object and others by objects in its environment. Each element of a physical surface reflects light independently; and in this respect two elements of the surface of an object, such as, for instance, a sheep, are no more related to each other than one of them is to a surface element in the animal's environment. Thus in the reflected light no trace is left of the units which actually exist in the physical world. To be sure, the refractory properties of our eye make waves which come from one point in the outside world converge upon one point of the retina. Also, the geometrical relations among the various points on the surface of an object are to a large degree repeated in retinal projection. But at the same time each local stimulus acts independently. Hence, so far as retinal stimulation is concerned, there is no organization, no segregation of specific units or groups. This is true in spite of the fact that on the retina a continuous object such as the sheep is represented by an equally continuous area, the image of the sheep; for in terms of stimulation the elements of this area are functionally as independent of one another as any one of them is of an element outside the image. In psychology we have often been warned against the *stimulus error,* i.e., against the danger of confusing our knowledge about the physical conditions of sensory experience with this experience as such. As I see it, another mistake, which I propose to call the *experience error,* is just as unfortunate. This error occurs when certain characteristics of sensory experience are inadvertently attributed to the mosaic of stimuli. Naturally, the mistake is most frequent in the case of very common sensory facts, in terms of which we tend to think about almost everything. And it is most persistent so long as any problems involved in these facts remain utterly unrecognized. Physiologists and psychologists are inclined to talk about *the* retinal process which corresponds to an object, as though stimulation within the retinal area of the object constituted a segregated unit. And yet these scientists cannot fail to realize that the stimuli form a mosaic of entirely independent local events.

Just when this has been fully recognized, the enormous biological value of sensory organization becomes apparent. We have seen that this organization tends to have results which agree with the entities of the physical world as present at the time; in other words, that "belonging together" in sensory experience tends to go with "being a unit" in the physical sense, and segregation in the sensory field with being divided from the point of view of physics. Thus in countless instances sensory organization means a reconstruction of such aspects of physical situations as are lost in the wave messages which impinge upon the retina. It is quite true that organization often forms continuous wholes and groups of separate members when no corresponding physical units exist. But when contrasted with the large number of cases in which organization gives a picture of objective facts, this disadvantage will rightly be regarded as negligible. If the sensory field consisted of mutually independent sensory grains, man would find it a hard task to orientate himself in such an environment. From this point of view, it would hardly be an exaggeration if we were to say that sensory organization is biologically far more important than the particular sensory qualities which occur in visual fields. Color-blind people are, on the whole, quite capable of dealing with their environment, although their visual experience has fewer hues than that of other people. With regard to the practically important similarities and differences among the stimuli, their defect is not a very serious impediment. Differences of hue are usually accompanied by differences of brightness; as a rule, the latter suffice for establishing the organization of the field upon which our behavior mainly depends.

Organization is no less important for scientific observation than it is for practical life. In Chapter I we have seen that a physicist's sensory experience is his only primary material. We may now add that this experience is important to him principally to the extent to which it is organized. The system which he investigates, his apparatus, its scale, its pointer, and so forth, are without exception segregated entities in his visual field. If they were not given to him as such specific things, research in physics would be all but impossible. When Behaviorists recommend to us the procedure of the natural sciences, they always forget to mention this phase of the "objective method." They should not do so, however. Even if we ignore visual experience, and consider physical observation as a series of purely physiological events in the physicist, we have still to recognize that these events are organized, and that research is possible only because of their organization.

Now it will also be clearly understood why the stimulus-response formula, which sounds at first so attractive, is actually quite misleading. In fact, it has so far appeared acceptable solely because Behaviorists use the term "stimulus" in such a loose fashion. In Chapters III and IV we have seen that, when the term is taken in its strict sense, it is not generally "a stimulus" which elicits a response. In vision, for instance, the organism tends to respond to millions of stimuli at once; and the first stage of this response is organization within a correspondingly large field. In many cases reactions of the effector organs will begin soon; but often even the first of these reactions depend upon the organization of the field as it develops at the time. Take eye-movements as an example. The laws of visually determined eye-movements refer to the boundaries of segregated entities, to the location of these entities in the field, and so forth. Apart from eye-movements, a man's actions are commonly related to a well-structured field, most often to particular thing-units. The right psychological formula is therefore: *pattern of stimulation—organization—response to the products of organization*. The operations of the nervous system are by no means restricted to primitive local processes; it is not a box in which conductors with separate functions are somehow put together. It responds to a situation, first, by dynamic sensory events which are peculiar to it as a system, i.e., by organization, and then by behavior which depends upon the results of the organization. Suppose that somewhere in a factory HNO_3 were produced out of its elements, and that in another part of the factory the acid were used to dissolve silver—would it be right to say that the silver reacts to nitrogen, hydrogen and oxygen? Surely, such a statement would be utterly wrong, because what happens to the silver depends upon the chemical organization of the acid, and cannot be understood as a reaction to those elements or to their sum. Similarly, we ought not to speak of behavior as though it were a reaction to "a stimulus" or to "some stimuli." The last expression, too, is at least ambiguous, because it might mean that the behavior in question results from several stimuli which operate independently at the same time.

Once I tried to convince a Behaviorist that when, in speaking of a male bird, he referred to a female as "a stimulus" he ignored the problems and facts of organization. All my efforts were useless. Although (or because) he treated sensory experience as something without any interest for psychology, he committed the experience error so persistently that he could not see why the female should *not* be called "a stimulus." How often have "a mouse," "a door," "the experimenter," and so on, been called "stimuli." The expression may be harmless when those who are fully aware of the problem of organization use it as an abbreviation. But when authors who have not yet learned to avoid the experience error use the same term, the consequences will be most unfortunate. Such people may never understand what we mean by organization.

A moment ago, I pointed out that, in establishing its specific entities with their boundaries, sensory organization tends to produce results which agree with the actual make-up of the given physical situation. How can this happen if the light waves which mediate between the physical objects and the eye are mutually independent events? Obviously, in the transmission of light something must be preserved that makes, on the whole, for the right organization. In actual fact, we already know precisely what is so preserved. Although the local stimuli are mutually independent, they exhibit formal relations such as those of proximity and similarity. In this respect the stimuli copy corresponding formal relations among the surface elements of the physical objects. These formal relations in the physical objects are preserved as corresponding relations among the stimuli, and since organization depends upon the latter it must also depend upon the former.

The fact that organization depends upon relations among the local stimuli makes it entirely clear that sensory organization cannot be understood in terms of local processes as such. Independent local facts are entirely indifferent to any formal relations which may obtain among them. On the other hand, we have no difficulty in understanding the rôle which such relations play in organization, if we assume that the organization of sensory fields pictures the self-distribution of processes in corresponding areas of the brain. Dynamic self-distributions maintain themselves by interaction among the local events. But we have seen that in all parts of physics interactions depend upon the "conditions-in-relation" as given in the various parts of a system (*cf.* pp. 68 ff.). Since the same holds for visual organization, we have every reason to believe that this organization results from the self-distribution of certain processes in the visual sector of the brain. As a matter of fact, a careful study of visual organization may sooner or later tell us quite specifically what physical processes distribute themselves in the visual cortex.

Some critics maintain that Gestalt Psychologists repeat the word "whole" continually, that they neglect the existence of parts of wholes, and that they show no respect for the most useful tool of scientific procedure, which is *analysis*. No statement could be more misleading. Throughout our discussion of organization we have found it necessary to refer to segregation as well as to unification. In physics also functional interrelation within a field is entirely compatible with relative segregation. We remember how oil in another liquid maintains its existence as a unit, in spite of the fact that at the common surface dynamic interrelations are intense. In psychology we may go so far as to say that one of the main tasks of Gestalt Psychology is that of indicating the genuine rather than any fictitious parts of wholes. All visual things are such genuine parts of the fields in which they occur, and most things have again subordinate parts. The very principles of organization refer to the segregation of such parts as much as to their unitary character. Analysis in terms of genuine parts is a perfectly legitimate and necessary procedure in Gestalt Psychology. Of course, it is also more fruitful than any analysis into local sensations which, as such, are surely not genuine parts of visual situations.

At this point a remark about another kind of analysis seems indicated. I may accept and describe a sensory field precisely as I find it before me. Such a description involves analysis in the meaning which has just been defined. I may, however, adopt a special attitude with regard to the field so that some of its contents are emphasized while others are more or less suppressed. Sometimes such an attitude gives rise to a change of organization. According to Gestalt Psychology, an analysis of this sort amounts to an actual transformation of given sensory facts into others (*cf.* Chapter IV, p. 69). An analytical attitude is not the only one by which a change of organization may be brought about. While we emphasize certain members of a field, we may intentionally keep them together and thus favor a particular kind of unification. Any change of organization which is produced in this fashion is again a real transformation of sensory facts.

According to Gestalt Psychology, such an attitude of the subject is associated with a pressure to which the processes of the given sensory field are subjected. To a degree the organization of the field may yield to this stress. Fig. 7, for instance, is normally seen as a symmetrical form. By emphasizing the lines marked "a," however, and keeping them together, one can for moments see Fig. 7a, the lines marked

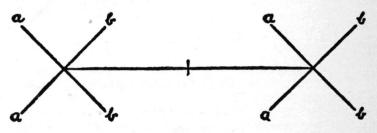

Fig. 7

"b" being more or less ignored. In the same way one can favor the lines marked "b" and so single out Fig. 7b. That such changes actually influence the sensory situation becomes particularly apparent if the point which is the objective center of Fig. 7 is considered. When the lines "a" are favored

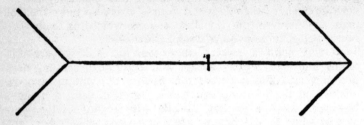

Fig. 7a

so that Fig. 7a results, the point is shifted to the right, as it also is, of course, when the lines marked "b" are not drawn at all. The point is shifted to the left when we single out Fig. 7b.

In some instances, sensory organization seems to change spontaneously, i.e., in the absence of any outside influence, simply because processes which pervade given parts of the nervous system for some time tend to alter the condition of

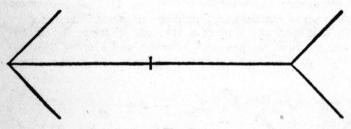

Fig. 7b

the tissue in question. We know that the same happens in electrolytical cells, in which the current polarizes the electrodes, and thereby establishes forces opposed to its own continuation. Fig. 8 shows an object formed by three narrow sectors. But after fixating the center of Fig. 8 for a while, most persons will suddenly see another pattern. Now the lines which in the first object belonged together as boundaries of a narrow sector are separated; they have become boundaries of large sectors. Clearly, the organization of the pattern has changed; and it tends to change again, as the subject beholds

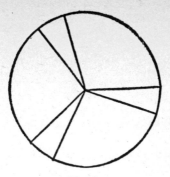

Fig. 8

now the narrow, and then the large sectors in alternation. If the subject fixates the center for a long while, the tempo of the changes is gradually increased. However, if now the pattern is turned in space, so that the sectors assume new positions, the organization becomes nearly as stable as it was at first. This fact may be taken as evidence for assuming that organized processes actually alter the conditions of their own medium, and that this fact is responsible for the reversals.[6]

[6] Since this was written it has been shown that the facts here under discussion are far more important than could be recognized at the time. Prolonged inspection of any specific visual object tends to change its organization. Moreover, other objects which are afterwards shown in the same region of the field are also affected, namely, displaced or distorted. Cf. J. J. Gibson, *J. of Exper. Psychol.*, *16*, 1933; W. Köhler, *Dynamics in Psychology*, 1940; also W. Köhler and H. Wallach, "Figural After-Effects. An Investigation of Visual Processes." *Proc. Amer. Philos. Soc.*, *88*, 1944.

VI

THE CHARACTERISTICS OF
ORGANIZED ENTITIES

WHEN THE GESTALT PROBLEM first arose, nobody could foresee that later it was to be closely related to the concept of dynamic self-distribution; nor were the facts of sensory organization immediately given the central position which they deserve. The actual starting point was the observation that sensory fields exhibit characteristics which are generically different from the sensations of traditional theory. It was Christian von Ehrenfels who, preceded by an observation of Ernst Mach, called the attention of psychologists to the fact that perhaps the most important qualitative data of sensory fields had been entirely overlooked in customary analysis.

While a sensation is supposed to occupy its place in the field independently, i.e., determined by its local stimulus alone, the curious thing about the qualities which Ehrenfels introduced into scientific psychology is their relation to *sets* of stimuli. Nothing like them is ever brought about by strictly local stimulation *per se*; rather, the "togetherness" of several stimuli is the condition which has these specific effects in a sensory field.

As an example we may take a glass of water in which soap is dissolved. The appearance of such a liquid is in German called *"trübe,"* which in English means something like "dim" or "turbid." However, if we isolate a small spot of the visual situation by looking through a small hole in a screen, the hole will be filled with a certain nuance of gray (which may have a bluish or reddish tint); the quality of "dimness" or "turbidness" will have disappeared. This characteristic occurs only as the property of a more extended area; it depends upon more than local stimulation. The same is true of the dimness or fuzziness which appears as a quality of things seen in a dark corner. Again, no local impression, examined separately, shows any fuzziness; but some extended areas do.

"Clearness" and "sharpness" as attributes of a field have the same translocal character. We may also mention the tactual characteristic of a surface which is called "rough" (the German *"rauh"*). There is no such character as roughness in any purely local experience of touch.

Ehrenfels' peculiar qualities occur in temporal extension as well as in space. For instance, the German word *"rauh"* is used just as readily with reference to certain auditory phenomena as it is for "rough" surfaces in the tactual field. When listening to rather rapid beats, or to the "R" of human speech, we experience this auditory characteristic. Naturally, since it depends upon beats, it must, and does, disappear when stimulation is shortened below a certain limit. Such words as "homogeneous" and "continuous" refer, of course, also to attributes of extended areas in space or of stretches in time.

From a functional point of view, these observations are not quite so surprising as they seemed to be at the time of Ehrenfels' discovery. We need not consider his qualities in order to learn that analysis in an extreme form will sooner or later make understanding of certain facts impossible: The processes which underlie our experience of a color are likely to be chemical reactions in which certain molecules are formed and others destroyed. Now the chemist can analyze such reactions; but there is a natural limit to this procedure, because at least one whole specimen of each atom or molecule which takes part in a given reaction, and also the whole dynamic event involved in their interaction, must be included. Beyond this limit the concept "this specific reaction" loses its meaning, .particularly in psychophysical theory, where colors are related to reactions. We are therefore compelled to recognize the occurrence of somewhat extended dynamic realities which would be destroyed by an analysis which goes too far. If this is so in chemistry, the same fact cannot surprise us when we face it in a sensory field.

The Ehrenfels qualities, which correspond to more extended dynamic events than color, originate at the same time as color does. We are assuming that those qualities and the common sensory attributes are, physiologically speaking, phases of the same total process-in-distribution. It would have been a superhuman achievement for Ehrenfels to have gone so far as to give in this fashion his new characteristics the same status as the common sensory qualities have. To him, his qualities represented experiences which are added to "the sensations" when these have first been established. In the school of Graz (von Meinong, Witasek, Benussi) there was at the time much discussion of *fundierte Inhalte,* a concept which implied not only priority of the sensations as compared with Ehrenfels' characteristics, but also a production of the latter by intellectual processes. Obviously, even those who were particularly interested in the new topic found it extremely difficult to recognize at once its radical consequences for psychological theory.

For the most part, Ehrenfels' qualities are characteristics of segregated entities in the sense in which this term has been used in the preceding chapter. "Simple," "complicated," "regular," "harmonious," are words which invariably refer to products of organization. When we call something "symmetrical," this something is certainly a segregated object. Similarly, "slender," "round," "angular," "clumsy," "graceful" are specific properties of things or extended events. From these instances there is only one step to such more particular shape-qualities as are given in the characteristic appearance of a circle, a triangle, a pear, an oak tree, and so forth. These qualities, too, occur only as attributes of specific entities. In German, the word *"Gestalt"* is often used as a synonym for form or shape. Ehrenfels, taking the case of shape as the most important and obvious among his qualities, used the name *"Gestaltqualitäten"* for all of them. As a consequence, not only the specific shapes of objects and figures are included, but also such qualities as "regular." Furthermore, I repeat, there are also temporal Ehrenfels qualities. The general definition of this term applies to the specific properties of a melody, for instance, to its "major" or "minor" character, just as it does to the "angularity" of a figure. Movements as visual facts have *Gestaltqualitäten* which are temporal and spatial at the same time. As examples may serve forms of dancing and the characteristic movements of animals such as "jumping" or "creeping."

At this point a general remark about terminology seems indicated. For Ehrenfels the new characteristics as such were objects of great interest. He did not recognize the much more general significance of organization, or the fact that it is for the most part the products of organization which exhibit the best examples of *Gestaltqualitäten* as their attributes. Now, in the German language—at least since the time of Goethe—the noun *"Gestalt"* has two meanings: besides the connotation of shape or form as an attribute of things, it has the meaning of a concrete entity *per se,* which has, or may have, a shape as one of its characteristics. Since Ehrenfels' time the emphasis has shifted from the Ehrenfels qualities to the facts of organization, and thus to the problem of specific entities in sensory fields. As a result, it is the meaning of Gestalt in which the word refers to a specific object and to organization that is now generally meant when we speak of Gestalt Psychology; and the problem of Gestalt attributes has become a special problem among many with which the Gestalt Psychologist has to deal. His hope is that the functional concepts which he applies to sensory organization will also be useful in the theoretical treatment of the Ehrenfels qualities. It thus becomes obvious that the introduction of a particular type of process is now the main tenet of Gestalt Psychology. Students who wish to make themselves familiar with this form of psychology will have to concentrate on extended events which distribute and regulate themselves as functional wholes. It stands to reason that such processes will have certain characteristics which they possess only as extended states, and that the same will hold for their parts. Such characteristics, it is assumed, will prove to be the physiological correlates of Ehrenfels' qualities.

From this point of view, even the segregation of specific entities in sensory fields appears as only one, though surely a highly important, instance among the various issues which constitute the subject matter of Gestalt Psychology. In fact, the concept "Gestalt" may be applied far beyond the limits of sensory experience. According to the most general functional definition of the term, the processes of learning, of recall, of striving, of emotional attitude, of thinking, acting, and so forth, may have to be included. This makes it still clearer that "Gestalt" in the meaning of shape is no longer the center of the Gestalt Psychologist's attention. For, to some of the facts in which he is interested the term "Gestalt" in the meaning of shape does not apply at all. Quite apart from psychology, the developments which occur in ontogeny, and certain other biological topics, will probably have to be treated in the same fashion. It is important to realize that this wide outlook does not imply vagueness. If the concepts of machine theory have so long prevailed without any adequate scrutiny, no objection can be raised against a discussion of the principles of dynamic distribution and regulation in general. By no means is it believed, however, that any of those larger problems can actually be solved by the application merely of general principles. On the contrary, wherever the principles seem to apply, the concrete task of research is only beginning; because we want to know in precisely what manner processes distribute and regulate themselves in all specific instances.[1]

[1] Köhler, "Gestaltprobleme und Anfänge einer Gestalttheorie." *Jahresber. ü. d. ges. Phys. herausg. von Rona.* 1924.

If in the treatment even of sensory fields an actual solution of our problems remains a task for the future, at least
the first steps can be taken at once. Here as everywhere, we
must first of all recognize what the essential questions are.
Now, no one fails to see, for instance, that visual depth as
determined by conditions on the two retinae, offers a fascinating problem. But to see the real issue in the case of *shape*
as a characteristic of segregated entities seems to be much
more difficult. The reason is the same as in the case of these
visual entities themselves (*cf.* p. 95). To repeat: when we
consider retinal stimulation, our thinking operates with the
concept of images, with the implication that an image is a
particular unit which has a shape in the sense in which perceived objects have shapes. Thus, many would say that the
shape of a pencil or of a circle is projected upon the retina.
Clearly, when spoken without caution, these words contain
the experience error. In the mosaic of all retinal stimuli, the
particular areas which correspond to the pencil or the circle
are not in any way singled out and unified. Consequently,
the shapes in question are also not functionally realized. Our
thinking may select and combine any retinal spots we wish;
in this fashion, all possible shapes, including those of the
pencil and of the circle, may imaginatively be imposed upon
the retina. But, so far as retinal stimulation is concerned, such
procedures are entirely arbitrary. Functionally, the shapes
of the pencil and the circle are just as little given in retinal
projection as are those of angels or sphinxes.

Some examples will serve to clarify the concept of shape
as a visual attribute. Occasionally, we see a map which is
meant to represent a country of well-known form. On other
maps we have often seen the shape of this country. And yet,
as now before us, the map exhibits areas with entirely unknown shapes. Suddenly, however, a radical change occurs
in our visual field: the unknown shapes disappear, and the
well-known shape of the country in question emerges in perfect clearness. Good instances for this observation are certain charts of ship captains, on which the sea tends to assume the appearance which the land has on ordinary maps.
Now, the contour of the land is the same on a maritime chart
as it is on a map of the usual type; i.e., the geometrical line
which separates land and water is normally projected upon
the retina.[2] None the less, when looking at such a map, say,

___

[2] Strictly speaking, this expression again involves the experience
error. In the mosaic of retinal stimuli there is, of course, no line
as a specific, unified and segregated, entity.

of the Mediterranean, we may completely fail to see Italy. Instead we may see a strange figure, corresponding to the area of the Adriatic, and so forth, which is new to us, but which happens to have shape under the circumstances. Thus, "to have shape" is a peculiarity which distinguishes certain areas of the visual field from others which have no shape in this sense. In our example, so long as the Mediterranean has shape, the area corresponding to Italy has no shape, and vice versa. This statement will seem less surprising if we again remember that the retinal stimuli constitute a mere mosaic, in which no particular areas are functionally segregated and shaped. When the nervous system reacts to this mosaic, and when organization develops, various circumscribed entities may originate, and be shaped, in

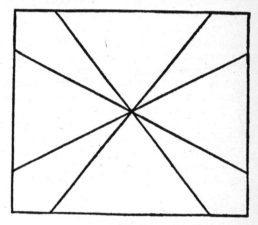

Fig. 9

our example; among others, the Italian peninsula or the Mediterranean. But unless we know about the principles of organization, we cannot predict which possibility will actually be realized. The stimuli as such do not tell us, and the instability of organization in the present instance makes it abundantly clear that they alone are not responsible for the presence or absence of shape in a given area.

Fig. 9, a variation of Fig. 8, or Fig. 8 may serve as a further example. With a constant pattern of stimuli, we may see in Fig. 9 two different shapes, either that of a cross consisting of four slender arms, or that of another cross which consists of the four large sectors. So long as the former shape is before us, the area of the latter is absorbed in the background, and its visual shape is non-existent. When the latter shape emerges, the first disappears.[3] It will be observed that, in both cases, the oblique lines are boundaries of the shapes which are seen at the time. They belong to the slender cross in the first case, and to the large cross in the second.

Thorough observations of this kind were first made by Rubin, who illustrated his point by a great many examples.[4] The fact that at a given time only particular areas of a field have shapes was shown conclusively, when subjects, who had seen one shape in a first presentation of such a pattern, did not recognize this pattern, if in a second presentation the other shape was seen. The latter shape had not been a visual fact when previously the former was perceived. As a result, the shape seen in the second presentation appeared entirely new and strange. Again, when one of the two crosses of Fig. 9 is seen, one does not at the time see other shapes which, from the point of view of retinal stimulation, might just as well be visually given. For instance, one does not see the shapes corresponding to Fig. 9a, 9b, or 9c.

In Fig. 10 are seen two unknown objects through which an horizontal line is drawn. When I now tell the reader that he has the number 4 before him, he will undoubtedly find it. But if he is not influenced by theoretical prejudices, he will confess that, at first, the shape of the 4 did not exist as a visual fact, and that, when it later emerged, this meant a transformation in his visual field.

In this example it will be clearly recognized that the existence of a particular visual shape goes with the existence of a corresponding visual unit which, when segregated, has the shape. Other shapes, which would correspond to a different organization in the same area, are for the time being visually non-existent. Thus, when we first look at Fig. 10, it is seen in a particular organization, which consists of two unknown objects and an horizontal line which runs through them. This means that one part of the 4 is absorbed by the object on the left side, a second fraction by the angular whole on the right side, and the rest by the horizontal. With the destruction of the 4 as a segregated thing, its shape is also dissolved. When sooner or later the subject actually sees the 4, the corresponding lines are more or less detached from their continuations. It is a general rule that visual shapes are given only so long as the lines or areas in question are set apart in the field. Any observations of puzzle pictures, of camouflaged objects, and

[3] Under certain unusual conditions both objects may be seen at the same time.

[4] *Visuell wahrgenommene Figuren*. Kopenhagen, Berlin, London, 1921.

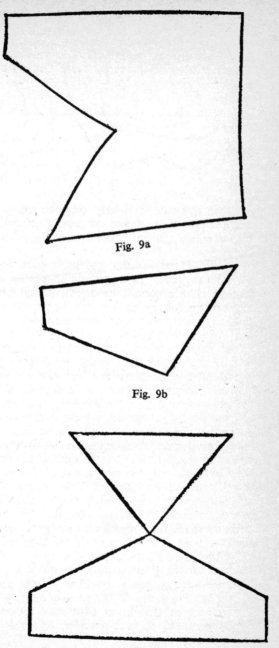

Fig. 9a

Fig. 9b

Fig. 9c

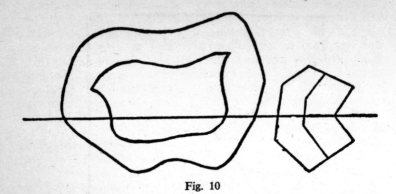

Fig. 10

so forth, confirm this rule. Similarly, one can easily convince himself that the visual existence of *partial* shapes depends upon the relative segregation of corresponding sub-wholes in larger entities.

The things around us are for the most part very stable entities. As a consequence, their specific shapes are regularly seen, so long as chance conditions or intentional camouflage do not interfere. It is for this reason that the problem of visual shape is so easily overlooked, and that many can still believe that "shapes are given in retinal projection." There is, however, no visual shape to which our discussion does not apply. In any part of the visual field which is shaped, processes must have particular characteristics which are responsible for the fact. These characteristics are not present in all parts of the field. If, on a clear day, we walk along a street between high houses, the sky is surrounded by the darker surfaces of the houses. Under these circumstances, do we see the bright area of the sky as shaped? As a general rule, we do not. The bright area has no shape of its own. In spite of the fact that it is surrounded by differently colored surfaces, this part of the sky remains "unshaped background." The contours remain edges of the houses; the houses have shapes; but the visible part of the sky has none. If we wish to see a circumscribed area of the sky as shaped, we may look through a hole cut in a screen, which we hold over our head. If the hole corresponds to the form of the letter H, the corresponding area of the sky will be seen as a bright H on a dark ground.

Students of Gestalt Psychology ought to be well acquainted with such observations, and with the consequences which follow. Just as a part of the visual field may either have a hue, or be achromatic, so a circumscribed area may be shaped or unshaped.

For some time to come it will be impossible to investigate the dynamics of visual processes in direct physiological observation. At present we can do no more than draw conclusions from a comparison of retinal patterns with visual facts. We then find that Ehrenfels was right in saying that shape is a translocal characteristic of certain areas. It seems to follow that the underlying processes must have a characteristic which is also translocal. Now, shape is an attribute only of entities which are set apart in the visual field. It therefore appears that when processes are relatively segregated from larger functional wholes they acquire at the same time the translocal characteristic which is responsible for the shape of the thing in question.

Naturally, since visual shape presupposes segregation of a corresponding visual thing, the existence of specific shape depends upon the same factors of stimulation as determine the organization of things. It can easily be shown that certain formal relations within the given pattern of stimuli are again decisive.[5]

After this discussion it will not be necessary to spend much time on the concept of experienced shape, or form, in the dimension of time. In the case of melodies, of rhythms, of seen movements, and so forth, we should merely have to repeat what has just been said in the case of simultaneously given shapes. The form of a musical *motif* begins at a particular point and ends at another; then another *motif* may follow. But, in a given case, there is no experienced form which extends, for instance, from the second tone of the first musical figure to the third tone of the next figure. Between the two figures there is what has been called a "dead" interval which corresponds, as empty time, to the mere extension or ground outside a visual shape. Again, when in a dark room a bright spot in motion describes the path of Fig. 6 (p. 90), we see certain forms of movement such as I, II, III. But we do not see other forms, not for example a form which corresponds to a fraction of I, the next horizontal stretch, and a

---

[5] Once K. Bühler tried to give an explanation of a very characteristic shape, that of the straight line. He assumed that all retinal points which form a straight line are anatomically connected in a special manner, and that this gives a straight line its particular appearance. This hypothesis has the character of a machine theory. I do not think that we can hope to solve our problem in this fashion. There are a great many highly characteristic shapes besides the straight line. Are we to assume that for each there is a special anatomical arrangement? Or, rather, a great many such arrangements for each single shape, since each may be projected upon many different parts of the retina?

fraction of II, taken together. Once more, experienced form
goes with the organization of corresponding wholes and sub-
wholes.

Since shape is an attribute of segregated entities, all our
previous remarks against the explanation by knowledge
acquired in the past apply here just as they do in the case
of those entities themselves. But so popular are the empiristic views that it will be advisable to mention a few more facts
which bear upon this point.

1. What is the effect of practice as to certain shapes upon
our visual experience in subsequent perception? Drawings
like Fig. 11 and Fig. 12 contain many combinations of geo-

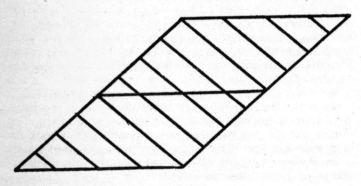

Fig. 11

Fig. 12

metrical lines which, when given alone, would make us see shapes other than those which we actually see. Thus, in both, the outline of Fig. 13 is geometrically present. If now we

Fig. 13

have a large number of such drawings which are ordinarily seen in a certain way, but which geometrically contain certain smaller figures, will training with regard to the latter change the way in which we see the former? More particularly, will this training disrupt the larger figures so that the practiced figures emerge with their specific shapes? Gottschaldt made such experiments.[6] Since past experience is supposed to affect organization automatically, i.e., independently of any knowledge about the presence of corresponding outlines, the subjects were not told to analyze, or to look for the practiced figures. The larger drawings were given simply for description. In about 90% of the cases, three previous exposures of the smaller figures had no effect upon the subsequent perception of the larger patterns. When, with new subjects, the number of previous exposures of the smaller figures was increased to 520, the result was still the same, the drawings being seen unchanged in 95% of the trials. Not even the few cases which showed a positive result can be explained by previous training as such, because the subjects who occasionally saw the practiced forms in the larger drawings had some suspicion as to the aim of the experiment, and actually asked the experimenter whether they should look for the practiced forms. Although they were not instructed to do so, they naturally took the test with an attitude of quite specific expectation. Hence, their positive results do not prove that past experience has an automatic effect upon subsequently seen patterns.

Gottschaldt's larger drawings were "difficult," in the sense that their organization was very stable. In some of these figures I cannot actually *see* the smaller figures, although I know not only that they are present but also where they

[6] *Psychol. Forsch.*, *8*, 1926. Figures 11-13 are reproduced from Gottschaldt's paper.

are located. But no objection can be derived from this difficulty of the larger figures, because in such an objection it would tacitly be admitted that very stable visual organization is stronger than any influence of practice. Surely, such larger drawings as Fig. 12 cannot be said to owe their stable organization to much pre-experimental practice in ordinary life. The shapes which we see in this pattern are by no means better known than Fig. 13. Those who claim that past experience has an automatic influence upon subsequent perception will have to support their theory by experiments of their own. If such an influence exists, it must be restricted to particular situations.

2. We do, of course, admit that given specific entities, with their shapes, readily acquire meanings. But when this happens, these entities are given first, and the meanings attach themselves to such shaped things later. I am not acquainted with any facts which show that, conversely, learning *builds* things and shapes. It is quite true that badly organized situations, in which specific entities and shapes are barely indicated, may be greatly clarified by the fact that these entities are well known. In this case, however, the main question is what factors established those entities in previous life. Obviously, conditions were then more favorable, and probably they were more favorable from the point of view of sensory organization. At any rate, such observations are far from proving that learning transforms so-called sensations into specific things. What is actually observed is merely that clear organization which has been experienced in the past tends to improve an inferior organization which is now given. And, to repeat, previous practice has no such influence, if the present situation is strongly organized in a different fashion. The number 4, for instance, has a well-known shape; but when Fig. 10 is shown to people who do not suspect the presence of the number, they are extremely unlikely to see it. It will not occur in their description of the pattern. One cannot object that in the past we have never seen the 4 in such an unusual environment. If practice has an automatic influence, this influence ought to be demonstrable precisely in such situations. Moreover, it is by no means the unusual character of the environment which prevents our seeing the 4 in Fig. 10. In Fig. 14 the 4 is seen at once, although in this pattern the environment of the number is no less unusual than it is in Fig. 10. Why, then, is it seen now? Clearly, in Fig. 14 the added lines do not tend to fuse with the various parts of the number so that this object is dissolved. In Fig. 10 conditions of organization are such as to favor the formation of

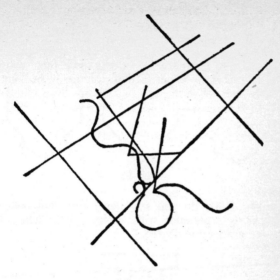

Fig. 14

other objects.[7] In Fig. 14 an equally strange environment contains no such conditions, and therefore the number remains a segregated visual thing.

I will give a few more examples in which well-known objects and their shapes are destroyed, because organization builds up larger entities. Fig. 15 may be described in various

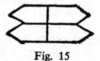

Fig. 15

ways; but no one would spontaneously mention the letter E in such a description. At the same time this letter is, of course, geometrically present, and the object which is actually seen is less known than the letter. Fig. 16 may be seen for months as an ornament, while the presence of two H's in it is never suspected. Similarly, under normal conditions the letter K is visually non-existent in Fig. 17. Of course, at this point the reader no longer observes under normal conditions. By now he is looking for letters in the analytic attitude which has

[7] *Cf.* particularly the condition mentioned in Chapter V, p. 85.

been discussed in Chapter V (p. 99). I must therefore ask
him to show Fig. 16 or Fig. 17 to more naïve friends with

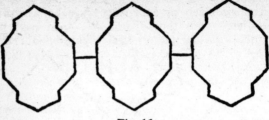

Fig. 16

the question: What do you see there? I do not believe that
their enormous experience with letters will influence the result to any considerable degree.

Fig. 17

3. Again, some will be inclined to derive visual shape from
tactual or motor experiences. This thesis is just as inacceptable as the corresponding interpretation in the case of
organization as such. Shape is a characteristic which experiences have, or fail to have. It is irreducible to other attributes. Thus, if visual entities appear shaped only because we
have certain other experiences at the same time, these other
experiences must have the shapes in question. Visual facts
may be capable of absorbing characteristics which do not belong to the original equipment of visual fields. In this case,
however, such borrowed characteristics must be natural citizens of the fields from which they come. As a consequence,
the hypothesis under discussion merely shifts the problem of
shape from one sensory field to another. Plainly, somewhere
it must be treated as such, without further shifting. This
reasoning applies also to our sensations of eye-movements,
which have repeatedly been mentioned in this connection. If
visual shape is a matter of eye-movements, then the kinesthetic experiences involved must be shaped in the sense in which
visual entities appear to be shaped. Once this is clear, it will
be admitted that such an hypothesis does not represent a

scientific gain. We may just as well acknowledge that shape is a visual attribute.

4. The best argument against any empiristic theories in this field is as follows. We readily admit that parts of a visual field can cause recall of experiences which have previously been associated with those parts. We then ask, however, what particular visual factors are responsible for the recall in each case. The answer is that, in ninety-nine out of one hundred cases, recall occurs because a particular segregated entity with its equally specific shape is given in the field. In other words, it is this shaped entity which is associated with other facts, and can therefore elicit these facts. This means that, if organization were absent, so that recall could be caused only by the color and brightness of "sensations," visual experience would for the most part not be sufficiently characterized to give rise to any specific recall. When referring to the automatic influence of past experience upon present vision, people are tempted to assume that this idea can also be applied to the phenomena which have here been interpreted as effects of sensory organization. From this point of view, a visual field would seem to contain shaped things, because certain previous experiences have been recalled. Those who reason in this fashion appear to forget that, as a rule, recall is caused precisely by such shaped things. They do not fully realize that, in a consistent application of their view, the visual field must be supposed to be entirely devoid of such things. It is easy to say: This or that is so because certain things have happened in previous life. But by now we need clearer and more specific statements. Nobody will deny that recall plays a tremendous rôle in mental life; but it can do so only because the sensory world as such is sufficiently endowed with specific attributes which it owes to organization. A mere mosaic of "sensations" would be unable to give recall the right specific directions. This difficulty, with which the empiristic interpretation is confronted, is further enhanced by the following fact: generally speaking, a shape remains the same independently of the color, the place, and the size of the area, which has the shape. According to empiristic views, this means that, irrespective of variations in these respects, the same previous experiences are always recalled. How can this happen when actually nothing is left that could serve as a constant cause for the same recall?

The fact to which I have just referred is called "transposing." Since Ehrenfels wanted to show that shape can never be explained in terms of sensations, he laid great stress upon the invariance of visual shape when the brightness, hue, size and location of an object are changed. To be sure, when the object is shifted too far toward the periphery of the field, its shape will be affected. Apart from this special case, however, the range within which objects can be transposed is enormous.[8] In this respect, forms in time behave just like shapes in space: a melody, for instance, may be given in different keys, and yet remain the same *qua* melody. Ehrenfels was entirely right when he said that in this fashion shape and temporal form are clearly established as phenomena *sui generis*. He also realized, however, that certain conditions must be kept constant if transposing is to be what the term implies. Relations among the stimuli involved must remain approximately the same when the stimuli themselves are changed. Thus we see once more that the same conditions as determine the segregation of specific entities in space and time are also decisive for their Ehrenfels attributes.[9]

There was a time when the remarkable behavior of *Gestalten,* particularly the invariance of their forms under conditions of transposing, was generally interpreted as proving that higher mental processes were involved (*cf.* p. 104). From our present point of view, however, sensory organization appears as a primary fact which arises from the elementary dynamics of the nervous system. So long as organization is regarded as an intellectual activity, we can not, of course, account for the rôle which organization plays in biology, particularly in ontogeny. It will also be remembered that Hertz has demonstrated the influence of organization on the behavior of animals who are not likely to specialize in intellectual processes. Apparently, Lashley has been the first to show that animals "transpose." Having been trained to choose, say, the darker of two gray objects, they shift their response when two other objects of the same class are presented. In other words, they choose the object which represents the dark side of the new pair, even if its particular gray has never been presented during the original learning. Without knowledge of Lashley's work, I repeated the same experi-

[8] With adults, one more condition must be fulfilled if transposing is not to affect a given visual shape. Most objects change their appearance when given a new orientation in space, and particularly when turned upside down. This fact, which reveals a curious anisotropy of the visual field in adults, does not seem to exist in early childhood.

[9] Wertheimer mentions, however, that not all relations among the stimuli are equally important in this respect. Some may be changed considerably without much effect upon a given shape, while even small alterations of others influence this shape at once.

ments with apes and chicks, and took special care to exclude several possibilities of indirect explanation. At present, there is no doubt that a chicken, trained to choose of two grays, I and II, always the darker, II, will afterwards, when II and a new (darker) gray III are given, in the majority of the trials not choose II but the unknown nuance III. The same experiments were done with apes, when the choice referred to the size or to the hue of objects. Several investigators have been able to confirm these experiments. It seems that animals react to such pairs as to unitary groups, either side of which has a particular character that depends upon its position within the pair. Thus II is the dark side of the first pair; but, in the new pair, III assumes this rôle; and since the animal has learned to choose the dark side of the pair rather than a more or less definite gray, it now tends to avoid the gray which it chose during the learning period, and to choose the new gray. It does not matter whether or not we assume that the chicken has visual experience. The difference between a choice which depends upon a more or less definite intensity of light and a reaction which depends upon a characteristic determined in a pair-unit is the same in both cases. It will be realized that here the stimulus-response formula is again quite misleading. It ignores the fact that between the stimuli and the response there occur the processes of organization, particularly the formation of group-units in which parts acquire new characteristics.

In order to prove that the concept of dynamic self-distribution explains transposition, we will now show that transposition occurs in physical systems. If all forces of a given dynamic distribution balance each other, their equilibrium will obviously not be disturbed if the intensity of all forces decreases or increases in the same proportion. Consequently, such dynamic states are largely independent of the absolute facts which obtain in their various parts. Assume, for instance, that the self-distribution is that of a current which flows through a conductor of a certain shape, such as an electrolyte which fills a vessel of this shape. The intensity of the current has no influence upon its distribution. Or also, if instead of ions like Na and Cl, K and Br or any others carry the electric charges, the distribution of the current is not changed. Or, take the electromotive phenomena which develop when two solutions (I and II) of different ionic concentration are in contact. Such phenomena depend upon the *relation* of the ionic concentrations, while the absolute concentrations have no influence. For example, if the solution II with a concentration of $1/20n$ is the electropositive side of the pair, as against I with a concentration, say, of ¼, then in a new pair with the concentrations 1/20n (II) and 1/100n (III) the new solution III becomes the electropositive side. In other words, to be the electropositive side of such a physical system is a property which a part of the system owes to its position in the whole system. In this respect, there is no difference between our electrochemical example and the case of two grays, one of which is the dark side of a pair.

Shape is probably the most important attribute of segregated things. But with the presence or absence of visual shape further characteristics are closely related. In Figs. 8 and 9 we observed a change of shape. At first one cross or star was seen, and then another. If such reversals are carefully observed, another change will be found to accompany the appearance and disappearance of the two shapes. When the slender cross is seen, the area of this cross has a character of solidity or substantiality; the cross has the density of a thing, while its environment appears as comparatively empty or loose. The contrary is true when the other cross appears. Now this cross looks solid and substantial, while the narrow angles, which have become parts of the background, are loose or empty. Since an area becomes solid when it has shape, and is in this sense a figure, Rubin has given the solid quality the name "figure character." He calls the looseness of the environment the "ground character." The term "ground" is particularly appropriate because the figure generally protrudes a bit in space. The unshaped environment is localized further backward, and actually seems to extend behind the figure as a homogeneous plane on which the figure lies. The sky above houses (cf. p. 110) has this character of a ground which spreads behind the houses as figures.

It seems that the character of solidity to which I have just referred occurs only as an attribute of segregated things. Clearly, it belongs to the general class of Ehrenfels qualities. Some psychologists will be inclined to derive this character from tactual experiences which we have when handling physical objects. But there is no particular reason why it should not also be an attribute of visual things as such. As a matter of fact, it may belong to the primary constituents of the meaning which the terms "thing" or "substance" have in common life. At any rate, figure and ground behave quite differently in the visual field. Color constancy, for instance, has been shown to be stronger for figure than for ground. The threshold for a patch of color has been found to be higher in the area of a figure than within a ground of the same objective color. On the other hand, after-images are more vivid when observed upon a figure than they are upon mere ground.

After these considerations some further statements will readily be understood which, without the preceding discussion, would perhaps be regarded as "mere philosophy." In experiments with animals "to be the dark side of a pair" was found to be the characteristic of an object which this object owed to its inclusion in a larger entity, the visual pair-unit. The same reference to larger wholes is implied in many terms which we continually use as banal words. We do not generally realize that the meaning of such words points beyond the local facts to which the words may seem to be attached. From a large list I will give only the following examples: The German *"Rand"* (in English "brink" or "edge") is such a word; again *"Anfang"* ("beginning"), *"Ende"* and *"Schluss"* ("end and "close"), *"Stück"* and *"Teil"* ("piece" and "part"), *"Rest"* ("rest" or "remnant"); also *"Loch"* ("hole") and *"Störung"* ("disturbance"). It will at once be seen that a place can appear as a "hole" only inasmuch as it constitutes an interruption of a larger entity, the other parts of which have the figure character. *Mutatis mutandis* the same holds for the meaning of "disturbance." It is by no means necessary to restrict the list to instances in which the words apply to sensory facts. In the case of thought processes an event is a "disturbance" only with regard to a larger and otherwise unitary whole which it interrupts. Without this reference the word has no meaning. Those who are acquainted with the theory of music will remember that a tone has the character of the "tonic" only within a musical development in which it plays a particular part. The same is true of the "leading tone" which points beyond itself not independently, but as part of a larger musical structure.

Similar cases can easily be found among the adjectives and verbs. *"Hohl"* ("hollow") and *"offen"* ("open"), "complete" and "incomplete" belong in this class, in that their meanings refer to specific experienced units in which these adjectives are alone applicable. In the realm of terms which designate events and activities we have, for instance: "starting" and "beginning," "ending" and "finishing," "desisting" and "interrupting," "proceeding" and "continuing," also "deviating," "bending," "retarding," and so forth. If we consider the meanings of such words as "hesitating" or "deviating," we find that their meanings presuppose the occurrence of larger coherent developments, changes of which are designated by these terms. The developments may be melodies, or the activities of other people as we see them, or thought processes

which take their course in a person. Essentially, the meanings of such words remain the same in all provinces of experience; for the principal phases of organization are not
restricted to any special fields.

VII

BEHAVIOR

IT WILL BE DIFFICULT to understand the following chapters unless we first solve a problem which seems to present serious difficulties to many people.

When referring to objective experience, I have repeatedly emphasized the fact that things, their movements and changes are given as *outside* or *before* us. At the same time I have maintained that objective experience depends upon processess in the brain. How, then, can this experience appear before us? About the facts as such there can be no doubt. To be sure, under certain conditions a sound may be localized in my head; but that tree over there I surely see as something far off, and the window, though much nearer, is still unquestionably outside. Functionally, however, the existence of these visual objects is a matter of processes in my brain, and therefore in me. The simplest physiological considerations prove this.

It seems advisable to discuss at once the physiological side of this problem. For the sake of simplicity, we will at first proceed as though the visual field were the only objective experience we have. Then one thing is immediately obvious. Although for the most part we have many objects before us, their totality appears as well-ordered in one visual space, so that any particular thing has fairly clear spatial relations to all the others. (This statement is a trifle superficial because it ignores the specific grouping of objects; but for our present purposes it will suffice.) The pencil on my desk is nearer to the book than to the lamp; the knife lies between the book and the fountain pen, etc.

Just as all other characteristics of the field are associated with physiological facts in the brain, so the relative position of experienced objects depends upon some kind of order in the processes which constitute their physiological basis. However, the mere geometrical location of these processes cannot be the correlate of seen spatial order. I take it for granted that whatever is experienced has a *functional* basis, in other words, that it depends upon actual physical events. If this postulate is to be applied to the facts which underlie experienced space, we are inevitably led to the concepts of field physics. In this part of science the consideration of what might be called "processes-in-extension" is regarded as a matter of course. The term which I have just used is simply another name for the self-distributed processes to which I referred in Chapter IV. In such processes, it will be remembered, local events occur, as they occur, only within the distribution as a whole. Therefore, the whole widely extended state of function is a unit. In units of this kind, distances may be measured in inches. But according to our postulate this is not the way in which the distances ought to be measured if we wish to find the correlate of experienced extension. Rather, we choose as this correlate the dynamic relations among the parts of the process, which maintain the parts as they are. These relations extend in a continuous fashion through the whole process, and it is their "functional geometry" which we suppose to be isomorphically related to the spatial characteristics of perceptual fields.[1] Of course, the dynamic relations in question operate in the tissue, i.e., in cells, fibers and tissue fluids, which occupy certain volumes of physical space. But we assume that, so far as our problem is concerned, only the dynamic relations count, while the geometrical distances and areas through which the dynamic order extends have no direct significance. It is true, to a considerable degree the dynamic order *depends* upon the geometry of the medium in which it occurs. For example, a great distance in terms of brain geometry is likely to be a great functional distance at the same time, and so on. But this dependence is far from being an identity. For, in the first place, the dynamic relations within the process are functional relations, while no geometrical relations are functions in this sense; and, in the second place, the functional extension to which I am referring depends not only upon the geometrical dimensions of the medium but also upon the laws of physics which determine the self-distribution. In the next paragraphs, relative localization of objects in visual space will be regarded as correlated with relative positions of corresponding local processes within the visual area of the brain. The preceding remarks are meant

[1] Quite recently, the concept of functional space has been more fully developed in: W. Köhler and H. Wallach, "Figural After-Effects. An Investigation of Visual Processes." *Proc. Amer. Philos. Soc.*, Vol. 88, No. 4, 1944.

to make it clear that when the expression "relative position of processes" is used it must always be understood in terms of functional rather than of purely geometrical relationships.

Let us return to the question which was raised in the beginning of this chapter. It will be advisable to consider a concrete example. In visual experience, the pencil over there is external to the book, and lies at a certain distance from it. Under these conditions there are two local processes in the brain, one corresponding to the pencil, and the other to the book. Moreover, the neurologists tell us that these processes occur in different places of the visual brain, and we must add that the functional relations between them are those which mean a certain functional distance. I now propose to show that the localization of objects outside ourselves follows directly from this consideration. My hand, for instance, appears, or may appear, in the same visual field as other visual objects. Plainly, just as this further visual object is external to the pencil and the book in visual experience, so the corresponding process in the brain must be external to the processes corresponding to the pencil and the book—both geometrically and in functional terms. The hand as a visual object must be given the same theoretical treatment as is given the pencil and the book; and the spatial relation between the hand and the pencil or the book must be considered in the same way as the spatial relation between the latter things. As a rule, my visual field contains, of course, more parts of myself than the hand: my arm, for instance, very often my feet, my chest and, though only in extremely peripheral vision, the tip of my nose. All these are visual entities, precisely as the book and the pencil. Thus, in my brain as a physical system, there must be processes which correspond to these parts of myself, just as there are other processes which correspond to such things as pencils, books, etc. Also, the brain processes which underlie the visual book, the visual pencil and all the other visual objects around me must be external to the processes which underlie the visual arm, feet, chest and nose. The reason is the same as in the case of the book and the pencil as external to each other: the physical book and the physical pencil are projected on different parts of the retina, and therefore cause processes in different parts of the visual brain. This holds also for the visible parts of my organism in their spatial relations to the outside objects. Their retinal locations differ from those of such objects, and consequently corresponding places in the brain are different from the places in which the outside objects are physiologically represented.

As a matter of principle, this is the solution of our problem. My body as an experience—in common speech we often call it "I" or "myself"—is to a degree a visual thing in the sense in which a pencil or a book are visual things. Now, just as the latter things appear outside each other, so "I" appear visually external to them, and vice versa. If their appearance in different places does not astonish anybody, because this separation can be understood in terms of the location of their physiological correlates in the brain, we have no reason to be surprised by the relative position of such visual objects, on the one hand, and the visible self, on the other hand. Thus, no special hypothesis is needed to explain why I am visually external to such objects, and they external to me. If there were any paradox in their appearance outside, i.e. outside of me, then exactly the same paradox ought to be found in the spatial relation, say, of the pencil and the book. People do not generally recognize this, merely because they fail to distinguish between the *body* as a perceptual experience and the *organism* as a physical system which, as such, never occurs in any experience. Of course, they also ignore the fact that the visual part of the self is physiologically caused by projection of parts of the organism upon its own retina, and by corresponding processes in the brain which have a particular location, a location in which they are *surrounded* by the processes corresponding to other visual objects. I do not believe that the confusion will ever end, unless we accustom ourselves to giving the perceptual self consistently one name, and the physical organism another name. I suggest that, just as I have done in these paragraphs, the former be called "body," and that the term "organism" be reserved for the physical system which is investigated by anatomists and physiologists.

When compared with this explanation, the idea that things ought to be experienced as being inside ourselves can surely not be defended. There is no more reason for this expectation than for assuming that the pencil ought to be seen within the book, or a cloud, or the moon. If somebody should object and say that, after all, the perceptual processes occur in the brain, and in this sense in my interior, what is the right answer? We have to answer that visual experience corresponds to the totality of self-distributed processes in the visual sector of the brain, and that all relations in visual space of which anybody can be aware rest on functional relationships within this totality. In such terms, other visual objects must appear outside the visual self. To the anatomical or geometrical location of any visual processes within the physical brain and skull, on the other hand, there never corresponds any experience whatsoever. Thus, this location can play no part in the determination of the places in which we see things. If somebody expects that seen things be experienced as being in the brain, he does not realize that the first half of this sentence refers to the visual field as an experience, whereas the second half, in which the expression "the brain" occurs, refers to a physical object in physical space. This means that he expects parts of visual space to be localized in relation to parts of physical space, which is an entirely impossible notion.

The fact that visual objects are so clearly localized outside the visible self makes everybody astonished when he first hears that things, colors, etc., depend upon events which occur "in himself." Of course, this statement is correct only if meant in a physiological sense so that "himself" refers to the organism, which is not part of our experience. It is far from being correct and clear for people who have not learned to discriminate between the physical organism and the self as a particular experienced thing. Surely, for the most part distant things do not appear at all to depend upon this particular experience, the self. And why should they? In visual experience a tree depends upon myself as an experience just as little as the brain process which corresponds to the tree depends upon the processes corresponding to the experienced self. Occasionally, we have seen in an earlier chapter, a certain influence will occur, and then be experienced; but, generally speaking, the tree and I depend upon each other just as little as any other segregated entities depend upon each other, when separated by a considerable distance.

Perhaps all this is too well known to be once more discussed at such length. Some years ago, however, a psychiatrist in Europe called this the most difficult problem among the questions which concern the mind in its relation to the body: How can things appear outside of us, when actually they are located in our interior?

So far we have considered ourselves and things exclusively as visual experiences. But the situation remains the same if we consider other experiences as well. Things and their properties may be experienced by touch instead of visually. Also, things are felt to be warm or cold; they smell, are heavy, and emit sounds. All these experiences are localized in one perceptual space, either with precision or merely in a vague fashion. More particularly, all have a location in relation to visual facts. Thus a voice may be heard as outside the window; a room as a visual scene may seem to contain the smell of a cigarette; and the cold surface of the glass in my hand is felt where the object is seen.[2] The fact that all sensory experiences appear in a common space may be explained in several ways. The reason may be the same as it is in the case of binocular vision, in which, notwithstanding the fact that two sense organs, the two eyes, are involved, all experience is located in one field. In this instance we know that the co-operation of the two eyes in giving us one field of vision is at least in part a matter of inherited factors. It is possible, though it has not been proved, that the same holds for the co-operation of vision, touch, etc., in giving us one sensory space in general. It is also possible that the experiences of the various sense modalities are localized in a common space because we have learned in early childhood how they must be spatially correlated. Besides these assumptions, which represent, of course, the nativistic and the empiristic possibilities in psychological theory, a third explanation must also be considered: in very early childhood the experiences of the various sense modalities may have been more or less adequately united in one space for *dynamic* reasons. Whichever interpretation is correct, all sensory facts do appear in one space, the space in which also the visual objects and the visual self are located. As a consequence, some non-visual experiences (as, for instance, most sounds) are, with the majority of the visual facts, localized outside. Other non-visual facts, such as those of kinesthesis, appear inside the self, but still in the same general space as contains the outside experiences. Inside we find, of course, also such subjective states as feeling tired, healthy, active, irritable, and so on. On the whole, we can say, non-visual data are fairly adequately localized with reference to visual phenomena. It follows that if the external location of visual objects offers no problem the same must hold for all instances in which non-visual facts appear outside the self.

After this preliminary discussion we can now turn to an old question. How does it come to pass that we ascribe to others experiences, more or less like those which we have ourselves? We seem to do so all the time, not only in general, but also quite specifically in particular instances. Obviously, therefore, our question refers to a fundamental fact in social psychology. But it is also a puzzling fact. For sometimes other people seem to recognize our experiences more clearly

---

[2] In this connection it does not matter whether the localization, say, of sounds in relation to visual objects, is invariably *correct*. If it is not correct, then the fact that we can compensate for the deviation is in itself a proof that both appear in the same space.

from without than we are able to observe them from within. For instance, I have difficulties in describing the inner experience of hesitation or lack of determination. Nevertheless others say that such states can be most clearly seen in my face. I am also inclined to believe them, since I know that facial expression very well from my observation of others. I think it was Nietzsche who once said that somehow the "you" is earlier than the "I." This applies first of all to our knowledge of character and personality. Our subjective experiences are far from giving us an adequate picture of our own person, while others often recognize its principal traits in a few minutes.

I do not believe that the things which other people *say* constitute our most trustworthy cues in this respect—as though their statements could be taken as descriptions of their experiences. For the most part people do not talk about their experiences as such. Also, we frequently ascribe to them pomposity or modesty, friendliness or coldness, when they do not say a single word about their feelings. In a foreign country we often recognize that others are provocative or kind, although their language may be entirely unknown to us. Even when we understand the words of other people, the *way* in which they talk may still be a better cue, than the meaning of their words as such. In some situations, a certain kind of silence can tell us more than any number of statements which might be made under the circumstances. The behavior of apes shows that they commonly understand each other quite well, although they have no language in the human meaning of the term. For these reasons language as a communication of meanings by words and sentences will hardly play a rôle in the following discussion. I am convinced that we shall nevertheless be able to deal with relevant phases of our problem.

The answer which philosophers have given to our question is well known: Since I cannot directly perceive what another person experiences, my only evidence with regard to his mental processes comes from his body. More particularly, it is events on the surface of this object which give me such information. But events of this kind have, of course, nothing in common with the actual experiences of the other person. Thus the only connection between my evidence and these experiences (which remain unobservable) is indirect. It is based on the fact that specific experiences tend to be accompanied by equally specific "expressive" alterations of a person's body. With this connection I have first become acquainted in my own case; I have found that my various experiences are correlated with certain movements and other changes in my body. After frequent repetition, this observation induces me to draw an inference by analogy when I perceive the same bodily events in others. I begin to believe that in their case these events may be taken as symptoms of corresponding mental processes. From the fact that this planet is inhabited by organisms, the inference is sometimes drawn that on another planet such as Mars, which in some respects resembles the Earth, there must also be living creatures. Clearly, this inference is of the same kind as the one which we are here discussing. Unfortunately, the astronomical parallel shows that inferences of this kind cannot be regarded as particularly reliable. Quite apart from this, it seems that the theory has little support in observation. In common life people simply do not proceed in this fashion, while at the same time they seem to understand their fellow men pretty well.

For this reason, psychologists suggest a different explanation. The starting point, it is true, they do not alter; it is again the statement that we find our own experiences accompanied by certain bodily events. But now comes the point at which the psychological explanation differs from the philosophical theory: According to the psychologists, constant repetition establishes strong associations between our experiences and accompanying bodily events. As a consequence, whenever such bodily events take place in others the corresponding experiences will at once be recalled. Moreover, the recall need not consist in the emergence of images and ideas; rather, it may assume the form of so-called *assimilation*, in which the fact which evokes the recall appears imbued with the recalled fact. Assimilation has been mentioned in other chapters. It is at work when the symbol + looks like adding, when a coffin appears imbued with the horror of death, and when a flag seems to have absorbed the particular virtues of a country. In the same way, we are told, bodily changes seen in others now appear as imbued with experiences which we frequently had when these changes occurred in our own case. As a result, friendliness may seem to be visible in other people's faces, or anger virtually audible in an animal's cry.

I need hardly point out that this is again an empiristic theory, and that it must be regarded with caution. If it were right, we should be unable to understand any behavior which has not frequently occurred in ourselves. Facts do not seem to agree with this conclusion. Do we never understand others as beings who are extremely different from ourselves? The characteristic manliness of Douglas Fairbanks used to impress me very much, although unfortunately I could not offer anything comparable. On the other hand, sometimes I see in the face of another person unpleasant greed in a version for which I hardly have counterparts in my own experience.

The philosophical interpretation of "social understanding" was no less empiristic than the psychological explanation is. Why do both take it for granted that our understanding of others must be an entirely indirect process? Obviously, both philosophers and psychologists assume that the characteristics of mental processes, on the one hand, and of observable behavior, on the other hand, are different in every respect. With this premise, the only possible relation between facts of the former and the latter kind will be an external, though regular, concomitance, and the empiristic consequences follow. But if the premise were correct, it ought to be easy to separate in our impression of other people such ingredients as have their origin in our own mental experiences of the past from those components which are mere facts of behavior. Incomparable facts cannot fuse into unanalyzable units. But if in a friendly-looking face we try to separate the friendliness from the characteristics of the face as such, we find the task quite difficult. So long as we consider the face as a whole, rather than as a mosaic of colored spots, the friendliness seems to remain an intrinsic characteristic of the face.

We have stated the premise which leads to empiristic interpretations of social understanding. But why has this premise been so generally accepted? Why do the theorists assume that mental processes and accompanying facts of behavior have nothing in common? The answer is fairly obvious. According to Descartes and many other philosophers, the materials and events of nature are *toto genere* different from the contents and processes of the mental realm. Few doctrines have influenced modern thought so strongly as this thesis has. Unfortunately, it has also been applied to the situation which we are here discussing. The behavior of other people, it has been argued, concerns their bodies. Consequently, the facts of behavior are physical facts and can, *qua* physical facts, have nothing in common with mental processes.

From what we have learned in previous chapters it must be clear that this argument is mistaken. Inadvertently, it uses the term "facts of behavior" in two different meanings. Whether or not the argument is correct when applied to behavior as a realm of physical facts, the problem of social understanding does not directly refer to behavior in this sense. It refers in the first place to perceptual facts which one person experiences in contact with other persons; for, both the bodies and the behavior of such other persons are given to the first person only as percepts and changes of percepts. It follows that theses about the nature of the physical world and its relation to mental processes have no place in a first discussion of our problem. Obviously, our first question must be how behavior as *perceived* can help a person to understand other persons. In trying to answer this question we need not at once make any assumptions about the nature of physical facts.

I do not, of course, deny that perceived behavior is related to changes which occur on the surface of the organisms in question, i.e., to physical behavior. I also admit that these physical changes are more directly connected with the mental processes of persons than are the events which we perceive when watching these persons. Nevertheless, since the behavior of others is given to us only in perception, our understanding of others must first of all refer to this source. Thus it seems that behavior as a realm of perceptual facts must also be our first subject when we try to solve the problem of social understanding. After all, we have to remember that sometimes percepts tell us more about facts than do the events which mediate between these facts and the percepts (*cf.* Ch. V, p. 94). Similarly, perceived behavior may tell us more about the mental processes of others than could be gathered from a study of their physical behavior.

Our problem is particularly interesting where it refers to the more subjective experiences of others such as their emotions and their thinking. Somehow these facts tend to express themselves in the behavior of people as we perceive it. Now, is it really true that behavior in this sense allows of no comparison with those mental facts? Or do mental facts express themselves in the more specific sense in which the term implies that the expression resembles what is being expressed? If the latter alternative could be supported by facts, the main reason for strictly indirect interpretations of social understanding would obviously be removed.

Under these circumstances, it will be our main task to compare subjective experiences with behavior as, at the time, perceived by others. We shall proceed slowly, however. In its efforts to classify human experiences, psychology has generally enhanced differences where closer inspection reveals striking similarities. As a matter of preliminary practice, we shall first consider such similarities in cases in which subjective experience is not involved.

Take the qualities of the different senses. For long it has been held that these qualities have nothing in common. And yet we can point at various examples which are at odds with this view. Brightness and darkness, for instance, are attributes of both auditory and visual experience. Again, if an

object which we touch appears cool, its coolness somehow resembles visual brightness; comfortable warmth is dark in
comparison. I have mentioned before that the German word
"rauh" ("rough") is used for certain auditory experiences as
well as for tactual facts. In English not only a surface which
we touch but also the sound of a voice and the taste of a
wine may be called "smooth." The German poet Morgenstern
once said of seagulls:

> *"Die Möwen sehen alle aus, als ob sie Emma*
> *   hiessen."*
>   (All seagulls look as though their name were
>   Emma.)

Morgenstern, I find, was quite right. The sound of "Emma"
as a name and the visual appearance of the bird appear to
me similar. Another example is of my own construction:
when asked to match the nonsense words "takete" and "mal-
uma" with the two patterns shown as Figs. 18 and 19, most
people answer without any hesitation.[3] In primitive languages one actually finds evidence for the thesis that the
names of things and events, which are visually or tactually
perceived, have often originated on the basis of such resem-
blances.[4]

After this preliminary exercise we can return to our main
problem, and compare subjective experiences with perceptual
facts. In this connection it will be interesting to know what

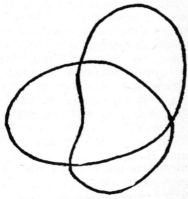

Fig. 18

[3] *Cf.* also Usnadze, *Psychol. Forsch.*, 5, 1924.
[4] E. von Hornbostel, *Festschrift Meinhof.* 1927.

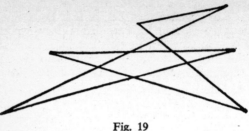

Fig. 19

words are being used with reference to subjective experiences. Most people will agree with the statement that if, in comparison with foveal vision, peripheral vision can be called "fuzzy," the same term also applies to most subjective experiences; in this respect they resemble facts in peripheral rather than in foveal vision. But if this is admitted, we have taken an important step; we have recognized that subjective experiences have at least something in common with certain perceptual facts. Klages has collected a large number of words which are used in the description of subjective experiences as well as of perceptual phenomena.[5] I will give only a few instances. Something arouses a "bitter" feeling in us. Again, one talks about being in a "soft" mood. "Sweet" love seems to occur in all countries, also "bright" joy and "dark" grief. In wrath there is something which many call "hot."

Often the terms in question refer to more *dynamic* characteristics. Thus, an expectation may be called "tense," an expression in which a subjective experience is compared with what we feel when we touch a taut string. A certain way of thinking appears to us as "straight," and everyone knows immediately what is meant when the term is used in this connection. Both "calm" and "restlessness" occur, of course, in visual fields; but often the same terms refer to facts in subjective experience. Again, we feel "attracted" by something, or are inclined to "reject" it. Sometimes our spirits are "high"; and sometimes they are "low." The reader will have no difficulties in continuing the list.

Some people will refuse to draw any conclusions from such facts. They will say that nothing can be inferred from mere analogies. I cannot accept this as an argument, however; for what we mean by an analogy is precisely a certain kind of resemblance. Moreover, when subjective experiences

[5] L. Klages, *Vom Wesen des Bewusstseins.* 1921.

are given names which also apply to perceptual facts, this
does not happen in a random fashion. If one such name is
applied only to particular subjective phenomena, and a second only to equally particular different ones, there must be a
principle which regulates the various applications. This principle must also be operative when, in a lively description of
inner facts, somebody invents a new such transfer of terms,
and again when others realize what he means. The only principle which I can discover is that certain experiences of the
inner and the perceptual worlds resemble each other.

The James-Lange theory of emotional life claims that
emotional experiences *are* sensory facts, namely, vague impressions which originate in our muscles, viscera, and so
forth. There may be some truth in this theory. But it
seems inadvisable to connect our present argument with
this or any other theory. It is quite possible to recognize
that certain perceptual and emotional facts resemble each
other, and yet to doubt that an identity can be postulated.
Moreover, the following discussion will, of course, be concerned with the perceptual characteristics which the behavior of other people exhibits. For the most part, these
characteristics are visual and auditory phenomena, which
play no part in the James-Lange theory. Thus we have no
reason to burden our investigation with arguments about
this theory of the emotions.

So far we have learned that, as a matter of principle, facts
of inner life and perceptual facts may have certain traits in
common. The main question which we have to answer is,
however, much more specific: Can the behavior of a person,
as perceived by others, resemble the mental processes of this
person? I will now describe a few instances in which observation seems to give a clear answer to this question.

In my presence two Russian scientists are talking in their
language about an issue on which they have for long dis-
agreed. I can observe their behavior as a matter of visual and
auditory facts; but I cannot understand their words. For a
while the scene is calm. Suddenly, however, the head of the
man to the left moves backward as though it were struck by
something, and from this moment both the tone of his voice
and the lines of his face exhibit a certain hardness. Soon
the other's behavior also changes; I am tempted to apply to
it the musical term *crescendo*. The same phenomenon now
begins to appear in the man on the left side. He, too, acts
and talks more and more intensely so that the whole scene
approaches a state of greatest agitation. But all at once I see
the man to the right looking at a placard on the wall, and

smiling. He says a few words to his colleague, who presently looks in the same direction. After a moment's hesitation his face lights up a bit, its hardness begins to vanish, and within seconds the scene is as smooth and calm as it was in the beginning.

These scientists happen to know my language, and are quite willing to explain what has happened. The man to the left tells me that a short while after the beginning of the discussion some unexpected words of the other man appeared to him as a personal offense, and that as a result he felt at first like withdrawing entirely into himself. The other man reports that quite abruptly the man to the left began to look hard as though he did not want to listen to further arguments, and that under this impression he, the man on the right side, could not help feeling more and more angry. The man on the left side now confesses that gradually intense irritation took hold of him also. Eventually I am told that the placard on the wall is the Russian translation of "Keep smiling." Since this advice helped, the scientists soon found their way back to a calmer state of mind.

It can hardly be denied that in this case the perceived behavior of two people and their subjective experiences have certain traits in common. As I see them, the two scientists form a group, the members of which direct all their activities toward each other. Subjectively, each feels that he directs his statements against the other, or that he defends himself against the other's arguments. Again, the movement backward of the man on the left side shows as a visual fact how he is struck by the other man's hostile remark, and the hardening of his face pictures the stiff inner attitude which he assumes as a consequence. The emotional *crescendo* in both which then follows is directly expressed in the visual and auditory *crescendo* of their behavior as I perceive it. Later, I see both directed toward the placard—as they actually are at the time. Eventually, I both see and hear how calm returns, while their emotions really subside.

The lesson which may be derived from this example is applicable far beyond the present instance. Many dynamic developments in subjective experience tend to express themselves in forms of perceived behavior which, to a degree, resemble those developments. Quite generally, both emotional and intellectual processes have characteristics which we also know from music, i.e., from auditory experience. *Crescendo* and *diminuendo, accelerando* and *ritardando* are obvious examples. But these terms are applicable not only to auditory facts but also to visually perceived developments. Hence, when such dynamic traits occur in the inner life of a person, they can be most adequately represented in his behavior as heard and seen by others. As a matter of fact, this happens all the time. When somebody is reminded of an injustice which he has suffered, he will, while his indignation grows, probably walk with increased speed. Thus the greater tempo and intensity of his emotional thinking are nicely rendered in the *accelerando* and *crescendo* of his movements as seen by others. Naturally, the same inner upheaval may express itself in an *accelerando* and *rinforzando* of vocal behavior. Or watch a person on different mornings. Sometimes his movements are even and calm; but sometimes his face and his hands appear unstable and restless. He need not tell you in the former case that he is well and at rest, nor in the latter that he feels restless; in a way, both inner situations are directly obvious to you. Similarly, hesitation and uncertainty tend to be accompanied by forms of behavior which, as perceptual facts, resemble those inner states. An observer may, for instance, see movements in various directions, each slowing down when it has hardly started, their sequence devoid of unitary organization. Furthermore, so long as human beings are not particularly inhibited, any sharp discontinuity in their experiences is likely to be followed by sudden events in their perceived behavior. In a moment of sudden fright human beings jump back or start. When a person experiences that flash by which new ideas sometimes come to us, he may stop in the middle of a sentence, and he may also strike his head. Thus his mental processes and his appearance to others exhibit the same discontinuity. Often the conduct of a man is seen as organized in a way which agrees with the organization of his actual planning and doing. Actions which flow from one determining source tend to appear as one coherent current of visual facts. On the other hand, when action as subjectively experienced consists of relatively segregated parts, the same articulation will probably characterize his perceived behavior. In discussing our problem, philosophers and psychologists may have concentrated too much on the expressive movements which accompany *emotions*. At any rate, equally relevant facts have virtually been ignored: behavior in the most *practical* sense of the word tends to be seen as organized in forms which copy the organization of corresponding inner developments. The reader will find further examples in a book in which I have described the behavior of apes.[6]

I now turn to observations of a slightly different class. In objective as well as in subjective experience direction may

[6] *The Mentality of Apes.* 1925.

involve *tension*. For instance, if my attention is attracted by a strange object such as a snake, this direction of my self goes with a feeling of tension. Naturally, a person who happens to be present will see my face and eyes directed toward the place of the object; but in the tension of my face he will also have a visual picture of my inner tension; and this tension will be referred to the same place. The objection may be raised that between my face and the snake there are no stimuli on which a perception of tense reference could be based. This argument is mistaken in that it ignores the facts of visual grouping. When somebody sees that my eyes assume a particular direction—and in this respect human eyes are astonishingly expressive—the parts of the field which lie in that direction will immediately be related to my eyes, my face, and my whole person. Grouping of this sort is no more enigmatic than are the instances of group-formation which have been discussed in a previous chapter. This holds also for cases in which the person in question is directed away from an object. Here again, the reference may be entirely obvious in an observer's visual field. As an example, I quote the following statements, which are taken from the description of a famous experiment:

"He started to reach for the head of the animal with the forefinger of his left hand but withdrew it suddenly before contact."
[Wool is presented to a child in a paper package.]
. . . "He then began to play with the paper, avoiding contact with the wool itself."

Both statements occur in Dr. Watson's report about his experiments with young children.[7] The first statement means that the movement of the finger is seen as directed toward the animal; no other interpretation can be given to the expression "to reach for." Objective methods of observation, as Watson understands the term, would not, of course, find any physical connection between the physical finger and the physical animal. Nevertheless, the author—who abhors the very notion of experience—is here so strongly influenced by a fact of visual grouping that for a moment he forgets his Behavioristic axioms, and reports in terms which make sense only from the point of view of perceptual experience. Actually, he is doing worse things; for, in using the expression "to reach for," he adopts the point of view of purposive psychology. In the second statement, the same observations apply

[7] *Psychologies of 1925.* 1926.

to the words "avoiding contact with." Obviously, if somebody "avoids contact" with an object, or if he "reaches for"
a thing, the psychological facts involved are excellently por-
trayed in the perceptual field of an observer.

In the last few examples it is the spatial rather than the
temporal side of perceived behavior which resembles the
inner experiences of a person. As a further instance of this
we may mention that people in a state of pathological depression tend to assume a drooping carriage, similar to the pos-
ture of a normal person in a period of extreme fatigue or sorrow. Just the contrary is seen in patients who enjoy a more
than normal euphoria or elation. Their bodies often show a
corresponding erectness, and in one case, which Dr. Janet once
described, the patient began to walk on tiptoe. These are
striking visual facts which again directly express mental
situations.

Many readers will be acquainted with the next example,
which I take from social psychology. A man in a leading
position, for which he is perhaps a bit too good-hearted, is
accustomed to treating his subordinates as friends. When he
finds himself obliged to censure one of them severely, and to
make him feel that friendly relations are over, such a man
may become a most suggestive object of observation. If he
has not already trained himself on previous occasions, he
will have the greatest difficulties in uttering the decisive
words. In spite of his serious intentions, he will not speak
these words, but rather others which do not go straight to
the center of the situation. If the other man is sensitive
enough, he may guess the whole truth from what he hears;
but what is actually said leaves something like a veil around
the main point. Seen from without, the official's conduct is a
picture of his inner perturbation. He is fully aware of what
he ought to do, but social factors prevent his behaving entirely according to this program. You may see him walking up
and down before the other man, as he finds himself constantly deflected from straight action. When he stops, his eyes are
worth observing. In the sensitive play of the eyes the inner
directions, but also the difficulties, of a person become more
easily apparent than elsewhere. Of course, it is rather easy to
look steadily into a man's eyes when saying nice things to
him which one does not entirely believe. In this case, the
social forces offer no resistance; on the contrary, they operate
precisely in that direction. But try to look into another's eyes
while you tell him what must come to him as a social shock.
For some people this is an extremely difficult task, particularly if in the past overt relations have been very friendly. The
man in our example may well intend to look into the other's

eyes; but his own eyes will either stop, say, at the mouth or the nose; or, if they actually reach the other man's eyes, they will at once again be deflected. Just as this official feels his intentions bending sideways, and his words avoiding the socially decisive step, so his behavior appears persistently deflected from its object, more especially from the other's eyes, where his very center as a person seems to be located.

The reason why such similarities are not familiar facts to the psychologist probably lies in the analytical tendency of our science. So long as we think of perceptual situations in terms of local nuances of brightness, hue, and so forth, we shall find no support for the view that behavior tends to resemble mental facts. But if we look upon behavior in a more naïve fashion, and allow grouping, direction, tension, and the like, to impress us as they naturally do, then that view will no longer surprise us.

A few words must now be said about the genetic side of our problem. *Why* does the perceived behavior of a person often resemble this person's mental processes? In many cases the answer is fairly simple. Take this example: While a pianist plays a sonata, he lives in a current of dynamic events which are clearly organized. As he experiences his own playing, he ends one musical phrase now, and begins the next one a moment later; he starts a *crescendo* as the Ehrenfels quality of one development, and a *ritardando* as that of another. Now, whatever the laws of motor innervation may be, the impulses which are conducted to his muscles surely depend upon the organization of the music as he has it in mind. Physically, the result consists of sound waves in the air, which are not organized, but mere sequences of mutually independent oscillations. Nevertheless, something remains in these waves which is on the whole sufficient for adequate organization of what the audience hears. Where he intends a *crescendo,* his playing results in a series of waves of increasing intensity. In the audience this gives rise to a unitary auditory development which again has the Ehrenfels quality of "swelling." Where the pianist ends a phrase, and then starts a new one, he gives the sound waves such relations of temporal proximity, intensity, and so forth, as are likely to establish the same articulation in the auditory fields of people in the concert hall. The situation is about the same as in the case of physical objects which appear as segregated things in visual experience. Although the light waves which these objects reflect, and thus the stimuli which impinge upon the retina, are not at all organized, formal relations among the stimuli are well preserved in the transmission. As a re-

sult, organization tends to establish the "right" things in perception. However, in our present example organization goes
further in re-establishing certain facts than it does in the
case of objects; for, what the audience hears tends to agree
not only with the pianist's nervous processes, but also with
his musical intentions and actions as psychological facts.
In order to understand this phase of the situation, we must
remember the concluding remarks of Chapter II. When the
pianist plays a phrase as a unitary development, are we to
assume that the corresponding brain processes constitute a
functional unit? Or are we to assume the contrary? Where, in
his experience, the phrase ends and, then, a new one begins,
are we to suppose that the corresponding processes in the
man's brain are uniformly coherent? Or are we to assume
that the temporal organization of these processes also exhibits
a discontinuity? Gestalt Psychology postulates that in both
cases the physiological organization is the same as the mental
organization. This view is also held with regard to all other
phases of organization. Hence, innervation projects upon the
pianist's muscles an organization which his mental processes
and their brain correlates have in common. In this fashion
the formal relations among the resulting sound waves are determined. But auditory organization in the people who listen
depends upon such relations. Consequently, their experiences
tend to be organized in a way which agrees with the organization of mental processes in the pianist.

Even if all this be true, does not our understanding of
other people remain an indirect process? To be sure, as we
see and hear them, other persons may often exhibit characteristics which resemble their inner experiences. Nevertheless,
such perceptual facts are not, for this reason, identical with
the inner experiences of those persons. At this point, therefore, the present analysis does not seem to offer a better solution of our problem than has been given by others. We also
seem to need a final step, an inference, which leads from certain perceptual experiences to the mental processes of others.
Similarity may facilitate this inference; but the inference, or
some other indirect process, appears to be necessary under
all circumstances.

I will now try to explain why I cannot accept this reasoning.
In doing so, I shall have to defend a certain form of Behaviorism—although not the Behaviorism which has been discussed in Chapter I.

If, on an evening, I think of the contacts with other people
which I have had during the day, I find that for the most
part it has not been particularly difficult to understand these

people. And yet I feel sure that during those contacts I have hardly been occupied with their inner experiences *per se*. Now that I think of it, I can of course try, and deliberately evoke pictures of the way in which Mr. X and Mrs. Y probably have felt on this or that occasion. I can also make this attempt when I am actually together with these persons. But during the effort I soon realize that this is an entirely unfamiliar procedure; plainly, I seldom do anything of the kind in normal social life. Moreover, the effort tends to disturb the way in which I naturally understand people, and which often seems to work much more satisfactorily. When understanding them in this fashion, I find myself concentrating mainly on people's voices and on their appearance; naturally also, when they talk, upon the content of their statements. But again, I seldom translate the content of these statements into terms of subjective experience. Rather, it is their words as such which seem to carry the meanings in question. Apparently, I always forget to take the final step by which we are supposed to enter other people's inner life.

Our analysis refers to understanding as it occurs under ordinary circumstances. At present we are not concerned with the epistemological questions which a philosopher would raise in this connection; nor do we consider the ways in which a psychologist would try to investigate the mental processes of others. The facts of social life which we are considering occur in the absence of any theoretical concepts. To a theorist, who sharply distinguishes between perceptual data and facts of subjective experience in others, a step from the former to the latter may seem to be entirely necessary if men are to understand each other. But in common life we pay no attention to the philosophical premises which lead to this conviction. First of all, in common life we are Naïve Realists. It does not occur to us to regard the things around us as mere perceptual counterparts of physical things. This also holds for the particular objects which we call other persons. As a consequence, all characteristics which things and persons owe to perceptual organization are commonly taken as characteristics of these things and persons as such. But we also ignore a second distinction: we draw no sharp dividing line between subjective phenomena in the narrower sense of the term and such perceptual facts as constitute human bodies. After all, why should we? In our own case, many subjective experiences seem to be vaguely localized within our bodies, and often virtually fused with some of their perceptual characteristics. In many cases it is extremely difficult to decide whether a given subjective fact is an affection of our body or of ourselves in the more restricted sense. Why should a different view be taken with regard to the bodies of others? These bodies, too, often exhibit characteristics which are in several respects exactly like subjective phenomena. Thus, so long as epistemological misgivings play no rôle, we take it as a matter of course that directions, tensions, efforts, excitements, and so forth, of other persons appear in or on their bodies.

This, it seems, is the reason why in the social contacts of common life the final step from perceptual facts to the mental processes of others is seldom taken. From the point of view of naïve phenomenology, it need not be taken. If I refer to the calmness of a man before me, I refer to a fact which I perceive. This "calmness" appears to be the same kind of state as I sometimes find, and sometimes fail to find, in myself. Under ordinary circumstances I am not interested in any other calmness which may be ascribed to the man. Similarly, if the man "gets excited," the *crescendo* which occurs before my eyes and ears is not, of course, a neutral sensory fact; rather, the dynamics of the perceptual event *is,* or *contains,* what I call the man's excitement. I do not ask myself whether something that belongs to a different world accompanies the impressive display. Such a question will arise only when I assume the sophisticated attitude with which philosophers and psychologists approach the situation. Naturally, in everyday life I never assume this attitude. Again, when I am aware of other people's "hesitation," "restlessness," "determination," "depression," "avoiding," "reaching for," and so forth, I am seldom tempted to go beyond the perceptual facts as such—which, I repeat, are far from being neutral facts. As I commonly use such terms, they refer to events in perceptual space.

May I invite the reader to make a simple observation before he criticizes these statements? It is not difficult to embarrass another person. I invite the reader to do so and, if he succeeds, to ask himself whether the embarassment of the other person is a perceptual fact, or something that happens in another world. Of course, during the observation the reader would have to abstain from any philosophical reasoning.

The present account needs amplification at one point. When saying that common social understanding refers to certain perceptual events, we seemed forced to assume that such events occur only on the surface of another person's body. And yet, as a matter of phenomenological description, this would not always be entirely true; for the events in question sometimes seem to emerge from the interior of the body. Does this observation contradict our analysis? The answer follows from another question. What is "the interior" from which those events seem to issue? Obviously, it is the interior of the body as a perceptual entity. Now, if events emerge from a volume which is surrounded by a certain surface, the volume and the surface clearly belong to the same world—which, in the present case, is the world of perceptual facts. Thus it is still the body as a percept, from the interior of which such events emerge. Consequently this observation is entirely compatible with our description of social understanding.[8]

Our analysis has a consequence which has so far not been mentioned. If the organism of a human being can emit stimuli which give rise to perceptual facts "with psychological ingredients," then there is no reason why stimuli which come from other sources should never be able to cause similar effects. Obviously, pictures of people, particularly those which we see moving on a projection screen, fulfill the necessary conditions. But quite apart from such banal instances, there are other events and objects which impress us in the same way. Few people can hear the rumbling *crescendo* of distant thunder as a neutral sensory fact; it sounds to most of us "menacing." As a matter of perception, various kinds of weather appear similarly imbued with psychological characteristics.[9] Thus we speak of "calm" and "restless," of "morose" and "friendly" days. Such terms are also used with reference to landscapes, to the appearance of streets in cities and villages, and so forth. To repeat, it would be surprising, and it would constitute a serious objection to our general argument, if only living creatures and their pictures exhibited Ehrenfels characteristics of this sort. Conversely, the frequent occurrence of similar phenomena in other parts of the perceptual world corroborates our thesis that no interpretations in terms of subjective experiences need be involved. Modern man does not attribute such experiences to a thunderstorm or to a landscape; and yet he hears menace in thunder, and sees friendliness in certain landscapes.

Occasionally, I must admit, the problem of social understanding seems to present difficulties which cannot be re-

[8] One might ask how an event can appear to emerge from the interior of a body when this interior is not visible. Similar facts of "transcendence" are by no means rare in perception. Since the problem concerns perception in general rather than our present investigation, we cannot discuss it here.

[9] In this case there is a complication. Weather affects us not only by stimulation of sense organs and subsequent perceptual organization, but also in a more direct biological fashion.

moved by our present analysis. Apparently, behavior does not always resemble the inner experiences which it accompanies. Is laughing, as heard by others, an adequate expression of the subjective facts which occur in the laughing person? I find it hard to answer this question. If the right answer were negative, indirect interpretations of understanding would for once have to be considered. But in view of the facts which we have here discussed, such interpretations would have to be greatly modified. For, if our descriptions are correct, i.e., if understanding is often quite direct, then any extension of this direct understanding by indirect processes will find its course more or less prescribed. More particularly, direct understanding will influence indirect understanding both in a negative and a positive sense. The facts of direct understanding will resist all indirect amplifications which do not fit those facts; and they will facilitate any indirect understanding which is in line with their own trend.

Quite apart from instances in which perceived behavior does not resemble the experiences of a person, direct understanding as such has its limitations. We cannot possibly maintain that the inner life of a person is entirely revealed in his behavior. Most people begin to conceal themselves early in life; and this holds particularly for their emotional life and their motivations. Actors, pianists, singers, and lecturers seldom look the stage fright which not a few of them nevertheless feel. To be sure, calmness which has merely been acquired as a social cover may sometimes fail to convince, just because it involves an effort. But it is undoubtedly true that innumerable passing events in the inner life of a person remain entirely hidden while he is in company. It would also be most astonishing if the stimuli which issue from a human organism were always to give rise to a fully adequate perceptual representation of those events. Much will often be lost, and much distorted. After all, the functional connection between the inner processes of one person and their perceptual consequences in another constitutes a tremendously complicated causal chain.

In maintaining that common social understanding is principally of the kind here considered, we have not decided whether understanding in this sense can be used as evidence in psychological work. On the face of it, it may look as though the answer to this question must be strictly negative. Have we not found that even thunder, the weather, and landscapes exhibit facts of the same sort? In these cases, nobody will take such facts as evidence concerning psychological processes. Thus it seems that we cannot actually rely on "direct understanding." Although this argument appears fairly impressive, I cannot regard it as entirely convincing. Quite a few perceptual facts concerning color, shape, movement, and so forth, are occasionally being used in natural science; and yet it is well known that the color, the shape and the movement of perceptual objects are often subject to influences which, under such conditions, make these facts useless to the scientist. For this reason they are trusted only in a preliminary way and, with notable exceptions, barely at all in actual measurements. In our connection, it seems advisable to follow, *mutatis mutandis,* this example, i.e., to trust immediate understanding, as here described, so long as in a given case there is no cause for suspicion. If we were to reject its testimony entirely, we might easily lose sight of facts which escape the more orthodox methods of psychology. However, no psychologist ought to rely on understanding in our sense who is not fully aware of its pitfalls.

These remarks do not, of course, refer to direct understanding as a remarkable phase of *perception.* Few perceptual facts are quite so interesting, particularly to the social psychologist; but also, few have been so consistently neglected.

VIII

ASSOCIATION

IF WE WERE to give no attention to direct experience we should be in great danger of constructing an artificially simplified system of psychology such as that of Behaviorism. On the other hand, it seems impossible to develop psychology as a science of direct experience alone. For this purpose the field of experience is too restricted. Quite obviously, the neural events which are accompanied by experience are only parts of larger functional structures. As such parts they depend upon facts to which experience as such has no direct access. How can one pretend to give an adequate theory of psychological events merely on the basis of experience, if the processes underlying this experience represent no more than a province within a larger functional whole? Nobody can understand a game of chess through watching only the moves in one corner of the board.

In the latter case, the observer would soon become aware of the fact that, all the time, important events are happening beyond the narrow field of his observation. For the moves within this field are obviously related to other facts which must lie beyond; particularly since certain moves come from there, while others disappear into that region.

Exactly the same is true of experience. For instance, when reading or talking about things which at the time are not present, we do not usually develop adequate images of such objects. Sometimes they may not seem to be represented by *any* experiences. When I am asked about my profession, I answer that I am a psychologist. But the actual experience connected with this word may be restricted to a feeling of familiarity and of knowledge available in a certain direction, in which I should have to move if more concrete and detailed data were needed. This readiness for transition in the right direction, while the object itself is not explicitly given, has been excellently described by William James. Probably it is one of the most common phenomena in experience. Its most conspicuous character consists in the fact that under such circumstances parts of actual experience are felt to point beyond this experience, toward something specific which, we feel sure, is there. Thus experience tells us about its own incompleteness. Nor should we be too much astonished by this observation. It is precisely what we have to expect if of a larger functional whole only a restricted part is represented in experience. The specific direction of which we are then aware corresponds to the fact that a part of the experienced field is functionally related to processes which have no experienced counterparts. Although they are not actually experienced, such processes must be highly specific. For, as a rule, our reading and talking go the right way, and thus prove to be adequately determined by those facts beyond.

Perhaps the simplest example of this is successive comparison in its different forms. After a few years of traveling I meet a friend, and my first idea is "How old he looks!" This does not mean that he looks particularly old on an absolute scale. I see older-looking men every day. Nor does it mean that an image of him as I knew him before is now reactivated and compared with his present appearance. Yet the statement somehow refers to the past; it represents an extreme form of what occurs in most cases of successive comparison. If, five seconds after a first tone, I hear a second one which has the same pitch, but is sufficiently louder, I can easily recognize this relation, although for the most part I do not actually recall the first when the second is given. (As a matter of fact, under the circumstances I have difficulties in evoking a more or less adequate image of the first tone, when I hear the second.) At the present time all psychologists seem to agree on this point.

But how can the relation be recognized if only one of the tones is actually experienced? The answer is that we do not experience the second tone as a separate fact. Rather, it appears with a specific reference "to that something in the past." [1] This reference has a direction or slope in the dimension of time, which may be upward or downward. Even if we take this for granted, however, our problem is not yet solved. Our judgments in such cases are usually quite accurate. Hence, what is left of the past, i.e., of the first tone, must be sufficiently representative of its loudness to make the second tone emerge with the *right* direction. On the other

---

[1] We may also say that the second tone has a characteristic which belongs to it as to the second member of a pair (*cf.* Chapter VI).

hand, this *trace* of the first tone cannot in all respects belong to the same class as the process which, five seconds before, accompanied the experience of the first tone. If it were of precisely the same kind, there would also be the corresponding experience—which, we have seen, need not generally be the case. Hence, only some *effect* of that first process can remain when the process itself has subsided. It is this effect which must represent the process itself. In fact, it must represent this process so well that the second tone appears with the right reference to the level of the first.

As to questions of detail, various hypotheses may be invented. But no theory will be acceptable which fails to assume the existence of some trace. I once developed a more detailed explanation of successive comparison, in which the nature both of the trace of the first tone and of the slope from the first to the second was indicated.[2] I concluded that experimentation on successive comparison can show us directly what happens to the trace of the first process when the process itself has ceased. So far such experiments make me believe that traces of this kind are preserved for a long time, and that they are probably identical with the physiological bases of memory.

All sound theories of memory, of habit, and so forth, must contain hypotheses about memory traces as physiological facts. Such theories must also assume that the characteristics of traces are more or less akin to those of the processes by which they have been established. Otherwise, how could the accuracy of recall be explained, which in a great many cases is quite high? Gestalt Psychology adds more particularly that any specific organization which the original processes, and the accompanying experiences, exhibit may be preserved in the traces. If it is preserved, it will, *qua* organization, exert a powerful influence on recall. Take the examples given in Chapter VI, where the concept of visual shape was considered. If a thing with its specific shape has often been perceived together with other facts, presentation of the same thing may later lead to recall of the facts. But if, with the same stimuli present, another thing with a different shape happens to be seen for some reason, there will be no recall. Thus, when the number 4 is shown in a certain environment (*cf.* Fig. 14, p. 115), it will easily cause recall of its name. But when Fig. 10 (p. 110) is shown to an unsuspecting subject, this name will not occur at all. On the other hand, once the sub-

[2] *Psychol. Forsch., 4,* 1923. More recently my theoretical assumptions have been greatly improved by Lauenstein (*Psychol. Forsch., 17,* 1933).

ject has found the 4 in Fig. 10, which means that 4 has now become a segregated thing, he will readily see it again in the future, and then recall the name. It follows that the traces of past experiences constitute neither an indifferent continuum nor a mosaic of independent local facts. Rather, they must be organized in a way which resembles the organization of the original processes. With this organization they take part in processes of recall.

The same property of traces may be deduced from the facts of recognition. When Rubin instructed his subjects to apprehend certain patterns in a particular distribution of figure and ground, they recognized them quite well if afterwards experimental conditions favored the same organization. However, if an area which had first been figure became ground in the second presentation, and vice versa, the subjects were confronted with new shapes which they did not, of course, recognize. And yet, the stimuli were exactly the same as in the first presentation. Here again the traces were shown to act in line with past organization rather than as mere aggregates of independent local facts. We may go further: in most cases of recall the activated material itself is obviously organized. That this is true not only of images but also of familiar motor "melodies" has been shown by Michotte and van der Veldt.[3] Individuals who have vivid visual images will admit that the image of a particular tree is detached as a figure from a dimmer environment or ground. To be sure, in free imagination and in dreaming we may behold scenes which differ widely from any experiences we have ever had before. Nevertheless, even the oddest creations of dreaming remain figures which exhibit the essential characteristics of organization.

In countless cases organization is so decisive that radical changes of the stimuli do not interfere with recognition or recall—provided the organization remains the same as before. Thus a melody is recognized in a changed key, in which not a single tone of the original may be preserved. Also, some days after we had heard a tune for the first time, we may find ourselves humming it in a key which, upon examination, proves to be different from that of the model. Here all factors excepting organization seem to be unimportant so far as recall is concerned. Similarly, an unknown figure which is seen today in red color, somewhat on the left of the point of fixation, and in a certain size, will readily be recognized tomorrow even though now it may be green or yellow,

---

[3] *L'Apprentissage du mouvement et l'automatisme.* 1928.

shifted to the right side, and in a different size.[4] Plainly, recognition and recall depend at least as much on the organization of past events as upon local effects of stimulation which, according to the mosaic theory, would be the elements of past experiences. We shall later come back to this fact.

From the present point of view, some observations can readily be explained which remain perplexing so long as the importance of organization is not recognized. In experiments on delayed reaction in animals it has been found that, after a delay of many seconds or even minutes, some animals are still able to choose the right object, say, from among three equal ones. And yet, at the time of the response the right object is no longer singled out by the particular cue which was given before the delay. Now, if during the delay the animal simply maintains his orientation toward the right object, his correct choice is perhaps not astonishing. But a real problem arises, if during that period the animal freely moves in his cage, and nevertheless afterwards makes the right choice. It has been said that in such a case the reaction of the animal depends upon some internal cue. This is true to the extent that without some after-effect of the original situation (in which, for instance, the right object was shown to contain food) correct responses would be entirely incomprehensible. Such an after-effect is, of course, an internal cue. But when, after the delay and after many random movements of the animal, this internal cue becomes operative, there must also be some characteristic in the right object, to which the cue refers. If we examine each object by itself, we can discover no such cue, because each object as such has the same characteristics as the others. None the less, they differ in one respect, namely, as to the rôle which each object plays in the group of objects. One constitutes the left end, one the right end, and one the middle or interior part of the group. If, after the delay, the animal reacts correctly, the only characteristic of the object in question which allows him to refer his cue to this object is the place of the object within the group of three.[5] Before the delay a particular event, such as the showing of food, served to single out one object. But this object was also characterized as occupying a specific position within the group of objects. Thus, if at the time that event became associated with the position of the right object within the group, the animal will after the delay respond to

[4] E. Becher, *Gehirn und Seele*, Heidelberg, 1911.
[5] The group may, of course, be larger. (*Cf.* O. L. Tinklepaugh, *The Journal of Compar. Psychol.*, 8, 1928).

this object. In other words, delayed reaction of this type depends upon the perception and recognition of a Gestalt characteristic. For this reason, delayed reactions as often investigated by animal psychologists cannot be understood without reference to the principle of organization. This becomes even more obvious if we consider the multiple choice method, which Yerkes has used with so much success. Here it is still more clearly the specific rôle of an object in a group which becomes connected with a response. Under these conditions, it is not particularly surprising that the response may remain correct, even if the position of the group as a whole, and therefore of all its members, is freely varied in the tests.

In the past, experimental psychology has not been greatly interested in the concept of memory traces as such. Investigators have been much more strongly attracted by another concept in the field of memory. When we say that the traces of organized processes are themselves organized entities, we do not seem to have mentioned the most important fact in memory, the fact that traces tend to become connected or associated. Association is commonly regarded as a bond between two experiences which enables us to recall the second experience when only the first is given again. Such a bond is said to be formed when two experiences occur together, and particularly, when their contiguous occurrence is repeated. The existence of traces is one basic factor of memory, habit, and so forth. Association by contiguity is a second such factor; and almost all the classical research on memory has dealt with this phase of learning and retention. Psychologists are proud of their work on association, because in this field both methods and achievements appear to be almost comparable to those of the natural sciences.

This pride is partly justified. On the other hand, we have gradually begun to realize that, with the excellent methods which are available, only a very special type of memory has so far been investigated, and that the results ought not rashly to be applied to memory in general. Moreover, there is one issue upon which these investigations have barely touched at all, because at first it is not readily recognized as a problem. Is it really true that the mere repetition of two contiguous processes establishes an association between them? Also, is an association a mere bond, which connects experiences in the way in which a string connects two objects? The concept of association to which these questions refer will be discussed in the following paragraphs.

The law of association by contiguity has been considered particularly satisfactory because it gives learning a purely mechanical interpretation. What could be more in line with the spirit of natural science? I must confess, however, that precisely from the point of view of science the law of association by contiguity appears to me as a strange statement. Two processes A and B happen to occur together and, whatever the nature of A and B may be, a bond is formed between them! I do not know a single law in physics or chemistry which could in this respect be compared with the law of contiguity. Once before, in Chapter IV, we have been concerned with this fact. When in physics two objects or events, A and B, become functionally interrelated, this interrelation and its consequences are invariably found to depend upon the characteristics of A and B. This is the case in astronomy, where the acceleration of one star by another is a function of mass. The same holds for electrostatics, where the direction in which interaction works depends upon the signs of the electric charges. In chemistry, atoms react or remain indifferent to each other depending upon their given characteristics. Conversely, there are no examples of interaction in which the nature of the interacting factors plays no part. And yet, in the classical law of association by contiguity, the nature of the things which become associated is tacitly ignored.

Obviously, at this point we are again confronted with the machine or mosaic theory. If, in the distribution of events within the sensory nervous system, interaction takes any part at all, results must depend upon the characteristics of the interacting processes. The mosaic theory of the sensory field excludes this possibility by assuming that local sensory facts remain indifferent to one another. As a consequence, the chances of peripheral stimulation alone determine the resulting pattern. We now recognize that in the classical concept of association the same view is taken for granted. All A's and B's are indifferent pieces in a mosaic. They do not interact. Any bond by which they may become connected must therefore be analogous to a string which we attach to two objects. In *such* a connection the characteristics of the objects do not matter.

At the present time, we may confidently say that this interpretation of associations is no longer tenable. Its weakness is apparent even if we consider only work that was done with classical methods.

In a series of syllables an A and a B, i.e., two contiguous syllables, are surely not indifferent to each other since neither A nor B is indifferent even to F and G and H, i.e., to more remote items in the series. If a subject is told to write down six syllables which we read to him quickly, he will usually be able to do so. But if, instead of six, we give him a series of

twelve syllables, his score will commonly be less than six.
Plainly, all members of such a series tend to disturb one another. How, then, can we say that they are mutually neutral? In the well-known technique of "paired associates," the
associations of a subject are tested by giving him single syllables to which he has to add the items which follow in the
series. His achievement as a whole is measured by the number
of cases in which his answers are correct. Essentially, this
procedure presupposes that associations within a series are
mutually independent facts which, because of this independence, allow of statistical treatment. This assumption cannot
be entirely correct; for it ignores the general interdependence of items in a series, to which I have just alluded. It is
quite true, if the interdependence is statistically the same in
all series, and if the problems under investigation are of the
common type, no great harm will be done. But as soon as the
nature of associations as such becomes a problem, we
must, of course, be much more careful.

As a second finding which seems incompatible with the
traditional view, we may mention certain changes which
syllables tend to undergo during learning. For the most part,
the series are read by the subject in a specific rhythmical
fashion, which consists of larger groups and subordinated
groups. At the same time the reading tends to assume a certain melody-character, in that the pitch of the voices goes
up and down as those groups begin and end.[6] Apparently,
this means that during learning, and most of all during the
first readings of the series, the material is being organized in
a specific way. But we know from previous discussions that,
if this is the case, the individual syllables ought to acquire
particular characteristics, characteristics which they owe to
their rôles in the organization. This consequence is perfectly verified in cases in which, after first learning a series as a
whole, subjects are shown the same items in another sequence. In the new order they look new and strange. Objectively, this influence of organization is most convincingly
demonstrated if, after learning to recite a whole series without any hesitation, subjects are shown single syllables for recall of the following items. Nagel found that under these
circumstances scarcely one-third of the syllables could be recalled, while nevertheless the series as a whole could be re-
cited with ease.[7] Within the flow of an organized series,

[6] Cf. the patterns given by Frings, *Arch f. d. ges. Psychol.*,
30, 1914.

[7] *Arch. f. d. ges. Psychol.*, 23, 1912.

given syllables do not seem to be the same things as they are alone.

Ebbinghaus and his successors chose nonsense syllables as the best material for the investigation of associations, because they wished to experiment under conditions in which no older, pre-experimental, associations would interfere with the new, experimentally established, bonds. If meaningful material were employed, they thought, such older associations would influence the results in an uncontrolled manner. Nonsense syllables seemed also to constitute a more uniform material than any other items. It would be unjust if we were to deny that psychology received a tremendous impulse from the work done with this method. It seems, however, that the early investigators used the technique in a somewhat one-sided manner. At any rate, the most valuable observations in the field were made when a certain narrowness of the original point of view was gradually overcome.

Some psychologists have criticized the method of Ebbinghaus because it does not actually investigate associations which are automatically established. This is a good cause for criticism in that the results of the method are commonly formulated as though the associations formed themselves spontaneously. Indeed, if the mere contiguity of syllables is supposed to cause their association, most experiments in which this material is used are far from testing associations in this sense. The subject is not simply exposed to a succession of syllables; rather, he is asked to memorize them. If he follows this instruction, it is not contiguity alone which establishes the associations, and this fact is not even mentioned when the results are formulated in terms of automatically formed bonds. Undoubtedly, this is a flaw in the procedure. The mistake is a grave one; for gradually it has been realized that without intentional memorizing the learning of a series of nonsense syllables is all but impossible.[8]

What, then, are the subjects doing when they try to memorize a series intentionally? No one was better authorized to give an answer to this question than G. E. Müller, who spent a large part of his scientific life on the investigation of association and retention. His answer was: "A series of figures, consonants, syllables, and so forth, is learned essentially in an activity of synthesis in which the members of the series are combined so that they become solid groups."[9] In an earlier chapter we have seen that such an attitude is capable

[8] Kühn, *Zeitschr. f. Psychol.*, *68*, 1914. Also Poppelreuter, *Zeitschr. f. Psychol.*, *61*, 1912.

[9] G. E. Müller, *Abriss der Psychologie*. 1924.

of establishing groups in perception, and that its effects may be just as genuine perceptual facts as any spontaneous organization is. From Müller's statement we can therefore conclude that intentional memorizing amounts to intentional organizing.

Though in the case of nonsense material and, most of all, of syllables such an activity seems to be virtually necessary, it is evidently not needed with certain other materials. Time and again we find ourselves recalling events when the facts which now lead to recall have surely not been intentionally combined with those events. It follows that while the nonsense material used in classical investigations satisfies certain conditions of exactness, it cannot teach us the whole truth about associations. When, instead of the classical material, we deal with the more natural experiences of everyday life, associations are not generally formed in that fashion.

But do all our experiences outside the laboratory associate themselves spontaneously? This again is not the case. We may hear a telephone number dozens of times together with a name, and may still remain unable to recall it when the name occurs again. In such a case conditions seem to be similar to those which characterize the association of nonsense syllables. Between the name and the number there are no specific relations; they do not tend to form a group spontaneously. Thus the suspicion arises that association occurs spontaneously where organization is spontaneous, and that association presupposes intentional combining where the material as such is unlikely to form organized groups.

This assumption is corroborated by the fact that meaningful nouns form associations much more readily than does nonsense material. In this case, of course, the nouns have long since been imbued with their meanings. Therefore, when subjects learn a series of nouns they find these meanings firmly attached to the words; and obviously it is these meanings which are now so easily associated. But why should they be? Most psychologists will answer that the meanings of the nouns adhere not only to these words but, as a consequence of previous associations, also to one another; in other words, that the process of learning has only to strengthen bonds which have existed for long. At this point a difference between Gestalt Psychology and Associationism must be emphasized. Let somebody read a few times the following pairs of nouns: lake—sugar, boot—plate, girl—kangaroo, pencil—gasoline, palace—bicycle, railroad—elephant, book—toothpaste. Learning of this series will be considerably easier than that of the same number of nonsense syllables. But can one really say that between lake and sugar, palace and bicycle, and so forth, there are strong pre-experimental associations which merely need some slight refreshing, and thus make learning an easy task? It seems to me that we cannot, since thousands of times the same words have occurred in other much more regular connections. Such stronger connections must exert an inhibiting influence on the weaker associations which, according to the explanation, make learning in this case so easy. Thus the explanation is not so plausible as it may at first appear. Gestalt Psychology offers a different interpretation. When I read those words I can imagine, as a series of strange pictures, how a lump of sugar dissolves in a lake, how a boot rests on a plate, how a girl feeds a kangaroo, and so forth. If this happens during the reading of the series, I experience in imagination a number of well-organized, though quite unusual, wholes. It may be that learning is here so easy because a material of this kind readily lends itself to organization. In order to exclude the possibility of frequent similar connections in the past, I had, of course, to choose strange pairs of nouns, the meanings of which can be organized into larger pictures, but do not do so quite spontaneously. If I am not mistaken, the combinations and sequences which are even more easily associated in everyday life are simply instances of entirely spontaneous organization.

On this ground, nonsense syllables must be regarded as the worst material that could be chosen if the essential nature of associations was to be discovered. Since such syllables do not spontaneously organize themselves in well-characterized and specific groups, the nature of spontaneous association cannot become apparent to the psychologist who makes use only of this material. Furthermore, since the series of syllables are built up at random, they teach us little about the fashion in which learning depends on what may be called the *structure* of a series. Even though it consists only of nonsense material which, to a degree, is homogenous, a series may be constructed in many different ways. Syllables may be put together as neighbors which fit each other phonetically, or just the contrary may be done. Some pairs may be constructed according to one principle, some according to another. The whole series may exhibit a specific structure; or it may be an indifferent series such as the ones which are commonly used. All these variations ought to be examined if we are to see whether or not organization is the essential fact which underlies association. From the trend of the foregoing discussion, we shall be inclined to say that it is.

As a last argument in favor of our thesis, we may mention

the fact that, if a series has been learned by combination of its members in pairs, subjects will readily recall the second members of the pairs when the first members are given, while recall will be quite difficult when the second members of pairs are presented and the following items in the series, i.e., the first members of the next pairs, are to be remembered. If we suppose that during learning the members of the series have been given as an objectively even sequence, this result is incompatible with the concept of association as it was once understood. Clearly, the conditions of association are not adequately described so long as conditions with regard to organization of the material are ignored. Strong association occurs only among such items of the series as become parts of well-defined groups. We do not deny that contiguity in space and time is a factor of great importance in association. But this factor does not seem to operate directly. In an earlier chapter we have seen that the factor of proximity plays a major part in the formation and segregation of sensory wholes. From what we have just stated it would follow, then, that contiguity in space and time favors association only because, under the name of proximity, it is a favorable factor in organization. Now, this condition is just one among many others which all have a favorable influence on organization, and since it now appears that organization is the really decisive condition of what is commonly called association, the rule of association may have to be reformulated accordingly.

To summarize: Where organization is naturally strong, association occurs spontaneously. In the absence of specific organization no association is to be expected, until the subject establishes some particular organization intentionally. Also, when the members of a series are well associated, they prove to have characteristics which depend upon their position in the whole series—just as tones acquire certain characteristics when heard within a melody. Finally, items of a series which constitute small solid groups are at the same time items which are particularly well associated.

After these preliminaries we can discuss the nature of the bond which is said to originate between the traces of processes when these processes become associated. The prevailing opinion is that association means increased conductivity of such neural pathways as connect the places of the processes and traces in question. With each repetition of these processes some event is assumed to occur in the tissue between them, which lowers its resistance. As a result, an excitation which reaches the place of the first trace will in the future spread toward the place of the second trace rather than to other parts of the brain. Thus the trace of the second process tends to be reactivated when the first process alone is given. This hypothesis is not entirely satisfactory. While it makes us expect that, after repeated presentations of a pair of items, excitation will travel along the connecting pathways and, perhaps, further increase their conductivity, it does not tell us why anything particular should happen to these pathways on the *first* occasion. The difficulty is serious, especially in cases in which the association is well established after only one presentation of the items.

We do not know what happens in recall. The only thing which we seem compelled to assume is some connection between the traces of two processes, A and B, so that reactivation of A leads to recall of B rather than of any facts with which A has not been associated. Now, in this respect two hypotheses are possible. If we believe that, in becoming associated, A and B remain two mutually neutral facts which merely happen to occur together, then some special bond, such as a particularly well conducting group of fibers, may be regarded as an adequate basis of the association. In full contrast to this view, we may, however, reason as follows: When an A and a B become associated, they are experienced not as two independent things but as members of an organized group-unit. This may perhaps now be taken for granted. But with this premise the neural situation cannot consist of two separate parts of which one corresponds to A and the other to B. Rather, the unitary experience indicates that a functional unit is formed in the nervous system, in which the processes A and B have only *relative* independence. If this is the case, we cannot expect two separate traces to be left when A and B are no longer experienced. Traces, we said, tend to preserve the organization of the original processes. Thus only one trace will be established, which represents the functional unit by which it was formed. And in this trace, A and B will exist only as relatively segregated sub-units. Consequently, by virtue of their inclusion within one trace, A and B will be just as well "connected" as they could ever be by means of a special bond. Such a bond is supposed to give the spreading of nervous activity the right direction from A to B. But the fact that A and B lie within a unitary trace (which is, of course, segregated from other traces) will have precisely the same effect.

It will be advisable to give our assumption a more radical formulation in which it can be more easily distinguished from the older view. According to our thesis, association loses its character as a special and independent theoretical concept. It becomes a name for the fact that organized processes leave traces in which the organization of these processes is more or less adequately preserved. I do not deny that associations are strengthened by repetition. But this need not mean that repetition increases the strength of a special bond. I also acknowledge the fact that sometimes, as in the case of nonsense material, a particular attitude of the subject is needed if an association is to be established. But, as we have seen before, everything points to the thesis that this attitude is one of active organization. If the subject succeeds, he now has correspondingly organized experiences; accompanying neural events must be similarly organized; and traces will be formed which again have the same organization. The only new problem which arises in this situation is that of the influence of intentions on organization. This problem is not related to questions of memory alone (*cf.* Ch. V, p. 99).

Some will be inclined to say that it does not matter whether we accept one theory of association or the other, since we are unable to look into the brain, and can therefore not decide which one is right. With such a view, the value of an hypothesis would be completely misunderstood. If an hypothesis has any specific content, it must also have specific implications; and these can be tested. In the present case, such implications are fairly obvious.

The old rule about association by contiguity, we remember, does not refer to characteristics of the A and B which become associated. This is natural enough, since in this rule association is tacitly supposed to be a connection like a string, by which things, equally indifferent to each other and to the connection, are forced into a kind of partnership. Organization, on the other hand, is far from being an aggregation which is forced upon mutually indifferent materials. In sensory experience, it has been shown, organization clearly depends upon the characteristics of facts in their relation to one another. Therefore, if association is a consequence of organization, it must also depend upon these characteristics. To a degree, this influence has been verified by observations reported in this chapter. But much more remains to be done. What we need are radical variations of the material which is presented for learning. Such variations are directly prescribed by the principles of Gestalt Psychology. Is it quite generally true that, other circumstances remaining the same, the strength of associations varies with the strength of the organizations in which the items lie? Also, we know the specific conditions upon which sensory organization depends.

Can it be shown that these conditions are just as essential with regard to association as they are in primary experience? [10] To be sure, not all rules which govern the behavior of associations can be derived in this fashion. Rules of sensory experience give us no direct information about the nature of traces as such. Nor do these rules inform us about the fate of traces in the course of time. On the other hand, when studying the nature of traces, we may at any time make observations by which certain problems in *perception* can be clarified. Perceptual organization occurs not only in the dimension of space but also in that of time. In the latter case, the behavior of traces is likely to be just as important as that of the present experiences involved. The rôle of traces in this connection will be more readily understood if their nature in general is better known.

A second implication of our hypothesis has practical as well as theoretical significance. This consequence refers to animal psychology. We have seen that nonsense syllables do not easily associate on their own account, because within series of such items well-characterized pairs and other specific groups are not spontaneously formed. But subjects who have great difficulties with such series may have good memories in everyday life. They may recall a great many events which they have never intended to commit to their memories. This reminds one of a strange contrast—which all animal psychologists must have observed—between animal learning as it occurs during laboratory experimentation, and habit formation in the same animals when living somewhere outside. I do not think that the reason for this difference is adequately stated if people refer to the "more natural" circumstances present in the latter situations. What does the term "natural" mean in this connection? Perhaps it simply means: favorable

[10] At the present time (1947) the answer to this question is partially known. Functional interrelations within a series of items have been shown to depend most strongly upon the nature of the material which is presented in the series. This holds both for interrelations which disturb learning and for those which faciliate the process. So far investigations have principally referred to the part which *similarity* of items plays in learning. Disturbing effects of similarity have been investigated by von Restorff (*Psychol. Forsch., 18*, 1933) and by several other psychologists in Germany and in America. The outcome of these studies is perfectly clear: series of nonsense syllables constitute a difficult material to learn, not so much because the items have no meaning as because in such monotonous series specific sub-groups do not spontaneously form. The positive influence which similarity of items has on their association has been demonstrated by the present writer (*Proc. Amer. Philos. Soc., 84*, 1941).

with regard to association; in other words, favorable from the point of view of organization.

Under the influence of the old concept of association, many experiments with animals, among others those on sensory discrimination, proceed in a way in which the concept of organization is completely ignored. For instance, on the rear walls of two alleys two objects are presented which the animal is expected gradually to discriminate under the influence of reward and punishment. On the floor of the alleys, in no connection with those objects, the wires are placed which punish the animal by an electric shock when his choice is wrong. Obviously, an electric shock, applied at this point, and the object, shown in another place, will not easily become parts of an organized unit. On the other hand, after a right choice the animal is fed somewhere behind the scene, i.e., in a situation just as separate from the right object as the shock is from the wrong one. A young Behaviorist once asked me whether, apart from vague concepts, Gestalt Psychology had anything specific to offer, which would matter in actual work. It seems to me that if we offer Behaviorism nothing but our criticism of his method, and suggestions toward a better one, it would be quite sufficient. In man, learning seems to depend on organization. It is highly improbable that the same rule does not apply to habit formation in animals. Therefore, when investigating sensory discrimination, we should, instead of separating the decisive factors, make every effort to facilitate their organization as a unit. Some years ago, I proposed the following procedure. The wrong object suddenly moves against the animal whenever he approaches this object. Such a technique would surely resemble the animal's learning in common life more closely than the traditional procedure does. The object would be much more likely to become imbued with "negativity." [11] Thus, much time would be saved. Quite apart from practical reasons, however, it seems to me a sound postulate of experimental science that conditions be varied in all respects. If Behaviorists could be persuaded to vary their experimental situations with reference to questions of organization, they would probably learn a great many new things about the nature of animal learning.[12]

[11] W. Köhler, *The Ped. Seminary, 32,* 1925.

[12] A most decisive step in this direction has been taken by K. S. Lashley (*Journ. Genet. Psychol. 37,* 1930), who introduced the jumping stand into the repertoire of animal psychology. The main merit of this apparatus consists in the fact that it virtually forces the animal to attend to the essential parts of the experimental situation.

My remarks apply to the formation of conditioned reflexes just as they do to other methods by which learning is being studied in animals. Some authors prefer the term "conditioned reflex" to that of "association." I do not find, however, that the former concept is clearer or more fundamental than the latter. In fact, what is called a conditioned reflex may be no more than a special case of association. The conditioned stimulus which becomes artificially connected with a reflex can probably evoke the reflex only because it has first of all become connected with the adequate stimulus which naturally arouses the reflex. This, of course, is an association of two sensory facts. Apparently, such an association may become so strong that, *via* the mere trace of the adequate stimulation, the conditioned stimulus alone can arouse the reflex. Now, if this association is the thing to be learned in conditioning, and if the association of two processes is only the after-effect of their organization, we must draw the same conclusion with regard to conditioning as we already have drawn with regard to ordinary association and to discrimination learning in animals. At the present time we seem to have no experimental evidence as to the question whether changes in the presentation of the conditioned stimulus, in its relation to the unconditioned one, influence the process of conditioning. In customary experimentation, a bell rings, for instance, just before food is given; but no attention is paid to the conditions which would either impede or facilitate organization of the two events. And yet, at this point animal psychology has an opportunity to test the value of two assumptions at the same time: First, is it true that conditioning involves the associating of two sensory facts? And secondly: Does conditioning depend upon factors of organization?

From the point of view which we have now reached, some of our previous discussions appear in a new light. We have made it appear probable that association depends upon organization, because an association is the after-effect of an organized process. Now, when the concept of organization was first introduced, we were at every step hampered by empiristic explanations, in which facts opposed to the mosaic theory are quickly discarded as mere products of learning. It has been shown, I hope, that as a matter of principle these facts do not allow of explanations in terms of learning, and that, therefore, organization must be accepted as a primary phase of experience. At present, we may go further and claim that, on the contrary, any effects which learning has on subsequent experience are likely to be after-effects of previous organization. For learning, in the sense in which the term has been used in this chapter, amounts to association, and, if we are right, association is an after-effect of organization. Consequently, any attempts to reduce the organization of experiences to the influence of associated meanings and the like involve a vicious circle. One cannot reduce organization to other factors, if these other factors can be understood only in terms of organization. I do not hesitate to repeat that experiences *are* quite commonly imbued with meanings. But this statement would be misleading if I were not to add, first, that for the most part it is organized experiences to which such meanings attach themselves, and secondly, that the facts of learning which are here involved derive again from the principles of organization.

IX

RECALL

PSYCHOLOGY INVESTIGATES three main topics in the field of memory: (1) learning and the formation of the traces which later enable us to recall, (2) the fate of these traces in the time between learning and recall, and (3) the process of recall itself. To be sure, recall plays a part in the investigation of *all* these problems, because the study of the laws of learning and of those of retention involves recall just as much as does the study of recall as such. But when interested in problems of learning, we can keep conditions constant with regard to retention and recall, so that only the conditions of learning are varied. If our problem refers to retention, the conditions of learning and those of recall will be kept constant, while those concerning the interval between learning and recall will be varied. In the study of recall there will be variation only of the circumstances which concern this event. Thus the three classes of problems are actually separable. In this chapter we shall be concerned mainly with questions of retention and recall, although we shall also consider certain facts which refer to learning and the formation of traces.

In Chapter VI, I mentioned certain experiments in which, after learning to choose one side of a pair, for instance, the darker of two grays, animals had to react to a new pair. The pair consisted of the "right" object of the learning period and of a new object. The new object was in the same relation to the "right" object as this had been to the "wrong" object of the original pair. The result was that in the majority of the trials the animals chose the new object, obviously because in the new pair this object played the same part as the "right" object had played during the learning period. In the changed situation the new object was "the dark side of the pair."

This result is not quite general, however. It depends upon the time which elapses between the trials with the old pair and the first trials with the new one. Once, when the learning had been completed, a chicken was given a new pair in single trials between choices with the old one, and this procedure was repeated until the trials with the new pair appeared statistically reliable. It was found that, under these circumstances, the animal chose the "right" object of the learning period quite as often as the new object. This fact can be explained as follows: When the chicken reacts to the objects, they will appear as a pair in which one gray is the dark, and one the bright side.[1] But at the same time one object will be seen as a more or less specific dark gray, and the other as a more or less particular bright one. So long as the pair is not transposed, both ways of seeing the objects are compatible with the direction of the training. On the other hand, if during the learning period the chicken reacts to the "right" object in terms of its rôle in the pair, and also as a more or less definite gray, the training will have two effects, which must conflict as soon as the new pair is introduced. For now the former product of learning will favor the choice of one object, and the latter, the choice of the other. Now, let us suppose that the two effects of learning are not equally persistent. If this happens, an increase of the interval between trials with the old pair and trials with the new one will favor the reactions which depend upon the more enduring product of training. Thus it follows from our experiment that the habit which depends upon the pair as a whole is more enduring than the habit which depends upon the grays as such. The pair as a whole is relatively less decisive only when the animal reacts to the new pair immediately after trials with the old one, i.e., at a time when the individual grays are still effective in memory. It seems to be a general rule that retention which refers to the organization of facts is more persistent than retention which refers to individual facts as such. Several psychologists have remarked that often we remain able to remember the general structure of things, when their more particular content is no longer available. This thesis deserves thorough examination, because work in this direction may help us to understand the psychological nature of concepts. In the case of the chicken, it was easy to examine our hypothesis. We gave the animal further trials with the new pair, when several minutes had

---

[1] Here, as always when talking about animals, I use terms such as "appearing" for the sake of simplicity. Whether or not the chicken has a visual field in the human sense of the word, such terms have a clear functional meaning in which alone we are here interested.

elapsed since his last trials with the old one. The result was that now the "relative" reactions clearly predominated.

In this field much remains to be done. In the beginning of Chapter VIII, I mentioned that successive comparison offers a way in which the fate of traces can be investigated. We have just learned about a second way. A third one, which is somewhat similar to the second, can also be derived from experiments with animals. I will discuss it as an example of the specific problems which are raised by Gestalt Psychology. When Yarbrough[2] investigated delayed action in cats he found that, if the animals had to choose between three objects, their reactions were no longer reliable after delays of only four seconds. With two objects, the delay could be increased to more than four times this amount. Why is the result so much better in the latter case? Examination of human subjects with a similar, though more difficult, task will give us an explanation. If 25 objects with individually identical properties are distributed before a subject in a semicircle, they do not all play the same rôle in the visual situation. Two objects, the first on the left and the first on the right side, have well-defined and highly specific boundary locations. To a degree, the object in the middle may also be regarded as specifically characterized, at least in the visual field of a human subject. But all the others amount to not much more than an indifferent filling of the arc. Now suppose that somebody points to one of the objects, and that, after a delay in which the subject does not fixate the object, he is told to indicate which one it was. So long as one of those particular objects is used in the test, the reaction of the subject will always be correct. But if the crucial object is in an indifferent position, and if the subject is not allowed to use indirect procedures such as counting, wrong reactions are quite likely to occur. Thus the subject may choose the sixteenth instead of the seventeenth object, or the eighth instead of the ninth, and if the delays increase, or if the subject is not sufficiently attentive, even greater errors may become frequent. This shows once more the dependence of delayed reaction upon the more or less specific position of the right item within a group, as demonstrated by Hertz with birds (cf. pp. 85 ff). The same principle can now be applied to cats who, after a delay, have to choose between three objects. If the cue given in the initial presentation refers to the object on the left side, the task of the animals concerns a highly specific place in the group. The specificity of this location is likely to survive in memory. The same is true if the object on the right side is the crucial object. In the case of the object in the middle, however, location within the group may be much less clearly characterized—for cats. When this object is singled out in the first presentation, its rôle within the group may be sufficiently clear for moments; but soon its trace is likely to lose its individuality, and to become part of the now undifferentiated interior of the group. It follows that the animals will less often react correctly when three objects, rather than two, are used in the experiment. Only if the experimenter were to give the three objects another distribution in space, so that all would have well-characterized locations, could the cats perhaps solve their problem again. The reader will be inclined to object that, with three objects, the probability of errors is *ipso facto* increased, and that therefore the behavior of the cats may have no relation to more or less specific locations within the given group. This objection could easily be examined by introducing precisely such changes of the situation as I have just mentioned. From the point of view of organization, this is not simply a matter of numbers, but also of distributions in space. Therefore, if the three objects were distributed in a way in which each plays a specific part, we should promptly discover whether an explanation in terms of mere numbers is acceptable. In Yarbrough's own experiments there is a result which contradicts this purely quantitative explanation. If mere number of objects, as against lack of sufficient specificity in the case of one object, were the condition which leads to failure with three objects, then the wrong reactions of the animals should be evenly distributed among the three objects. Actually, this was not the case. After a long delay (beyond 4 seconds) some cats never chose the object in the middle. All their reactions were directed toward the first object on the left, or the first on the right side. This is just what may be expected if our explanation is correct, whereas the fact cannot be understood without reference to organization. We may conclude that, with cats, the traces of past events undergo an exceedingly rapid transformation, in which the less clearly specified parts of groups deteriorate. When this has happened, subsequent behavior will obviously be determined by the simplified organization which alone is left.

A similar observation was made by Mr. Tinklepaugh and me when, using another method, we did some experiments on delayed reaction with a monkey. A very large square on the ground was covered with sand some inches high. Before the animal's eyes certain marks were made on the sand such as, for instance, a small hill of the same material or, in another experiment, a straight line which was drawn on the surface with a finger. After this preparation, food was buried in the sand in a place which, for a human subject, was clearly characterized as having a specific position *near* the mark. We wished to see whether the animal would use the mark in remembering the place of the food; for, without a mark in the homogeneous surface, his previous reactions to buried food had not been very clear. The monkey, who had watched our preparations, was not released until some time had elapsed. When allowed to approach the sand, he immediately went to the mark itself, and tried to find the food there. He never searched in the neighborhood of the mark. Further observations are highly desirable; but one explanation seems so probable that I do not hesitate to mention it here. Just as in the case of delayed reaction as investigated with cats, the reaction of the monkey depends upon a trace in which the organization of the visual field is represented. In this field the hill or the line are outstanding features. On the other hand, the location of the place of the hidden food is much less specifically given. We may therefore assume that a simplification occurs, which is analogous to the one observed in Yarbrough's experiments. In the monkey, the trace of the field will also be transformed during the delay, and in this change all less defined parts will again be at a disadvantage. As a trace, the situation will be so obscured that virtually only the outstanding mark with a vague reference to hidden food is left. The method which we used with this monkey may, of course, be further developed. It may then become an accurate instrument for the investigation of the fate of traces in animals.[3]

Thus traces are by no means rigid entities. Rather, they are imbued with dynamic tendencies; and these tendencies seem to be stronger in animals than they are in man. From this point of view, the study of delayed reaction in animals is likely to assume great significance for general psychology. It is always advisable to investigate first of all the most pronounced forms of phenomena.

In such observations, behavior which depends upon memory traces is used as an indicator of changes which these traces undergo. There are, however, other situations in which the traces are well preserved, while under the circumstances in question recall is nevertheless difficult or even impossible.

[3] In the meantime Mr. Tinklepaugh has made considerable progress in this direction. His "substitution method" is an excellent technique for studying the characteristics and the fate of traces. (*The Journ. of Compar. Psychol., 8,* 1928.) *Cf.* also W. Köhler, *Psychol. Forsch., 1,* 1921.

Some examples of this kind have been mentioned in the preceding chapter. We will now treat others which also show that recall depends on very specific conditions.

If the term association expresses the fact that the trace of a unitary experience is itself a unitary fact, it might seem to follow that, once such a unitary trace is formed, any group of stimuli which corresponds to a considerable fraction of the original situation will cause recall of its other parts. Actually, this does not follow, because between the characteristics of an organized experience and the corresponding stimuli there are by no means point-to-point relations. The organized process depends upon the whole set of stimuli and their "characteristics-in-relation" in a fashion which cannot be analyzed into independent effects of local stimuli. For this reason, a fraction of the original set of stimuli does not es-

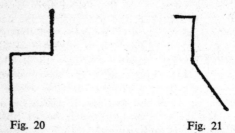

Fig. 20   Fig. 21

tablish a process which has actually been contained in the original process. Rather, such a fraction causes a process which differs in certain respects from the corresponding part of the original event. As a consequence, the process which is now given may have no equivalent counterpart in the unitary trace of that event, and may for this reason be unable to cause recall of its other parts. For instance, Fig. 20 is unlikely to evoke the missing lines of an H although, geometrically, Fig. 20 is the larger part of an H. Nor will Fig. 21 cause recall of the missing lines of an R. When seeing an H or an R, we have not, of course, seen Fig. 20 or Fig. 21 as actual visual shapes. Thus the traces of the H and the R contain no parts which correspond to the lines given in our Figures, and recall does not occur. We must conclude that recall is restricted to instances in which the process now given and a part of the original unitary event are sufficiently similar. This will be the case only when the present process corresponds to a *natural* part, or sub-whole, of the original organization. Thus U.S. may be expected to cause recall of A., and the stars, recall of the other parts of the American flag. In both cases the part which is now given resembles a relatively independent part of the original experience. Obviously, similarity is the principal condition. If we draw a profile from the nose downward to the chin, this line does not correspond to a complete sub-whole of a face. None the less, since such a line looks not too different from the same line as part of the whole profile, the process corresponding to that line resembles parts of the process which underlies the profile as a visual shape, and also the corresponding traces. Hence, recall is quite likely to occur.

Generally speaking, however, recall cannot occur so easily as is being assumed in current empiristic theories. It seems to be restricted to a rather narrow channel between a Scylla and a Charybdis. Association is necessary for recall, and association presupposes a sufficient degree of unification in the sense of organization. Recall, on the other hand, can occur only if the process which is now given resembles some region within the organized trace of the whole experience. Thus, if a part of the original situation is too thoroughly absorbed within the larger organization, stimulation which corresponds to this part will be unable to cause recall. Between these limiting conditions, one of which is imposed by the nature of association and the other by that of recall, there is only a narrow range in which recall can actually occur.

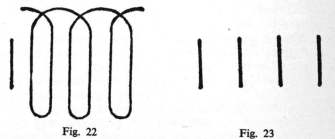

Fig. 22   Fig. 23

In order to demonstrate this fact, I made the following experiment: Subjects were shown pairs of figures. After a while parts of these drawings were presented with the instruction to recall the missing parts. Now, in a case like that of Fig. 22, for instance, either the vertical at the left was presented, or Fig. 23. Geometrically, Fig. 23 represents a much larger part of the original pattern than that single vertical does. And yet, when the vertical was presented, correct recall was much more frequent than it was when Fig. 23 was shown. From the point of view of Gestalt Psychology this is not at all astonishing. Fig. 23 gives a visual experience which does not occur as part of Fig. 22. In Fig. 23 even the first vertical on the left has lost its tendency to recall Fig. 22, because in Fig. 22 the vertical is segregated as something apart, while in Fig. 23 it is the left end of a set of parallels.

This last point introduces a further restriction to which the possibilities of recall are subjected. An aggregate of stimuli may become unable to cause recall, not only when separated from other stimuli with which it was originally combined, but also when given together with stimuli which were not present at the time of the original presentation. This condition, too, may lead to experiences to which no part of the trace in question corresponds. We realize once more that not only the organization given at the time of the association matters, but also the organization at the time of (expected) recall. When given again in a certain environment, a pattern of stimuli may constitute an excellent basis for recall. However, a pattern will not often be repeated in precisely the environment in which it occurred when the association was formed. Now, quite apart from the cruder obstacles which have been considered above, even a slight change of the surrounding field may make a given pattern unable to cause recall of associated items, simply because the change introduces a new organization in which the experiences corresponding to that pattern are no longer present. That this is true can be deduced from Nagel's experiments (*cf.* p. 158). In a well-learned series of nonsense syllables each item, though embedded in the whole series, would seem to be a thing by itself. But if one such syllable is given alone for recall of the following syllable, this change of environment is often sufficient to make recall impossible.

The same influence of organization upon recall has been demonstrated in a surprising form by Shepard and Fogelsonger.[4] These psychologists made their subjects learn pairs of syllables. Some of these pairs had identical second members. Between the first occurrence of such a syllable and its repetition in another pair there was an interval of 25 minutes. At the time of the test the first syllable of a pair was given, and its partner had to be recalled. But where two syllables had, at different times, been followed by the same second syllable, both were presented together in the test. So long as organization is ignored, one must expect that in the latter case the partner of the two presented syllables will be more easily recalled than a second syllable which has been associated with only one first syllable; for two associations which operate in the same direction are generally supposed to reinforce each other. Actually, however, just the contrary was observed. The fact that two syllables were given seemed

[4] *Psychol Rev., 20*, 1913.

to inhibit recall. The disturbance was particularly striking when both syllables were presented simultaneously, but it was also observed when they were given in rapid succession. The explanation seems to be that, during learning, the subjects had always been given a single first syllable together with its partner; that when, in the crucial cases, two syllables appeared before them, these objects would at first look unfamiliar in the new grouping; and that, as a result, neither could immediately evoke the partner common to both. This explanation was confirmed by qualitative observation. The subjects reported that recall became possible only through an attitude of analysis, in which one of the syllables was sufficiently isolated. It follows from our explanation that any extraneous syllable, which has never occurred during the learning, but is presented with a first member of a learned pair, must have the same disturbing effect. The authors found this to be the case. Thus the explanation seems fully verified. Our conclusion is that even a very slight alteration of circumstances will sometimes make recall difficult.

A similar result was obtained by Frings [5] in his work on inhibitions, although his problem referred to learning rather than to recall. In classic experiments it had been shown that, if a syllable A has become associated with a syllable B, the same A cannot so easily be associated with a third syllable C as could a neutral syllable. Also, when A has been associated with C as well as with B, A is slow in causing recall of either B or C. The competition of the two associations has an inhibiting effect. Frings was able to show that under certain circumstances these inhibitions disappear completely. His subjects were asked to learn series of syllables, the instruction being that the syllables should be read and memorized in rhythmic groups of the anapaest type, in which, after two less accentuated items, a third one follows with the main accent. In such a group the first syllables naturally form a sub-whole. In the test these two syllables were presented, and the third was to be recalled. Now, if a group like (ac)d occurs in a first series, and a group like (bc)e in a further series, one expects the association between c and e to be inhibited, because c has first been associated with d, and is now to be associated with e. Similarly, once the associations (ac)d and (bc)e are formed in spite of this inhibition, the subjects should have difficulties in recalling d, when ac is given, and e, when bc is given. From the point of view of organization, however, we have to realize that in

[5] *Arch. f. d. ges. Psychol., 30,* 1914. These experiments were planned by Bühler.

(ac)d the syllable c is a member of the sub-whole (ac), whereas in (bc)e it is a member of the different sub-whole (bc); and that therefore c is not quite the same thing in both cases. We may also say that in the former case not c, but rather the sub-whole (ac), has been associated with d; and again, that in the latter case (bc), not c, is associated with e. On this ground neither learning nor recall should be inhibited. The experiments confirmed this view. When a syllable c occurred in two different sub-wholes, there were no inhibitions. It is particularly interesting, however, that inhibitions occurred immediately when a subject was fatigued at the time of learning, and therefore unable to grasp the syllables in the prescribed rhythmic complexes.

We have shown that, because of the facts of organization, experimental findings may differ considerably from what the classic laws of association and recall make one expect. And yet, the most radical limitation of these rules has so far not been considered. But this further point cannot be introduced until a more general topic has been discussed, a task to which we will now turn.

On various occasions we have mentioned that everybody experiences his self as a particular entity among many other objects. Consequently, in the brain there must be processes not only corresponding to objective experiences, but also others corresponding to the experienced self. The processes which represent the self differ in many respects from those which correspond to outside objects; but there must also be characteristics which both have in common. This follows from the fact that sometimes the self interacts with outside experiences in precisely the same fashion as one outside experience interacts with another. Two examples will suffice to corroborate this point.

When a physical object moves, the corresponding visual thing will as a rule also be *seen* as moving. There are, however, instances in which, while objectively one object moves, and another is at rest, visually the former remains almost or entirely stationary, but the latter moves. This happens not only as an occasional illusion. "Induced" movement, as the phenomenon has been called by Duncker,[6] occurs under quite specific conditions and is always observed when these are realized. Thus, when clouds are passing the moon in a certain direction, the moon is often seen to move in the opposite direction. When a point on the window of a moving railroad car is fixated by a passenger, the objects outside

6 K. Duncker, *Psychol. Forsch., 12*, 1929.

begin to glide backward. Any change of its spatial relations
to other things may have this effect upon an object which
is physically at rest. Now, precisely the same tends to happen
to the self when its spatial relation to outside objects is
changed. For instance, when our environment is turned
around us, we soon feel ourselves turning in the opposite
direction. Here the induced movement of the self is mediated by visual experiences. Michotte and Gatti have shown
that the same effect is produced when a person holds two
objects in his hands, which by some device are slowly and
at the same rate moved toward one side. Here again, the subject feels that his body turns in the opposite direction.
Thus the self exhibits the phenomenon of induced movement
exactly as outside objects do.

As a second example, I choose the fact that, just like any
other object, the self may become a member of perceptual
groups. Naturally enough, if I put my hands on a table,
while another person does the same on the opposite side of
the table, I see four hands in two pair-groups. But the whole
self may enter a group in the same fashion. If somebody
accompanies me along a street, and if ahead of us another
pair is walking, I feel (and partially see) myself as a member
of one of two groups.

In the preceding chapters the concept of organization has
been applied to outside experiences. But our present examples show that actually organization concerns the whole
field, which means that the self is included. In other words,
I maintain that certain general principles of function apply
as much to the self as to objects in a more common sense.
At first, this statement may sound a bit disturbing, because
traditional thought tends to give the self a unique position.
Does not the self alone preserve its identity while almost
everything else in the field is freely changeable? Notwithstanding this identity, are not the states of the self far more
intensely varied than objective experience is? I will admit
that these are important facts, which are bound to have a
strong influence upon any organization in which the self
participates; but it does not follow that when we consider
the rôle of the self in experience the concept of organization as such is no longer applicable. At times those facts
confer upon the self a central position within the total
field; but even this is by no means always the case. After
all, in many situations experience includes other persons, and
there are circumstances under which such people occupy a
more conspicuous position in the field than the self does.

When studying behavior in the perceptual sense of the
word, we became acquainted with a kind of grouping in

which dynamic reference plays a decisive part (Ch. VII). It will be remembered how Watson, the Behaviorist, described the behavior of a child. He saw the child referred to an object, a fact which involves not only that in his visual field the child and the object in question were members of a pair-group. This particular group was also characterized by a dynamic relationship which extended from one of its members to the other. Similarly, when a dog barks, the action of the animal will often be perceived as obviously referring to a particular object at which the barking is directed. Quite generally, there are no more convincing group-formations than those which exhibit dynamic factors in this sense. We have also seen that the reference may be of two kinds. It is either positive, i.e., directed toward the object; or negative, as it is, for instance, in the attitude of avoiding. In both cases we will use the expression *bipolar organization*, which is meant to distinguish such dynamic instances from those of ordinary pair-groups.

But the discussion in which we became first acquainted with bipolar organization made it also clear that in this respect, no less than in others, perceived behavior tends to picture the experiences of the perceived creature. In other words, bipolar organization occurs not only when we observe what others are doing. Rather, anybody may find himself directed toward, or away from, particular objects in a way which involves the same kind of dynamic pair-formation. In fact, apart from states of lowest vitality, there is hardly a total field from which bipolar organization is absent. The self is virtually always directed toward something or away from it. The most striking instances are those of intense emotions and motivations. But attention in general may also serve as an example. In the case of vision, its direction tends to coincide with that of fixation; but this connection is by no means rigid. Actually, attention as a reference to particular things is experienced in its purest form when, while fixating a given point, we concentrate on one object after another in the periphery of the field.

Obviously, bipolar organization resembles situations in physics in which lines of force or directed processes refer one part of a field to another. In Gestalt Psychology the various directed attitudes of the self are not interpreted as "instincts" which reside in the self *per se*. Rather, they are regarded as *vectors*, which depend both upon the self and upon given objects, or more precisely, upon the relation which obtains at the time between the characteristics of the former and those of the latter. This is, of course, entirely in line with the way in which physical vectors between objects depend upon the "characteristics-in-relation" of these objects. The various states of the self which are here involved are to a high degree determined by physiological conditions within the organism. Studies of special appetites, of sexual behavior, and so forth, have made this perfectly clear. Even when the adult has well-established forms of conduct with regard to a particular vector, his habitual activities in this respect are not likely to appear unless conditions within the organism are favorable. On the other hand, under the most favorable internal conditions action may be strong even when quite adequate objects are not present. In spite of all this, it remains equally true that the strength of psychological vectors is also a function of the objects which are offered. The very best investigations in the field leave no doubt about this point.[7]

Our comparison of bipolar psychological organization with field action in physics is meant quite seriously. In fact, we are inclined to assume that when the self feels in one way or another referred to an object there actually is a field of force in the brain, which extends from the processes corresponding to the self to those corresponding to the object. The principle of isomorphism demands that in a given case the organization of experience and the underlying physiological facts have the same structure. Our hypothesis fulfills this postulate. In the next chapter we shall mention further facts which point in the same direction.

The play of psychological vectors, the sources from which they spring, the stresses which some parts of the field suffer under their influence, the various changes which are so caused, and eventually the cessation of vectors and stresses when certain results have been obtained—all this is the major study of psychology, as it is the major content of life. We cannot deal with these problems in the present chapter. For our immediate purposes we have, however, learned an important lesson in these paragraphs: when using the concept of organization, we have to apply it to the self as much as to other parts of the field.

---

[7] In the case of some vectors we do not know of particular physiological conditions which determine the interior side of bipolar organization. For instance, after being alone for long periods, most persons will feel a strong "drive" toward social contact, even with strangers. In some respects this vector operates in a way which is quite similar to the need for food, drink, or a mate. Could it be that prolonged lack of social contact and, as a consequence, of sufficiently interesting "objects" establishes a particular condition in the nervous system, and that, in a general way, this state is comparable to lack of food, water, and so forth?

We may now return to the discussion of memory and re-call. Has the fact of bipolar organization any consequences in this part of psychology? An obvious consequence is as follows. We have found that association means the survival of unitary traces when organized processes have occurred. Now, if the self forms particularly strong functional units with objects to which it is referred by vectors, then not only outside experiences but also this operation of vectors, togeth-er with corresponding states of the self and corresponding objects, must be expected to leave such traces in the nervous system. In actual fact, we do of course remember our for-mer attitudes when certain situations are again given, just as we can remember these situations when the attitudes once more arise.

But something more important follows from the fact that vectors operate in psychological situations, and that their op-eration has after-effects. The following experience is quite common: I have a task which, perhaps, I do not like, but which is urgent. In the course of the day, however, I find myself occupied with many other things. I talk with friends, I read a book, and so forth. But time and again something like a pressure makes itself felt in my interior, and upon ex-amination this pressure proves to issue from that task. The pressure amounts to a persistent tendency of the task to be recalled, and thus to enter the present field of action. Clear-ly, the phenomenon can mean only that the trace in ques-tion still contains a vector. It is in connection with such ob-servations that important experiments, first made by Lewin and Zeigarnik, can best be understood.[8]

The subject is given a sequence of simple tasks. He has for instance, to copy some lines from a book; to continue an ornament, the principle of which is given in a sample; to solve a simple mathematical problem; to name twelve towns, the names of which begin with the letter L, and so forth. In some cases he is allowed to finish his work, in others the ex-perimenter interrupts him before the work has been com-pleted. After a series of such tasks, only one half of which have been completed, the subject is asked in a casual way whether he can remember the tasks. The report which is given under these circumstances tends to be exceedingly in-teresting. The first tasks which the subject recalls usually be-long to those which have been interrupted, and generally many more of this class are remembered than of the other. When in one such experiment 32 subjects were examined, 26 recalled more interrupted tasks than completed ones; for all

[8] Cf. Psychol. Forsch., 9, 1927.

subjects taken together the superiority of the former tasks amounted to 90%. Care was taken to eliminate the influence of particular properties of the individual tasks: tasks which were interrupted with some subjects were completed in the case of just as many others. Of a series of 22 tasks, 17 were more frequently recalled after interruption than after completion. When the same experiment was repeated with other subjects, the superiority of recall for interrupted tasks was on the average again 90%. In a third experiment in which the subjects were children, it was 110%.

The explanation given by the authors points to the fact that, when trying to solve a problem, the subject is in a state of tension which refers to his work, and that this tension tends to persist until the solution is accomplished. If the work is interrupted before completion, the trace of the situation will contain the tension. And just as, during the work, the tension keeps the work going, it still operates in the same direction when, after interruption, the situation has become a trace. Since recall would be the first step toward completing the task, the outcome of the experiment is quite understandable.[9] If this explanation is correct, it must have verifiable consequences. I will mention only one. We cannot expect that under normal conditions tensions in traces will be preserved forever. It seems much more probable that they gradually disappear. This was actually found to be the case. When recall was examined after a delay of 24 hours, the superiority of the interrupted tasks had considerably decreased.

These facts refer to recall as depending upon the characteristics of the original situation. Another problem concerns the question to what extent recall is influenced by vectors given at the time of recall itself. In this connection, many experiments on memory are open to serious criticism. In Chapter VIII we have seen that when subjects actively memorize nonsense material, results cannot be interpreted as though they referred to automatically formed associations. Similarly, when in the test subjects are given a syllable with the explicit task to recall the next, results may differ widely from those which would be found in a test of spontaneous recall. In this case again, the common experimental procedure is far from fitting the classic law concerning association and recall by contiguity. If we wish to follow the obvious meaning of this law, we must give the subject a syllable without any in-

[9] In passing we may remark that at this point a certain relationship between findings of experimental psychology and Freudian concepts is to be acknowledged.

struction, and in a situation in which nothing makes him suspect that he is to recall an associated item. The question would be whether under such circumstances this item is spontaneously recalled. For the most part, experimenters do not proceed in this fashion; rather, they ask for recall. Now, just as a subject can be directed toward parts of his present field, he can also be referred to things which lie beyond this field, for example, to things and events of the past. This is an attitude which we commonly assume when we try to remember the name of a person or of a place. The attitude is bound to have an influence upon recall. But although in the law of association this factor is never mentioned, it is quite generally introduced in experiments which refer to the law. There are few investigations in which this inconsistency has been avoided.

Some time ago, many psychologists would have said that automatic recall is one of the principal motors of mental life and of behavior. At this point great caution seems now indicated. Experimental evidence is opposed to such a view. It has been shown that recall does not occur unless particular conditions are fulfilled. The most important work in this field has been done by Lewin.[10] Among his experiments there is one in which this problem was directly examined. He made his subjects learn pairs of syllables either in the usual fashion or by a new procedure which I cannot here describe. After a large number of repetitions, which were distributed over several days, the subjects were given single syllables with the instruction to read them, and then to wait. Occasionally, a first member of one of the previously presented pairs was shown. From the traditional point of view, one would expect the second member of such a pair to be immediately and automatically recalled. In general, however, this was by no means the case. Even when the instruction was changed to "tell me the first thing that occurs to you after reading each syllable," the result remained on the whole negative. It is interesting to examine the exceptions, in which recall of the associated syllable did occur. When a subject is instructed to wait passively, his attitude is not well defined. After some waiting, one attitude or another will almost always develop. For instance, if a syllable appears as familiar, there will be a tendency to identify and to examine the item in terms of the past. Now, as soon as the subjects

[10] *Psychol. Forsch., 1* and *2,* 1922. Somewhat similar experiments had been made before by Poppelreuter (*Zeitschr. f. Psychol., 61,* 1912), who was also the first to raise the criticism mentioned in the text.

began thus to be directed to the old context, recall occurred quite frequently. This was by no means spontaneous recall, since it would not have occurred without that particular tendency in the subject.

As a basis for recall, it does not suffice if the subject is just somehow directed to the present object. In Lewin's experiments a vector toward the item as belonging to events of the past was necessary; otherwise, recall did not occur. Similar facts can easily be observed in common life. For instance, well-known objects are strongly associated with their names. Nevertheless, when walking along a street, and being successively directed to a great many things, we are for the most part far from recalling their names. If the objection is raised that objects are associated with a great many things besides their names, and that all these various associations inhibit one another, this very argument admits that innumerable strong associations do not normally lead to corresponding recall. Unfortunately, this fact is constantly being ignored in empiristic theories. But when do associations actually become effective? Suppose that the reader is walking with me along a street, and that he has just accepted my statement concerning the lack of recall where the names of common objects are concerned. Chances are that immediately afterwards any number of known objects along the street will be given their names by the reader. This clearly proves that the mutual inhibition of several associations cannot be the main factor which prevents recall in such a situation. For, where are these inhibitions now? The decisive point is, of course, that our conversation has given the reader an attitude not only toward names as such, but also toward naming as a special form of recall. As a consequence, corresponding associations begin to operate at once.

These are revealing observations. For facts to be important, the laboratory environment is not strictly needed. We ought never to have believed that it is mainly spontaneous recall which keeps mental life and behavior going. At any moment we find ourselves occupied with some work, or some problem, or the subject matter of a conversation, and so forth. Under these conditions dynamic relations between the self and its objects tend to develop in a coherent and consistent fashion, which gives the terms "working," "solving our problem," "defending a thesis," and so on, their obvious meanings. Occasionally, this may seem to be a somewhat optimistic description of life. For instance, when I return to my manuscript, my working may not at once be quite coherent. At first even a faint noise may deflect me from my task, and one slight disturbance after another may have the same effect, until eventually a continuous flow of coherent operations is again established. But what about recall when this fortunate state of affairs again prevails? All the words and concepts which occur in my work are associated with other words, concepts and situations, most of them entirely unrelated to the present task. Such associations belong to very different epochs and interests in my life. Now, if each were automatically to cause the corresponding recall, my mental scene would soon become a chaos of incoherent items. Actually, the work continues as a self-contained chain of operations which tends to approach the end I have in mind in an orderly fashion. Even if in the beginning practically anything may deflect me from my course, soon I am so well directed that after a temporary distraction I find myself at once returning to the main road. Spontaneous recall of one thing or another may account for some such disturbances, just as do accidental noises; but it cannot explain the consistency with which the work itself proceeds. Compared with the vectors by which under such circumstances the self is referred to its task, spontaneous independent recall must be a factor of secondary importance.

This has been convincingly demonstrated in some of Lewin's experiments. I will describe his observations in a slightly simplified manner. To begin with, his subjects had again to learn pairs of nonsense syllables. Afterwards they were shown certain further syllables with the instruction that in each syllable the first letter was to be put in the place of the last, and vice versa. The result had to be pronounced, and the time which was required for the operation was measured. The reader will notice that here we have, in a simple form, precisely the situation which I have just described. The subject is working on a specific task. Now, if among the syllables the first one of a previously associated pair is given, corresponding recall would bring about a wrong reaction. Any tendency in this direction would at least inhibit the right response so that in such a case the time of the operation would be increased. On the other hand, if a syllable which is now presented is again the first member of a previously associated pair, but if at the same time the syllable which the subject is to form happens to be identical with the second member of that pair, any tendency to recall this syllable should facilitate the correct response, and the time of the operation should be shortened. To the author's surprise nothing of the kind was observed. There were no wrong responses corresponding to independent and spontaneous recall. Also, where any tendency of this kind would have inhibited the subject's response, the time of the operation was as a rule not raised above the average. Again, where such a tendency would have accelerated the response, the time of the operation was the same as in the case of control syllables.[11] Clearly, under the circumstances of these experiments vectors operate according to the accepted instruction, however strong the associations may be which connect parts of the given situation with extraneous material.

Dr. Lewin realizes that, to a degree, this fact can be explained in terms of a principle which has been discussed in the beginning of this chapter. We remember that if an A has been associated with a B, presentation of A will not lead to recall of B, in case the characteristics of A are no longer the same as they were when the association was formed. We also know that these characteristics will be altered if, although the stimuli corresponding to A are given again, A is part of a changed organization on the later occasion. Now, when during learning a syllable is read in a natural way, it is taken as a simple unit. But if the subject later obeys the instruction, according to which the first and the last letters of the syllable have to change places, he will apprehend the syllable in terms of this task. As a consequence, it will appear in a changed organization. For instance, its two crucial letters will now be seen as outstanding parts. This may suffice to make the syllable unable spontaneously to evoke its partner. The explanation seems to be corroborated by the observation that for the most part Lewin's subjects did not realize that known syllables were shown among the new ones. It will be advisable to make similar experiments with other materials, the characteristics of which are more specific than those of nonsense syllables, and less likely to be perceptibly changed in a new field. Neither Dr. Lewin nor I feel convinced that an entirely adequate theory of these facts is so far available. In some of Lewin's experiments the subject's attitude toward the syllables was virtually the same in the test as it was during the learning. None the less, there was no recall so long as the subjects tried to follow the instruction. At any rate, if objects do not generally cause recall of their names (*cf.* above pp. 181 ff.) this cannot always be explained by the assumption that the objects in question are sufficiently changed by their present environment.

In further experiments Lewin did succeed in causing recall, and also inhibitions, by previous associations which

---

[11] From these results it follows that we cannot, as N. Ach has proposed, measure conation by the strength of opposed associations which just balance the conation.

operated against a given task. This was achieved by giving a particular total situation. Suppose that in the case of several syllables recall leads to the same result as the procedure which the instruction actually demands. If under these circumstances the subject succumbs to the temptation to rely upon recall as the easier way, his attitude may inadvertently and completely become one of recalling. Once this direction has been established, the next syllable will tend to elicit its partner, even if in this case recall gives a result which is at odds with the task. In this fashion not only errors by recall but also inhibitions of the correct performance were at last actually demonstrated. This would almost seem to show that previously established associations cannot influence a given field unless a corresponding vector is at work.

I hesitate to accept this as a general thesis. To be sure, psychological theory has gone much too far in assuming that, when strong associations have been formed, recall will happen spontaneously, and irrespective of what the present situation may be. On the other hand, are we to suppose that during our whole lifetime no recall occurs unless it is supported by a vector in this directon? It may be advisable to hold our judgment *in suspenso* until future investigations have further clarified the issue.[12] In the meantime, precisely if vectors should prove to play a tremendous part in recall, the appearance and the disappearance of such vectors would become particularly important problems of psychology. Vectors arise and they persist, but they also change and disappear, for many reasons. It may safely be assumed that in the study of such events we shall find ourselves once more confronted with problems of recall. We do not know very much about recall of vectors as such. But the possibility that vectors which once have been active can again be elicited by recall deserves serious attention.

For this and for other reasons no exaggerated conclusions ought to be drawn from the preceding discussion. It is true, current theories of habit, association and recall do not realize how many conditions must be fulfilled if a well-organized situation is to be seriously affected by recall which

[12] Since this was first written, von Restorff and the present writer have made a special study of the conditions upon which recall depends (cf. *Psychol. Forsch., 21,* 1935). Our experiments seem to leave no doubt as to the actual occurrence of entirely spontaneous recall. But they have also confirmed the view that recall can be both facilitated and all but prevented by various conditions of organization.

does not fit this situation. It is also true that we are barely beginning to recognize the more essential problems in this field. Again, it is fortunately true that in millions of cases recall does not occur, although it ought to do so according to widely accepted views. Nevertheless, recall in general remains one of the most frequent and most important facts in mental life. If, in writing these pages, I am not continually deflected from my task by accidental recall, it is also a fact that I could not write a single word, if the effects of past training were not operative at each moment. All the time English words are arising from somewhere—by recall. In writing, my hand moves across the paper in forms which easily arise from a store of acquired skills. It would be ridiculous if we were to deny such facts and their relevance to the business of human living. The problem is merely to explain why, on the whole, recall remains restricted to instances in which it makes sense with regard to given total situations and their organic development.

This is a chapter of critical evaluation and of unsolved problems. Thus one more question may here be raised, a question which was many years ago discussed by von Kries, but which is still largely ignored in psychology.

Suppose that two items A and B have been associated. How does a process A—or A′ which is similar to A—bring about recall of B? In some textbooks the fact is given an easy explanation in terms of machine theory: At the time when the association was first formed, the process A traveled along a particular path in the nervous system, and at practically the same moment B was conducted along another path in the neighborhood. It is assumed that when A and B arrive in the brain, something happens to the fibers which connect the places of arrival so that these fibers are henceforth better conductors. From this point of view, recall will occur in the future when a new process A (or A′) travels along the path of the original A to the same final station. For this place is now especially well connected with the terminal station of the path of B. Taking the line of least resistance, the excitation will spread to the place of B and reactivate its trace. Everybody knows illustrations such as Fig. 24, which contains the whole functional scheme of the explanation. Clearly, this is a typical machine theory, in which recall does not depend upon the characteristics of the processes which have been associated. If A (or A′) causes recall of B, this happens only because processes of the type A are conducted along given paths to a place which is particularly well connected with another place, the place in which B is represented by a trace.

Fig. 24

For two reasons this scheme cannot explain recall: 1. If a process X, which is quite different from A, should happen to be conducted along the path of A, it would also take the line of least resistance, spread to the trace of B, and reactivate it, even though X has never occurred together with B. One cannot object that the explanation is to be applied only to such processes as have before occurred together. In the explanation itself such a restriction is not mentioned; nor can we deduce from the explanation why there should be a restriction. Thus the scheme does not explain what seems to be an essential condition of recall. 2. If a new process A (or A') happens to start from another point of the sense organ, and therefore to travel along another path, it will not be conducted to the place which has previously been connected with the place of the trace of B. As a consequence, there is no reason why under these circumstances the effects of A should spread to the place of B rather than to any other part of the brain. This means that in such a case A cannot cause recall of B, although A and B are associated. Actually, however, if at the time when the association was formed A started from one region of the retina, a like process A (or A') will generally cause recall of B, even though A now issues from another region on the retina. So much has been shown by E. Becher.[13] It seems to follow that the nature of A rather than its location in the nervous system is decisive for recall.

If it be argued that between the new path of A and the place of the trace of B there may also be some highly conductive path, I must answer that with this argument the original explanation is sacrificed. For now it is no longer pathways made highly conductive by association which are

[13] *Gehirn und Seele*, 1911. Lashley has done similar experiments with rats. I can confirm his findings. For anatomical reasons Becher's experiments still seem to me to be more conclusive than observations in animal psychology.

responsible for correct recall; rather, reference is made to fibers which are exceptionally good conductors for unknown reasons. And why should only A, which has actually been associated with B, be lucky enough to find such a convenient path from its new place to B? The same might just as well happen to any processes D, E, F, and so forth, which have never been associated with B, but might find by chance a good path to B, so that B would be recalled.

The weakness of the whole assumption lies in the fact that it makes recall depend upon the location of processes—as though a process of a given kind always traveled along the same route. But in the visual sector of the nervous system, for instance, a given process may be conducted along certain fibers at one time, and along other fibers at another time. Neither given colors nor given things and shapes have particular places to which their occurrence is restricted. As a matter of fact, in vision the correlation between various kinds of processes and particular locations is approximately zero. This excludes any possibility of explaining correct recall in terms of special anatomical places and connections.

Under these circumstances it seems natural to solve the problem in dynamic rather than in machine terms. The similarity between a new A (or A') and the old A must play a part in the fact that the new A will cause recall of B from virtually any place. Now we know that similarity is a factor which strongly favors pair-formation in perception, even when the members of the pair are not immediate neighbors. The same factor may favor a specific dynamic interrelation between a new process A and the trace of an old A. If this happens, the place of A will no longer play a decisive part in the process, and A will be able to cause recall of B, wherever A may be located.[14]

[14] The results of the investigation quoted in footnote 12, p. 184, are in complete agreement with this interpretation of recall.

X

INSIGHT

IF ASSOCIATION, HABIT AND RECALL are not the facts by which
the course of mental life is principally determined, what
other factors are more important? To this question there is
an answer, which is seldom clearly formulated, but nevertheless implicitly accepted by most people. We will call it the
layman's conviction. The layman believes that he often feels
directly why he wants to do certain things in a first situation,
and certain other things in a second. If he is right, the forces
which principally determine his mental trends and his actions are for the most part directly given in his experience.
Not all psychologists share this view. Many still believe that
people do one thing or another, because on a first occasion
certain nerve paths are particularly good conductors and, on
a second, certain other paths. From this point of view, persons in whom the right nerve paths happen to be best
conductors in a given situation ought to be grateful for their
luck. For, why should variations in the conductivity of pathways be regularly correlated with the characteristics and,
therefore, the demands of given situations?

The layman's belief springs from everyday experience.
The defenders of the other view seem to believe that their
view alone is compatible with the spirit of science. Whom are
we to follow? I confess that I prefer the layman's conviction.
In the treatment of sensory processes, the data of unprejudiced description have proved to be better guides than the
postulates of machine theory. In trusting the former, the
theorist of sensory function has now established contact
with the natural sciences in a way never attained by those
who thought that only the machine principle was scientifically
acceptable. After this lesson I feel justified in adopting the
view of common experience also with regard to the total field
in which the self as well as its objects plays a part. This means

that here again certain functional notions, which were allegedly prescribed by science, are now rejected. It is hoped that, just as in the realm of sensory function, confidence in direct observation will eventually be rewarded by a much better contact with science.

After specific things, groups, events, the self, and so forth, have been recognized as natural parts of the total field, we could make no worse mistake than that of falling back upon atomism at this level. We cannot be satisfied with discussing certain segregated entities in one chapter, others in a second chapter, the self in a third, and attitudes in a fourth. The ways of actual life do not coincide with those of neat enumeration and classification. If we bring together the members of one class, we are likely to cut in the process the live bonds of dynamic interrelations. Perhaps the most interesting dynamic relations occur between members of altogether different classes. In an anatomical museum, it may be instructive to see together hundreds of hearts; but in physiology, the function of a heart is related to that of a lung rather than to that of another heart. If experienced things are exhibited as one class, selves as a second, and attitudes as a third, one might be tempted to believe that, from the three classes, individual specimens could be chosen *ad libitum,* and then be put together so as to give a total field. Clearly, this assumption would be altogether childish; there are certain rules about the things, selves, and attitudes which can be parts of one field. To see this, one need not be a Gestalt Psychologist. But even the statement which has just been made misses a particularly important point, and is to this extent deceptive. Is it merely from empirical rules that we learn about the facts which can be included in one total field? The layman is convinced that there is more in this than a mere rule. He maintains that he feels how many of his attitudes grow from things and situations as *adequate* responses. Thus we return to our starting point. The kind of experience which the layman claims to have plays hardly any explicit part in the scientific psychology of our time. I feel that I must take sides with the layman; that, for once, he rather than our science is aware of a fundamental truth. For the layman's conviction is likely to become a major issue in the psychology, neurology and philosophy of the future.

In our next discussions, obvious and almost commonplace observations will have to be considered. It is not our fault that, to a deplorable degree, such observations have disappeared from psychology as a science, and must therefore be rediscovered. Later we shall see that precisely such obvious phases of human experience may express fundamental facts of brain dynamics.[1]

Occasionally, I find myself in the attitude of "admiring." But admiring never occurs as a fact by itself. It always is "of something." Nor is there ever the slightest doubt as to the object to which the attitude refers. For instance, last night in the concert hall, it was an *alto* voice which sounded "admirably" serious, calm and confident. Unquestionably, this was the object of my admiration—not the nose of my neighbor, nor the back of the conductor, nor any of the thousands of other objects and events which I had before me. Admiration, like other attitudes, has a direction. In my example, it was directed toward the person from whom the singing came. Now, do I mean by this that the admiration merely extended to that person and stopped there, as though it were comparable to a long stick which extended between me and that place? If this were the case, the admiration would be no more than a third thing between two others, and a causal relation between the voice and the admiration could only be hypothetically assumed. Possibly, this relation could also be verified in appropriate investigations; but surely, it could not be directly experienced. Actually, of course, in this situation I did directly experience, first, that my admiration was related to the singing rather than to any other thing, and secondly, that admiration was the natural answer to such a way of singing. As a consequence, I needed no indirect criteria, no scientific investigations, no coefficients of correlation, in order to know about the connection between the singing and my admiration. As a matter of fact, my experience told me more than any scientific induction could. For induction is silent as to the nature of the functional relation which it predicates, while in the present example a particular fact of psychological causation was directly experienced as an understandable relationship.

Some weeks ago I saw my little child smiling for the first time, and I was charmed. How did I know that my feeling was concerned with the smile? If my experiences represented an aggregate of feelings, events and things, some of them directed and some not, but all distributed in a certain way, merely as a consequence of histological circumstances, then I could only make guesses about possible functional relations among the various components of the aggregate. Potentially, a change of any component might be followed by

[1] The present discussions are, of course, closely related to the concept of bipolar organization as explained in Chapter IX.

any kind of change in any other part; and the only way in which the actual functional connection could be discovered would be that of varying conditions systematically, until certain possibilities are eliminated, and others statistically verified. In the present case, for instance, only frequent concomitance of a smile on a child's face with the experience of being charmed would allow me to assume that there probably is some connection between the two. Even so, I could not be quite sure until all other factors have been sufficiently varied and proved to be irrelevant. To what extremes have we come in psychology, if it is necessary seriously to discuss such a thesis. In my particular experience, one side of the child's face happens to look a little darker because of a shadow. According to the strange view which we are now considering, I might have referred my feeling to this shadow rather than to the child's smile. Such a wrong hypothesis could have been prevented only by a sufficient number of opposed instances.

After a long walk, on a hot summer day, I drink a glass of cold beer. While I do so, I feel coolness and a characteristic taste in my mouth. Also there is great enjoyment. Now, is it necessary for me gradually to learn that in such a situation the enjoyment refers to the coolness and the taste? That it has nothing to do with the spider which I see on the wall, or with the size of the chair before me? Surely, no such learning is needed. I am no more directly aware of my enjoyment as such, and of the touch and the taste by themselves, than I am of the fact that the enjoyment refers to just this coolness and taste. My pleasure is also felt to be an adequate reaction to these facts. Between the pleasure and its sensory basis I experience what is called in German their *"Verständlicher Zusammenhang,"* which may be expressed in English as "understandable relationship."

The same may be said of many cases in which the attitude of the subject is *negative.* For two weeks I have been busy carefully preparing a set of instruments for certain experiments. This morning I find them completely disarranged, and feel angry. If now I were to say: here is the window, there the table, in one corner the instruments, in another a chair, and near the door myself in an attitude of anger—would this enumeration be an adequate description of the situation? Most certainly, it would not. I am sure that, for instance, the door has no connection whatever with my anger. On discovering the disturbed arrangement, I know immediately that it is this fact which makes me angry. And again, not only is this particular reference inherent in my experience; the anger is also felt to be natural under the circumstances.

One beautiful night in Tenerife, when I was calmly working at my desk, I was suddenly frightened as I had never
before been frightened. All at once the house was vio-
lently rattling and shaking—my first experience of an earth-
quake. Could there be any question as to the fact that it was
this sudden upheaval rather than anything else which frightened me? Obviously not. Once more the emotion was felt as
caused by a particular experience. Quite generally, we
need not gradually learn that unexpected intense events are
followed by fright, as though *a priori* a friendly face or the
smell of a rose might just as well be followed by fright. When
fright suddenly overtakes us, it is always felt to spring from
particular facts.

After sitting for half an hour in a restaurant which is full
of smoke and talk, I feel restless and ready to leave. Clearly,
this restlessness refers to the given situation. I know about
the reference not because of a rule discovered in previous
life, according to which in my case such conditions have
regularly been followed by a state of restlessness; rather, I
experience directly, *hic et nunc,* how these surroundings disturb and confuse me. Such conditions I feel to have this
effect necessarily; the causal connection is part of my experience.

Two days ago, I was very much depressed, because I
could not hit upon a satisfactory presentation of what I conceived to be the main point of this chapter. Under these circumstances, were there two separate facts, the state of depression as such, and besides a certain intellectual situation?
And could a possible connection between the two be assumed only on the basis of statistical evidence? Such questions sound most artificial. When I was trying to solve my
problem, I clearly felt my depression as based upon that difficulty. Also, precisely this depression was felt to be adequate
in view of such a situation.

If in all these examples my inner reactions are experienced
as following from the nature of given situations, in certain
other instances events in the environment are felt to follow
from my attitudes. For example, I can look at Fig. 1 (p. 83)
in a passive way. Under these circumstances I see the pattern as two groups of dots. But if, while I look, something
makes me think of oblique lines, the figure is likely to be
transformed into three pairs of dots, each of which forms
a kind of oblique line from a lower dot to the right to a dot
higher up to the left. If this transformation really occurs, it
is felt to originate in my particular mental attitude at the
time. Suppose that I scratch my head or hum a tune while in
Fig. 1 the organization changes. Such activities are surely not

felt to have any connection with the transformation.

Or take this instance. What is the name of that town on the Santa Fe Railroad? Here it comes. When I am searching for a name, this operation does not occur as a thing apart; nor does the place in which the forgotten name must be hidden constitute a thing by itself. Rather, the searching is felt to be directed toward the place of the hidden name. When eventually the name emerges, this fact is felt to be achieved by the stress of the searching. Now, I have not gradually learned that in such a situation searching *per se* happens to be related to the emergence of a name. I have also not gradually learned that in such situations a noise outdoors is an irrelevant fact.

I hold my arm horizontally for a while. Very soon the arm will not remain in this position unless I make a special effort. At the time, I experience, besides this effort, the blue sky, a lark's song, the arm as a visual thing, a smell of moist ground. There is also a particular feeling in the lifted arm, a feeling which grows more intense as the minutes go by, something like a downward pull in the arm. Geometrically or logically, all these experiences allow of many different combinations in pairs. My effort could be related to the lark's song, to the smell, to the color of the lifted hand and to the blue of the sky. Actually, however, my effort is not something apart that could be equally well related to any of these experiences. Rather, it is felt to keep the arm horizontal against that downward pull. The nature of the pull is felt as requiring precisely such an effort, if the arm is to remain in its position; and the nature of the effort is experienced as compensating for just this pull. If somebody should describe the situation most thoroughly in terms of local data, with their places, with their directions (if they have any), with their locations in time, and even with their relations as to place, distance, succession or simultaneity, similarity, and so on— he would still never mention the main characteristic of the situation, which is the dynamic relationship between some of its parts.

In discussing a somewhat similar case, David Hume emphatically defended the opposite view. I do not know how my arm is lifted, he said, when I wish to raise it. There can be no more than a mere succession in time, since I do not know the nature of the mechanism which actually raises the arm. This is a strange argument. It is entirely foreign to the analysis of pure experience which Hume had promised to give. In this connection, when we talk about the arm, we must, of course, take it as an experienced thing, not as a physical object which moves in physical space. Whatever the innervations and contractions of the muscles may be in this case, a phenomenological analysis has here to deal with an intention, on the one hand, and with an experienced movement of the experienced arm, on the other hand. The problem is whether the intention is felt to be as extraneous to the arm's movement as is the color of a cloud or the brown of the arm's skin in the same situation. At this point the great philosopher seems to have slipped, and inadvertently to have made use of a logical trick. In doing so, he has obscured this issue for whole generations.

In order further to clarify the import of the present discussion, I will now consider an objection which I derive from an observation of my own. One might say that, after all, such experiences of "depending upon," "being the natural outcome of," "being based upon," and so forth, do not actually prove that the connections in question are necessary. For instance, many years ago I used to be greatly impressed by the overture to *Tristan and Isolde*, and at that time I should have described my enjoyment as the direct and understandable outgrowth of just this kind of music. I cannot possibly say, however, that my reaction to Wagner's overture is still the same. Frankly, I am tired of it. I could almost go so far as to say that now dislike appears to me to be a perfectly natural response to the music. Now, does this change really affect the account which I have given of my earlier reactions? We can easily show that there is no contradiction whatsoever. It is quite true, in exactly the same physical situation, exposed to precisely the same sound waves, a given person may today feel that being delighted is the only adequate response, and yet some time later be disgusted when hearing the same composition. A simple way to achieve such an alteration consists in giving people the same sequence of sounds a few hundred times each day.[2] But what happens under these circumstances? We must distinguish between melodies as physical facts and melodies as auditory experiences. After a few hundred repetitions, most melodies have, as experiences, no longer the same characteristics as they had in the beginning. They now sound empty and stale. Repetition affects them in the same way as it affects even the best anecdotes and jokes. It follows that changes of responses when objective conditions are constant are entirely compatible with our main thesis. This thesis refers to understandable relations between experienced facts and experienced inner responses. As soon as, with the same stimuli, the experienced material changes, we can no longer expect the same responses to appear as natural and adequate. On the contrary, it would make

[2] K. Lewin and A. Karsten, *Psychol. Forsch.*, 10, 1927.

us suspect our thesis, if under such circumstances the responses remained the same.

There is a further reason why music which I enjoyed many years ago, may now no longer please me: in the meantime *I* have changed a great deal. How can we expect that in a changed self the effects of a given composition will be the same as though the self had not changed? Effects depend not only upon given causes but also upon the characteristics of the system in which the effects take place. This holds for experienced causation just as it does for causation in physics.

Quite generally, however, I must again insist that awareness of causal relations in the psychological field must be distinguished from statements as to the more or less regular coexistence and concomitance of psychological facts. A given experience of the former kind has its observational import quite irrespective of what may happen in other instances. Just as I can be perfectly sure that I now see a certain flower as red, though, if I should later become color-blind, it would look gray—so a given experience of causal dependence must be accepted as such, even if further experiences in similar situations do not exhibit the same characteristic.

It is an old rule in science that nothing makes positive statements more acceptable than a frank acknowledgment of instances to which the statements do not apply. I do not wish to deny that in countless cases we are very far from experiencing how one fact is brought about by others. Let a subject observe a movement which repeats itself in a given part of the visual field. When afterwards he sees the negative after-image of the movement, it will surprise him—provided that this is his first contact with the phenomenon. His surprise proves that the after-image is brought about by conditions of which he is entirely unaware, or which are not felt to be causally responsible for this effect. Again, many subjects will be greatly surprised when after prolonged fixation of the center of Fig. 8 (p. 101) a new shape suddenly appears before them. They do not feel why just this transformation occurs. Once I had a physicist as a subject in a certain experiment with this pattern. He was asked to signal all the transformations one way or the other which occurred while he fixated Fig. 8. In this experiment the pattern consisted of bright lines in an otherwise completely dark room. The effect was that when the observations were completed the physicist asked me how I had managed to change "the objects" so quickly and so often, although my place had been at a distance of several yards, and I did not seem to have moved at all. He did not in the least suspect that events in his own organism were alone responsible for the transformations.

Everybody knows that so-called moods may change without our being aware of the causes. Just as we may suddenly feel that we have caught a cold without realizing where and when, so we sometimes feel irritable, when no cause for this mood is experienced. To be sure, the irritation tends soon to find something on which it can discharge itself, and then the something in question will probably appear as an adequate object. But before this happens, we can do no more than guess what the hidden cause of the mood may be; for at first the mood has no experienced reference to any particular object. Actually, some meteorological condition which affects our organism, or disturbed digestion, may be responsible. We are not directly aware of such influences.

From this example two lessons may be derived. In the first place, it corroborates the view that, while dynamic relations may be experienced, effects may also be conspicuous when no experience points at their causes. The second lesson is that both kinds of determination may be united in a single event. For when we are in an irritable mood, and now discover something that more or less fits this inner situation, the object in question will at once appear as an entirely adequate cause for intense anger. And yet, our reaction may be greatly exaggerated by the hidden causes which have made us irritable long before this occasion.[3]

I do not see, however, that the fact of hidden determination in some cases can serve as an argument against experienced causation in others. In the case of cholera and plague, certain germs are known to be the principal causes of the diseases. In diabetes this is not the case. Would anybody use

[3] At this point a remark about psychoanalysis seems indicated. According to the analysts, people often do not know at all why they behave in one way or another. Their actual motivations may be quite different from those which, they believe, are operating. Now, we can admit that some such instances occur in normal life, and that there may be many more under pathological conditions. I doubt, however, whether observations of this kind justify the general pessimism which is so often derived from them. We have no reason to suspect innumerable experiences in which the layman is clearly aware of his motivations. To this I should like to add that we ought to distinguish between two things: in some cases the Freudians may be right, while in others people merely fail to *recognize* their inner states. I am inclined to believe that many observations which the Freudians interpret in their fashion are actually instances in which recognition does not occur. Recognition, which operates with perfect ease in perception, is surprisingly sluggish in the case of inner processes. Incidentally, this is true whether or not the inner facts in question *deserve* to remain unrecognized.

this "negative instance" as an argument against bacteriology? We may therefore calmly accept a similar dualism in psychological causation.

In spite of all our examples, however, is not experienced causation often simply a product of learning? If, in my mail, the address on an envelope is in a certain handwriting, the fact makes me happy, whereas, if I find a certain other handwriting in the mail, precisely the opposite is true. Let us ignore the graphological and aesthetic phases of the situation, and suppose that it is chiefly my acquaintance with the writers which makes one handwriting look attractive and the other disagreeable. In both cases I feel that my responses are sensible in view of the given objects. Nevertheless, these responses seem to have been learned. The same words and letters would not be felt as being adequate causes of my reactions if no corresponding "conditioning" had occurred. For a moment, this observation may make us suspicious of many statements in the preceding paragraphs. Actually, however, such facts are by no means at odds with our main argument. In the present example, a certain handwriting has become imbued with the friendly experiences which I have had with a certain person, and another with the unpleasant facts for which a different person has been responsible. As these persons themselves, when present, would arouse corresponding responses, so their handwritings do now; because they are charged with one meaning or the other. It is a mistake to believe that in such instances emotional responses have gradually become connected with the handwritings. Rather, the connection which has actually occurred consists in the fact that the visual appearance of certain words and letters, written in one way or the other, has become saturated with positive or negative experiences of the past. Being so saturated, the handwritings now are adequate causes of the emotional responses which I have described. It is not astonishing that they are felt to be such causes.

At this point a further remark seems to be indicated. When I am thirsty, I am inclined to think of a refreshing drink. This object of my thinking is, of course, brought into the field by recall. It is clear, I hope, that this fact has no relevance to our present problem. However the recall may have been brought about, once the thought of the drink is part of the field, this object is felt to be a most adequate cause for my desire, and the desire to be directly understandable in view of such an object. The mere fact that something has entered the field by a process of recall is irrelevant to the question in what kind of relation this object is experienced within the field. This must be emphasized, because we are so accustomed to explanations in terms of learning, habit, recall, and so forth, that once a situation is shown to owe *something* to the past and to recall we tend to give up further thinking. And yet, even if all parts of a situation owed their presence to processes of recall we should still have to ask this question: Are any of these experiences now felt to be causally related?

We have returned to the layman's conviction. Psychology and the epistemology of science show a tendency either to ignore this view or to attack it as though it implied a serious danger. David Hume has often been mentioned as the man who is responsible for the hostility. But it seems to me that this great figure in the history of human thought is only the most eminent representative of a trend which has also been present in Greece, more than two thousand years ago, and which springs from a strong need for clearness.[4]

There is a particular sort of clearness which the layman's conviction and my statements in this chapter do not fit too well. This ideal of clarity would be achieved if the world could be conceived as an enormous number of equal and unequal pieces, which have merely formal relations as to position in time and space, to similarity, etc. That this is a true picture of experience was tacitly taken for granted in Hume's famous analysis of causation, so that eventually he did not prove more than he had implicitly presupposed from the outset. He had no difficulty in gathering examples which seemed to corroborate his thesis that causation is never experienced; because in a great many cases we really do not feel at all how one thing is determined by others. And since he did not discuss other cases, it appeared to many that the truth of his view had been demonstrated beyond all argumentation. It seems to be common belief that Hume was the greatest Empiricist of all time. But in reducing the world of experience to pieces among which only formal relations obtain, he was entirely dominated by certain intellectual premises and ideals. He was great, but he was not in a strict sense an Empiricist. Empiricists do not, or ought not to, take so much for granted.

In his Radical Empiricism William James laid great stress upon the fact that "the relations between things, conjunctive as well as disjunctive, are just as much matters of direct particular experience, neither more so nor less so, than the things themselves."[5] As I see it, this view is an obstacle in our

[4] For instance, in some of Plato's discussions about the characteristics of the truly real world the same tendency is unmistakably present.

[5] *The Meaning of Truth,* Preface.

way rather than an aid. Neither is it helpful when James, though attacking atomism in the treatment of experience, clearly fails to recognize what we have called organization (Ch. V). In a way, namely, in a purely logical sense, relations can be considered among all parts and fractions of a given field—if we are interested in this possibility. But such ubiquitous relations are entirely unfit to make us understand why in a given case a particular attitude is experienced as arising "because of" an equally particular event or object in the field. In a given situation this is, for the most part, a unique relation. And while this dynamic relation is actually experienced, the host of formal relations to which James refers is generally not at all experienced. Moreover, such formal relations obtain, of course, also between a given attitude and any other item in the field. Under these circumstances, it seems more important to realize the great difference between relations in these two meanings of the word than to emphasize that the formal type can be predicated everywhere.

It is only fair to mention that in some places James approaches our problem from another side, as when he writes about our "sustaining a felt purpose against felt obstacles, and overcoming or being overcome";[6] also where in his description "the experiencer feels the tendency, the obstacle, the will, the strain, the triumph, or the passive giving up, just as he feels the time, the space, the swiftness or intensity, the movement, the weight and color, the pain and pleasure, the complexity, or whatever remaining characters the situation may involve." [7] This is something quite unlike a network of formal relations which spread indifferently all across the field. The stress is not placed precisely where I have tried to place it; but there is no doubt that at times William James was most anxious to give felt determination its share in the description of experience.[8]

When we discussed purely sensory organization we had no particular opportunity to introduce the concept of experienced determination, because the simpler effects of sensory organization do not for the most part tell us much about the way in which they are brought about. I do not maintain that sensory fields are devoid of experienced causal connections. For instance, the perceptual situations given in paintings are likely to contain convincing examples of such dynam-

[6] *Some Problems of Philosophy*, p. 213.
[7] *A Pluralistic Universe*, p. 376.
[8] Since James' time similar views have been defended by several authors whose names will be found in the bibliography at the end of this chapter.

ic relations, and the same holds for many perceptual situations in common life (*cf*. Ch. VII). It remains nevertheless true that the most intense experiences of this kind occur in the total field, and refer to dynamic relations between the self and certain objects. Under these circumstances, it seems advisable to restrict the next discussions also to causal relations in which one of the terms is the self.

The direct awareness of determination as described in the preceding paragraphs may also be called *insight*. When I once used this expression in a description of the intelligent behavior of apes,[9] an unfortunate misunderstanding was, it seems, not entirely prevented. Sometimes the animals were found to be capable of achievements which we had not expected to occur below the human level. It was then stated that such accomplishments clearly involved insight. Apparently, some readers interpreted this formulation as though it referred to a mysterious mental agent or faculty which was made responsible for the apes' behavior. Actually, nothing of this sort was intended when I wrote my report. It is to be hoped that no such misunderstanding will arise from the present discussion. Intentionally, the concept of insight has now been introduced on the basis of entirely common and simple facts. No question of inventions or other outstanding intellectual achievements is here involved, and, far from referring to a mental faculty, the concept is used in a strictly descriptive fashion. I will not deny that, from a philosophical point of view, it makes all the difference in the world whether or not the determination of certain experiences can itself be experienced. But for the moment it appears to me more essential that the concept as such be clearly understood than that such further consequences be at once fully realized. I have also tried to make it quite clear that, taken in its basic sense, the term insight refers to experienced dynamics in the emotional and motivational fields no less than to experienced determination in intellectual situations.

Several times I have remarked that in common experience nothing can be more obvious than insight, i.e., awareness of determination as described in this chapter. Scarcely a single total field lacks this characteristic entirely. And yet, among the psychologists only a small minority seems fully to realize that this is one of the most important psychological concepts. It is true, many will express themselves in terms which imply that insight occurs in their subjects' or their own experiences. It may be, however, that this happens only because the layman's conviction is embodied in certain forms

[9] *The Mentality of Apes.* 1925.

of language, which the authors use without being clearly aware of the implications. As a result, insight does not occur among the concepts which they actually use in their theories. For to make use of the language of the layman is not the same thing as to see how much good psychology this language contains. There are also those to whom Hume's analysis of experience and the concepts of the nineteenth century represent a framework which will never be seriously affected by further developments. In their eyes, the content of this chapter must, of course, be sheer mysticism. Suppose that a representative of this group is riding in a bus in which he has to stand, because it is crowded. At a certain moment a heavy man chooses the feet of our Humean as a good place to stand on. As a matter of principle, the Humean would have no way of deciding whether the pretty face of a girl in the bus or the man's conduct is the cause of the anger which he, the Humean, now feels. He might find out by experimentation and induction, or he may have learned to connect such things correctly in the past. But if his theoretical convictions are right, he could not possibly tell without such indirect evidence.

Do Behaviorists belong to this class? Most probably they would decline to enlist in either class, because so far our problem seems restricted to the field of experiences, of which they refuse to take any account. But, actually, it does not matter. What Behaviorists call scientific procedure is under all circumstances the inductive technique, which alone is admitted by the strict Humeans.

Our discussion can, however, be transferred from the field of experience to that of brain physiology. It will be remembered that in Chapter II we decided to use experience as an indicator of the processes which mediate between outside conditions and the overt behavior of the organism. This procedure was based on the principle of isomorphism, i.e., the thesis that our experiences and the processes which underlie these experiences have the same structure. Thus we assumed that when the visual field exhibits a thing as a detached entity, the corresponding process in the brain is relatively segregated from surrounding processes. In another chapter we found that, for the sake of consistency, we had to postulate particular processes in the brain which underlie our experience of the self in its various states. Now, just as in experience the self is surrounded by objects, so the processes which correspond to the self must occur in the midst of processes which are the correlates of these objects. But we have experiences not only of objects around us, and of the self with its various states, but also of psychological causation, in which states of the self are felt to be determined by parts of the environment, or occasionally events in the environment by activities of the self. From our point of view, there is only one way in which such facts of experienced determination can be represented in the brain: we have to make use of what the scientist calls *field physics*. In other words, when the self is felt to respond to the characteristics of a certain object, then in the brain the processes underlying the experienced self must be affected by the processes which correspond to the object. More particularly, the specific characteristics of the processes corresponding to the object must somehow be represented in the area in which the processes underlying the self occur, and under the influence of this "field" the processes corresponding to the self must change in one way or another. Conversely, a particular attitude of the self with regard to an object must have a physiological counterpart which extends to the locus where this object is physiologically represented, so that the process corresponding to the object can change under the influence of the self's field. In the former case, the changed state of the self would not exist independently; rather, it would be established and maintained by the field of the object. In the latter case, the same would be true of the change in the object which would be caused and maintained by the field of the self. If we have any confidence that basic functional concepts of physics are applicable to brain dynamics, this view of the situation represents the simplest way in which such hopes can be realized.

To make this point perfectly clear, I will return to one of our former examples. When, on a hot day, I enjoy a cool drink, my pleasure is felt to refer to the taste of the drink and my thirst, but not, for instance, to the spider on the wall, nor to the size of a chair before me, nor to thousands of other things in my environment. In the brain, more particularly in a part of the brain in which certain "self-processes" occur, there is under these circumstances a particular process B, the process which underlies my experience of thirst. Now, when I begin to drink, another process A, which corresponds to the coolness and the taste of the drink, develops precisely in the part in which before only the process corresponding to my thirst took place. In terms of the present theory, A at once begins to exert an influence upon B, an influence which depends upon the characteristics of A in their relation to those of B. The change which is thus established makes itself felt as pleasure. This change, I assume, is determined by A just as directly as the temperature of a surface is determined by the rays of light which fall upon it, or as the growth of a dwindling fire is determined by a fresh supply of oxygen. In other words, the taste of the drink and my pleasure are not experienced as separate facts, but the latter as caused by the former, because the corresponding processes in the brain are causally related in precisely this fashion. Insight as here defined is no more than an expression of this fact. Naturally, the same interpretation must be given in instances in which, conversely, a particular attitude of the self is felt to modify an object.

Once it is formulated, the present theory is so simple that it may almost appear as banal. But this impression disappears as soon as we remember how the same situation would be treated according to now accepted ideas. Once more machine theory and dynamic theory appear in sharp contrast. Neither in reflexes nor in conditioned reactions, nor even in associations (as usually conceived) have the qualitative characteristics of a process any influence beyond the locus of this process. The effects of events in one part of the brain upon the situation in other parts are always mediated by sufficiently conductive pathways. There is first a process A as such, then transmission of nerve impulses along certain paths as a second event, and eventually an effect in a place B, a third fact, which is brought about by those impulses rather than by the particular nature of A. With the same A as a starting point, if another path happened to be a better conductor, a different process C rather than B would be thrown into action. The occurrence of A affects B only because of historical conditions as given at the time when A is active. Suppose we could change the arrangement of nerve fibers a bit. Perhaps, if this were done in the right fashion, a cool drink would make a thirsty man disgusted and angry.

It may be that this physiological interpretation has never been expressly formulated. If so, it ought to have been done; because no other interpretation can be derived from the concepts which are now widely accepted in neurology and psychology. Why is the theory of direct field action never considered? Why, if we prefer to deal with psychological terms, is insight as a fundamental and commonplace fact of mental life mentioned only by a few? Why do we discuss as many psychological problems as we possibly can as though machine concepts were the only ones acceptable in science? I do no more than derive the consequences of this situation. The sharper we contrast machine and field theories the more hope can we have for the future of our science.[10]

[10] The interpretation of insight in terms of field action is at odds not only with current neurological views. It also suggests

I do not believe that our description of certain experiences in the total field has so far been quite complete. It is quite true that emotional reactions are commonly referred to their causes in just this fashion. But our very examples tell us that more is involved than mere emotions. Take the restlessness which overcomes a man who for some time has been sitting in an overcrowded, noisy restaurant. He has not only a feeling of strong dislike of his environment, but is also anxious to leave. In other words, he wants to move away from what he feels to be the cause of the trouble. Moreover, in his experience this impulse toward a certain action follows from the given situation just as directly as does his displeasure. Thus the man has insight both in emotional and in motivational causation.

Our life is full of trivial instances of this kind; but it is equally obvious that impulses toward the most important actions may also arise in a way which we can thoroughly understand. The *how* and the *why* of such actions are often no more hidden than is the way in which our feelings are aroused. Here I will consider only examples which belong to the more simple variety.

On a beautiful morning I am sitting quite contentedly in full sunlight. But after a while I feel too hot; at the same time a tendency to move away from my present place arises. A place in the shadow of a tree in the neighborhood looks pleasant; and immediately the impulse away from the sunlight becomes a tendency toward the shadow. Just as at first the characteristics of one place made me inclined to move away from it, so now the properties of another arouse an impulse of approach. In both cases there is insight: we

that certain theses which are widely held by philosophers of science cannot be entirely correct. According to these authors, all concepts in science which imply causation are merely auxiliary concepts, and ought not to be used in a strictly empirical description of the physical world. Observation in physics, these authors say, offers no experience that corresponds to causal nexus. If this were true, the concepts "force" and "field" would have a place in science only as convenient mathematical tools, and as a consequence we could not correlate our experience of direct inner determination with field action in the brain. In discussing this problem, we have to realize that the scientists do not actually disprove causal nexus in physics; they merely state that observation as now used in science is never observation of causal nexus as such. In other words, so far as science is concerned, the concepts of causation, force, and field remain nondescript—from which it follows that any evidence of a different sort may serve to give such concepts a meaning.

feel how in the first case a certain tendency develops from the nature of the given situation, and then, how another part of the field further determines the direction of the impulse. The reader will remember that for our present problem it is entirely irrelevant whether the thermic properties of the shadow are known to us by previous learning or in a more direct way.[11]

A similar description may be given in the case of fright. When a sudden event is felt to cause fright, a very strong impulse to move away from the event arises at the same time. And again, this tendency to increase the distance between the frightening fact and the self is experienced as being the direct outcome of this fact just as the fright itself is. We noticed before how, in Watson's description of a child's behavior, the overt act of withdrawing from an uncanny object is not only a datum in the observer's visual field, but also a picture of what happens in the child's own experience.[12] Does anyone believe that the child feels his fear of the object, and the impulse to withdraw his hand, as two unrelated experiences? Or that, in his fear, the child might just as well feel a tendency to embrace or to swallow the disturbing object? A Humean would have to insist that this is the case. As to the fact that in this instance the object has become dangerous only through previous learning, I will once more remark that the way in which a certain characteristic becomes part of the field has no relevance to the rôle which it plays in this field (cf. p. 197).

Just as an impulse of withdrawal arises directly from certain situations, so the opposite tendency is felt to be adequate in other situations. I have mentioned the case in which a shadow attracts a person who has for some time been

[11] I do not forget that subordinate parts of our organisim show reactions which are in a way similar to those here described, and yet belong to the reflex type of movement. Stimulated by a prick, the foot will be withdrawn by a reflex. But from such facts no objection can be derived against our description of other facts. In some of its activities the organism undoubtedly resembles a most practical machine; at the same time in others, namely those in which the self is involved, experienced causation and corresponding field dynamics may play the most decisive part. There is no reason why both kinds of function should not occur in the same system.

[12] Incidentally, here we have an instance of organized events in *perception* which tell us something about the causal relation between certain parts of the field (cf. p. 200). At least the reference of the withdrawal to a particular object was obvious in Watson's observation.

exposed to the sun. Similar instances are so frequent that it seems almost superfluous to give special examples. The child whom Watson saw reaching for an animal's head undoubtedly felt "attracted" by that interesting object. When in Spain the toreador has acted in a particularly skillful and bold fashion, the admiration of the crowd often drives them so strongly in their hero's direction that, unable to enter the arena themselves, they bend forward, and reach toward him as far as possible. Sometimes the tension becomes so great that hats, handkerchiefs, and the like, are thrown down in the direction of the impulse. Have these people gradually been conditioned to connect approach rather than other tendencies with admiration—as though frowning or shaking the left leg could equally well have been coupled with admiration by proper conditioning? Sometimes I feel that, whether we are Introspectionists, Behaviorists, or whatever else, the chief dividing line among contemporary psychologists would separate those who acknowledge direct determination as explained in this chapter from those who admit only "connections" in the sense of machine theory.

As a last example I choose a simple practical situation. For some purpose I wish to break a wooden board. I press against it, and while I feel my effort against the resistance of the board, I also see and feel how the board yields in the direction of the pressure. Are we really to believe Hume when he maintains that in my experience the yielding of the board is as unrelated to my effort as the color of the board or, say, the movement of a cloud? Actually, I feel how the board yields under my pressure just as I feel myself yielding when a friend of mine and I measure our strength by pressing hard against each other's shoulders, and I lose the battle. Moreover, once the board begins to yield, I immediately feel a tendency to increase the pressure, and again this new tendency is experienced as following from the change in the board's resistance.

What is the common content of these examples? Between certain facts or events in our environment and our responses we experience not only formal relations but also specific causal relationships. Imagine the following were to happen as a mere sequence: first, I feel uncomfortable near a hot radiator (but I do not know, until I gradually learn, that my discomfort refers to the heat); secondly, as a further experience, entirely unrelated to the first, I feel an impulse to move in a certain direction (but I do not know, until I learn, that this direction means "away from the heat"); and, thirdly, again as an unrelated fact, I find myself moving in a direction which actually increases the distance between the radiator and me (though I do not know, until I learn, that the direction of this movement has any reference to that object, or to the tendency which has been experienced a moment before). I find it almost impossible to enumerate these experiences in a way from which causal references are as entirely absent as they would be if the Humeans were right. Human language, with its implications and references which all the time point from one word or sentence to another, must be a most annoying instrument to any follower of David Hume. As we read the words of the preceding sentences, insight is at once built up, however we may try to prevent its intrusion. What I want to express is, of course, that according to Hume no experience can ever require that another happen. And yet, it seems that precisely this is what certain experiences always do.

Now that the concept of insight has been applied to experienced motor tendencies and to actual movements, I will once more return to the functional concepts which prevail in our time, and thus make the dynamic or field view clearer by contrast. Consider the machine theory in its strictest form. According to this theory, the sequence: feeling hot—feeling a tendency toward moving in a certain direction—actually moving in this direction, is brought about by the way in which centers of the brain are connected by pathways. Feeling hot has a cortical correlate somewhere in the brain. From this point particularly well conducting fibers lead to another place, the excitation of which is accompanied by a tendency to move in a certain direction. This place again is connected by excellent pathways with a further place, the place in which actual innervations of certain muscles start. Evolution has done an admirable job in establishing these nervous connections. They are such that, as a matter of fact, the second link in the chain is a tendency to move away from the place of the heat, rather than to sneer or to swing one's arms back and forth. Similarly, the connection with the right center of innervation happens to be properly arranged. For while this connection actually makes us move away from the heat, with other connections we might, in the same situation, begin to laugh, or we might slap our forehead. As a result of our action, we do feel satisfaction. But that, too, is merely a matter of connecting pathways, which guarantee that the brain center for the feeling of relief rather than the center, say, for despair is thrown into action. At any rate, if this interpretation of human actions were right, we could never understand any of the sequences which occur in our lives. For instance, if in the same situation, but with different connections, the feeling of intense heat were followed by a tendency to pinch one's nose, and this tendency by a rapid movement toward the source of heat, and this again by any feeling of whatever kind, such a sequence would be just as understandable as the actual one. For the latter would also be a *mere* sequence, to which such terms as understanding or insight could never be applied. How could they be applied, since from this scheme the first prerequisite of understanding is absent? This first prerequisite is direct participation of the nature of first facts in the determination of subsequent facts, in other words, dynamic or field determination of sequences rather than determination by the geometry of connecting tracks.

After this discussion it will hardly be necessary to come back to the thesis which explains such sequences by the formation of secondary connections, i.e., associations and conditioned reactions. According to the Associationists, associations are blindly formed in the sense that the nature of given events has no influence upon their association. Furthermore, once an association is formed, corresponding recall is supposed to be again a matter of best-conducting pathways, just as is a reflex sequence. As a result, everything that has just been said about a reflex sequence holds also for explanations in terms of associations or conditioned responses. In behavior, any sequence could be as well established as the actual one, if the proper objective sequence were repeatedly given. The outcome of the process would again depend only on the conductivity of pathways. Thus the terms understanding and insight would once more be inapplicable.[13]

Our next task consists in giving our own interpretation of such sequences. We have offered a physiological interpretation of the way in which emotional states are felt to be referred to their experienced causes. This interpretation will now be

[13] At about the time when this book was first written, Professor Thorndike introduced a modification of the concept of association, a modification which he then extended to the Law of Effect. The Law of Effect claims that biologically advantageous effects of movements strengthen the connections, the operation of which has led to these movements, and thus to the effects. Originally, it was tacitly presupposed that any sequences, irrespective of their nature, were in this way strengthened, if only they were followed by a biologically favorable result. According to the new view now held by Professor Thorndike, the "belonging" of given events facilitates their connection. Is "belonging" a fact which depends upon the characteristics of the events in question, and can thus give us insight? This is not the case. If we follow Thorndike, "belonging" need not be more than the experience that a first event "goes with" a second event.

amplified so as to include our motor tendencies and subsequent actual movements.

A positive or negative emotional state, we have said, is felt to spring from the nature of a fact inasmuch as the physiological correlate of the emotion is directly brought about by the processes which represent this fact. Thus, in our example, the discomfort of a person is felt by him to be caused by excessive heat, because the cortical correlate of the thermic experience changes the state of certain parts of the brain in a way which, in experience, means discomfort. But the tendency to move away from the heat is felt to be caused by the heat just as directly as the discomfort is. Consequently, we must again give an interpretation in terms of physiological field action. In other words, the process which underlies the feeling of discomfort is not the only direct effect of the heat as represented in the brain; rather a vector develops at the same time, and no less directly. This vector extends from the processes which represent the heat (and its source) to the part of the brain in which the correlate of discomfort is established, and its sense of operation is that of tending to increase the distance between the two. If now the subject actually moves away from the source of heat, what happens in the brain? As the objective distance is increased, the corresponding distance in the brain also grows, which is precisely the change implicit in the sense of the vector as given the moment before. It will be seen that with this interpretation we once more follow the principle of isomorphism. For, in experience, the actual movement is felt to agree with the tendency to move, which accompanied the discomfort; i.e., the person in question has insight with regard to the relation between his tendency to move in a certain direction and his actual movement.

I am ready to admit that these remarks are far from giving a complete account of the facts under discussion. Even if we disregard the question precisely what kind of vector is operating under such circumstances, we have not explained why the presence of such a vector in the brain tends to be followed by movements which are in line with the direction of the vector. It seems that during the first months after birth a child is not able directly to perform such movements as would correspond to his interests in particular objects. We must therefore ask ourselves how agreement between experienced tendencies (or corresponding physical vectors in the brain) and actual movements is gradually realized. Some will assume that between the two facts there is no natural relation whatsoever; in other words, that originally any tendencies (and corresponding vectors in the brain) can be followed by any imaginable movements of the limbs. If this were true, the right sequences would have to be learned entirely and without exception. Another assumption is that the direction of actual movements tend to coincide with that of experienced motor tendencies (or corresponding cortical vectors); and that in early childhood this agreement is not yet realized merely because the maturation of the nervous system is not completed at the time. Certain observations favor the second rather than the first assumption. Even so, at present we seem unable to say how the direction of a cortical vector would bring about corresponding direction of an actual movement—as it would have to, if the second assumption were correct.

Clearly, it is one of the major tasks of field theory to find the right answer to this question. In the meantime, it must be emphasized that, even if the right movements had to be learned, this learning would occur under the influence of given cortical vectors. Among all movements which might occur in a situation those which have a certain direction would be singled out by the fact that their occurrence is in line with the direction of the prevailing vector. For this reason only such particular movements would reduce the tension which at the time exists in the brain. One would expect this fact to have considerable influence on the process of learning. But, to repeat, we are not yet convinced that it is merely learning which establishes the right relations between situations, vectors and movements. At this point, just as at many others, it seems to be the natural fate of Gestalt Psychology to become Gestalt Biology.

BIBLIOGRAPHY

Chapter I

W. S. Hunter: *Human Behavior.* 1928.
K. Koffka: *The Growth of the Mind.* 1924. Second edition, 1928.
J. B. Watson: in *Psychologies of 1925* (Ed. by C. Murchison).
A. P. Weiss: *A Theoretical Basis of Human Behavior.* 1925.

Chapter II

K. Koffka: *Principles of Gestalt Psychology.* 1935.
W. Köhler: *Dynamics in Psychology.* 1940.
W. Köhler: "Die Methoden der psychlogischen Forschung beim Affen." *Abderhaldens Handbuch der biologischen Arbeitsmethoden,* VI, D. 1921.
W. Köhler: *The Place of Value in a World of Facts* (Ch. IV). 1938.

Chapter III

M. Bentley: *The Field of Psychology.* 1924.
D. Katz: *The World of Color.* 1935.
K. Koffka: "Gestalt Psychology." *Psychol. Bull.,* 19, 1922.
K. Koffka: *The Growth of the Mind.* 1928.
K. Koffka: *Principles of Gestalt Psychology.* 1935.
W. Köhler: "Akustische Untersuchungen III." *Zeitschr. f. Psychol.,* 72, 1915.
W. Köhler: "Uber unbemerkte Empfindungen und Urteilstäuschungen." *Zeitschr. f. Psychol.,* 63, 1913.

Chapter IV

K. Koffka: *The Growth of the Mind.* 1924.
W. Köhler: *Gestaltprobleme und Anfänge einer Gestalttheorie.* 1924.

W. Köhler: "Komplextheorie und Gestalttheorie." *Psychol. Forsch.* 6, 1925.

W. Köhler: *Die physischen Gestalten in Ruhe und im stationären Zustand.* 1920.

W. Köhler: *The Place of Value in a World of Facts* (Ch. VIII). 1938.

W. Köhler: "Zur Theorie der Regulation." *Arch. f. Entwicklungsmech, 112,* 1927.

M. Wertheimer: *Drei Abhandlungen zur Gestalttheorie.* 1925.

M. Wertheimer: "Untersuchungen zur Lehre von der Gestalt, I." *Psychol. Forsch., 1,* 1921.

Chapter V

W. Köhler: "Bemerkungen zur Gestalttheorie." *Psychol. Forsch., 11,* 1928.

W. Köhler: "Komplextheorie und Gestalttheorie." *Psychol. Forsch., 6,* 1925.

W. Köhler: *Die physischen Gestalten in Ruhe und im stationären Zustand.* 1920.

W. Köhler: in *Psychologies of 1925* (Ed. by C. Murchison).

M. Wertheimer: "Untersuchungen zur Lehre von der Gestalt, II." *Psychol. Forsch., 4,* 1923.

Chapter VI

E. von Hornbostel: *Festschrift Meinhof.* 1927.

L. Klages: *Vom Wesen des Bewusstseins.* 1921.

W. Köhler: *Die Methoden der psychologischen Forschung an Affen* (Cf. Ch. II).

W. Köhler: *The Place of Value in a World of Facts* (Ch. IV). 1938.

Chapter VII

W. Köhler: *Die physischen Gestalten in Ruhe und im stationären Zustand.* 1920

W .Köhler: *Psychol. Forsch., 4,* 1924.

E. Rubin: *Visuell wahrgenommene Figuren.* 1921.

W. Sander: *Ber. ü. d. 9. Kongress f. exper. Psychologie.* 1927.

M. Wertheimer: "Gestalt Theory." *Social Research, 11,* 1944.

M. Wertheimer: *Psychol. Forsch., 4,* 1924.

Chapter VIII

M. Bentley: *The Field of Psychology*. 1924.
G. Katona: *Organizing and Memorizing*. 1940.
K. Koffka: *The Growth of the Mind*. 1924.
R. M. Ogden: *Psychology and Education*. 1926.
O. Selz: *Die Gesetze des geordneten Denkverlaufs*. 1913.
J. van der Veldt: *L'Apprentissage du mouvement et l'automatisme*. 1928.

Chapter IX

E. Becher: *Gehirn und Seele*. 1911.
W. Köhler: *Dynamics in Psychology* (Ch. III). 1940.
J. von Kries: *Die materiellen Grundlagen der Bewusstseinserscheinungen*. 1901.
K. Lewin: *Psychol. Forsch.*, *1* and *2*, 1921, 1922.
K. Lewin: *Vorsatz, Wille und Bedürfnis*. 1926.
W. Poppelreuter: *Zeitschr. f. Psychol.*, *61*, 1912.

Chapter X

W. Benary: *Psychol. Forsch.*, *2*, 1922.
W. Dilthey: *Ideen über eine beschreibende und zergliedernde Psychologie*. 1894.
K. Duncker: *The Pedag. Sem.*, *23*, 1926.
K. Duncker: "On Problem Solving." *Psychol. Mon.*, *58* (*5*), 1945.
T. Erismann: *Die Eigenart des Geistigen*. 1924.
K. Jaspers: *Psychopathologie*. 1921.
K. Koffka. *The Growth of the Mind*. 1924.
K. Koffka. *Psychol. Forsch.*, *9*, 1927.
W. Köhler: *Arch. f. Entw. Mech.* 1927.
W. Köhler: *Mentality of Apes*. 1925.
W. Köhler: *Die Methoden der psychologischen Forschung an Affen*. 1922 (Cf. Chap. II).
W. Köhler: *The Place of Value in a World of Facts*. 1938.
K. Lewin: *Vorsatz, Wille und Bedürfnis*. 1927.
M. Wertheimer: *Productive Thinking*. 1945.
M. Wertheimer: *Schlussprozesse im produktiven Denken*. 1920.
A. N. Whitehead: *Science and the Modern World*. 1925. New York: New American Library (Mentor Books, No. MD-162). 1948.

INDEX

℗   ⓜ

Quality Reading from PLUME and MERIDIAN

☐ **FREUD AND HIS FOLLOWERS by Paul Roazen.** "A monu-
mental study of one of the most influential men of modern
times, his disciples and opponents."—*Los Angeles Times*
"A distinguished and poignant study, penetrating and comprehensive, magnificent in scope and achievement. . . ."
—*Kirkus Reviews*   (#F440—$5.95)

☐ **COCAINE PAPERS by Sigmund Freud. Notes by Anna Freud.
Edited and with an Introduction by Robert Byck, M.D.** This
book traces the history of cocaine in the nineteenth century,
including a wealth of previously unpublished and unavailable
writing both by and about Freud. Personal letters and the
early dream analyses reveal Freud's significant course from
experimentation with cocaine to the writing of his master-
piece—*The Interpretation of Dreams.*   (#F431—$4.95)

☐ **THE DOUBLE: A Psychoanalytic Study by Otto Rank.** An examination of the concept of a duplicate self down through
the ages in myth, fable, legend, and literature by one of
the great pioneers of psychoanalysis. Using art to explore
the primal depths of the mind, Otto Rank perceives the im-
agined twin as a reflection and attempted resolution of eternal
and agonizing inner human conflicts.   (#F505—$3.95)

☐ **THE WILL TO MEANING: Foundations and Applications of
Logotherapy by Viktor E. Frankl.** One of the most important
books of Europe's leading existential psychologists, the
founder of logotherapy. Drawing upon his many years of
professional practice and the concentration camp experiences that helped shape his views, the author outlines his
invaluable therapeutic techniques.   (#Z5118—$2.95)

☐ **IDLE PASSION: Chess and the Dance of Death by Alexander
Cockburn.** A unique investigation into the history and psychology of chess that reveals it as a mirror image of all
man's obsessions and desires. Includes analyses of chess
masters from Paul Morphy to Bobby Fischer, the literature
of chess, and psychoanalytical theories about chess as expressed by Freud and others.   (#Z5109—$2.95)

In Canada, please add $1.00 to the price of each book.

Buy them at your local bookstore or use coupon on
next page for ordering.

PLUME and MERIDIAN Books of Special Interest

☐ **SIN, SICKNESS, AND SANITY: A History of Sexual Attitudes by Vern Bullough, Ph.D., and Bonnie Bullough, Ph.D.** Extensively researched, far-reaching in scope, this fascinating work is a comprehensive summary of our knowledge of past sexual attitudes, as well as an appraisal of the causes and direction of of the sexual revolution today. (#F472—$4.95)

☐ **THE PSYCHOTHERAPY HANDBOOK edited by Richie Herink. With a Foreword by Daniel Goleman, Senior Editor,** *Psychology Today.* This unique guide brings together clear, concise articles on more than 250 varieties of psychotherapy practiced in America today, making it by far the best single overview of a complex and crowded field. Each article, provided by a leading authority, gives definitions of the therapy, its history, techniques, and applications, plus reference lists for further reading. (#F525—$9.95)

☐ **POSITIVE PARENTHOOD: Solving Parent-Child Conflicts through Behavior Modification by Paul S. Graubard.** A practical problem-resolving procedure that not only will reduce strife to make your parent-child relationship happier and more relaxed, but also will promote independence and responsibility. (#Z5176—$3.95)

☐ **THE DEVIL: Perceptions of Evil from Antiquity to Primitive Christianity by Jeffrey Burton Russell.** Combining superb scholarship with rich psychological insight, this major study examines the evolution of both the philosophic and the physical image of evil. The text and illustrations also explore the myriad ways in which evil has been embodied by the imagination. (#F504—$5.95)

☐ **A PSYCHOHISTORY OF ZIONISM by Jay Y. Gonen.** A brilliant, psychological analysis of the political, cultural, emotional, intellectual, religious, and militant forms of Zionism. "With rich and convincing detail, it reveals more than a bookshelf of standard Mideast analyses."—*Publishers Weekly* (#F441—$3.95)

In Canada, please add $1.00 to the price of each book.

Buy them at your local bookstore or use this convenient coupon for ordering.

THE NEW AMERICAN LIBRARY, INC.
P.O. Box 999, Bergenfield, New Jersey 07621

Please send me the PLUME and MERIDIAN BOOKS I have checked above. I am enclosing $_____(please add 75¢ to this order to cover postage and handling). Send check or money order—no cash or C.O.D.'s. Prices and numbers are subject to change without notice.

Name_____

Address_____

City_____State_____Zip Code_____

Allow 4-6 weeks for delivery.
This offer is subject to withdrawal without notice.